Writing and Marketing Shareware

Revised and Expanded 2nd Edition

TRADEMARKS

Writing and Marketing Shareware

Revised and Expanded 2nd Edition

Steve Hudgik

Windcrest®/McGraw-Hill

SECOND EDITION
FIRST PRINTING

Library of Congress Cataloging-in-Publication Data

Hudgik, Steven C.
    Writing and marketing shareware / by Steven C. Hudgik.— Rev. and expanded 2nd ed.
        p.   cm.
    Includes index.
    ISBN 0-8306-2552-6 (p)
    1. Shareware (Computer software)   I. Title.
QA76.76.S46H83   1991
005.1'068'8—dc20
                                                91-19702
                                                CIP

TAB Books offers software for sale. For information and a catalog, please contact TAB Software Department, Blue Ridge Summit, PA 17294-0850.

Acquisitions Editor: Brad J. Schepp
Book Editor: Orda Jim Hackney
Production: Katherine G. Brown
Book Design: Jaclyn J. Boone
Cover: Sandra Blair Design, Harrisburg, PA   WP1

This book is dedicated to the Association of Shareware Professionals (ASP) and all ASP members. They are a group of dedicated programmers and business people who are always willing to give their time and resources to help new authors trying to get started or to help promote the shareware concept. They have worked hard to bring shareware the recognition it deserves and to protect the shareware marketing concept.

Contents

Acknowledgments

In writing this book I have had a lot of help and I appreciate that help very much. This book could not have been completed without the support, cooperation, and assistance of many people.

I want to express my sincere thanks to the over 350 shareware authors, distributors, users, and magazine editors in five countries that responded to my mail survey.

I would also like to thank the 45 shareware authors and dealers that allowed me to interview them on the phone and also the ASP members that provided feedback, answered questions, and asked questions in the ASP forum on CompuServe.

Many thanks also go to the ASP for establishing a forum on CompuServe where even nonmembers can drop in, "listen" to conversations, ask questions, and learn how to become successful shareware authors.

To the shareware dealers and many unknown users that have put up with my experiments with various methods of encouraging the registration of shareware, I would also like to say "thank you."

Bob Falk, whose help and encouragement helped me complete this book, has my sincerest appreciation.

To Lance Rose, whose help in reviewing the legal section of this book was invaluable and who also provided many good suggestions for improvements, I must say "thank you."

I must also thank Jeannine M. E. Klein, who edited the first version of this book and, in the process, taught me a lot about writing.

A great deal of thanks go to Nelson Ford for writing the *Programmer's Guide*. Parts of this book were derived from the *Programmer's Guide* by Nelson Ford, who is the owner of the Public (software) Library. If you would like a free copy of PsL's monthly newsletter, write to: PsL, P.O. Box 35705, Houston, TX 77235.

I would also like to thank my family for putting up with my ignoring them so that I could finish this book.

Preface

This is a marketing book. It shows you how to successfully market your software using shareware.

I wrote this book because I believe in shareware. Shareware is the only risk-free way for users to find the software they need. Shareware brings fresh ideas, new approaches, and innovation to software—forcing all software publishers to be more responsive to the user's needs. I believe in shareware as a way for small software publishers to get started. In fact, shareware is the only business I know that you can start up with very little money and grow into a multimillion dollar business!

I originally planned for this book to be about 150 pages. As you can see that plan did not work out. After talking with both successful and beginning authors, I realized there were more questions and more topics that needed covering. I have tried to provide all the information you need to start a software publishing business. As a result, this book covers a broad range of topics. It is also an excellent summary of how to run a direct marketing business. (Yes, shareware is direct marketing.) But there is more to each topic than what I have included here. There are books solely devoted to each of the individual topics: goal setting, advertising, marketing, running a mail-order business, writing software documentation, etc. I hope you keep reading and learning. In running a business, there is always more to learn.

Please do not take what I write here as absolute rules, or even limit yourself to the suggestions I have offered. Business is a dynamic, changing environment. The software business can be even more dynamic than other businesses, and change comes almost every day. Pay attention to what is happening in your targeted market. Take any software ideas you have and experiment with them. Then, build your business around the idea that best fits that market.

This is a marketing book. It covers a wide range of activities that are necessary to get any product or service to the consumer: product design, packaging, advertising, publicity, customer support, telephone etiquette, and much more. Specifically, it covers software marketing.

Marketing rule #1 Know your market—that is where your customers are. Your target *market* is a *specific* group of people who need your product or might need it in the future. For example, the target market for tennis balls is people who play tennis. You do not try to sell tennis balls to golfers. For software, the target market for DOS utilities is everyone who has an IBM-compatible computer. The target market for Loran locator software is much smaller—primarily airplane pilots. So remember: know your customers and target them.

What are my qualifications for writing this book? To start, I am a successful full-time shareware author. I have been writing public domain software since 1983. I have been marketing my software using the shareware method since 1985. The list of software I currently have in circulation includes:

MS-DOS shareware

Home Insurance (Home Inventory)   Play 'n' Learn
Your Financial Advisor   Home Money Manager IIa
For Record Collectors   For Sports Card Collectors
For Jazz Record Collectors   For Comic Book Collectors
For Classical Record Collectors   For Photographers
For Antique Documents   Book Minder
For Business Card Collectors   Professional Book Minder
For Film & Video Tapes   For Stamp Collectors
For Coin Collectors   The Information Index
For Memorabilia Collectors   For Gun Collectors
Your Menu   For Legal Case Notes
Shareware Mailing List Manager   ZipBase

MD-DOS Freeware

PC Bartender

CP/M Public Domain

Personal Asset Manager   Home Money Manager I & II
Home Loan   Home Insurance
Holiday Manager

Although I have written a lot of code, my true strength is marketing. I read and study business and marketing books. I have been a marketing consultant for the past five years and have helped several small businesses get their start. I have a Master of Business Administration and Bachelor of

Science in Electrical Engineering, but what has more value is real-life experience. My real-life experience includes over 10 years as a Senior Client Manager (sales and marketing) with a Fortune 500 company. I was the top salesman in 1988 with over $20 million dollars in sales, and I received their Flame of Excellence award in 1989.

I have run my own business since I was 12 years old. In high school, while other kids went to parties, I formed a company to provide the music for those parties. I paid for my college education by running several businesses. I cannot help it! It is in my blood. I love running a business and making it a success. And although I have made a lot of mistakes along the way, I have learned from my mistakes.

I have told you who I am and why I am qualified to write this book. Does that mean this has to be a good book? No. I have read many poorly written and useless books by highly qualified authors. You are the one who will decide whether this book is worthwhile. So I leave it in your hands. You decide. If you do not feel the information in this book is of value to you, or you find some parts useful but disagree with others, please write and tell me what you think. If you feel I have missed important points, or if you have a question, please write. If this book gives you the start you need to form a multimillion dollar corporation—*please write*. Whatever the situation, I would like to read your comments. My address is:

Steve Hudgik
c/o HCP Services, Inc.
P.O. Box 974
Tualatin, OR 97062

Thank you, and I wish you success!

Introduction

Shareware is exploding. Over 25,000 shareware authors have written more than 85,000 programs. Major software publishers, such as Lotus Corporation, are moving toward the shareware concept by providing copies of their software on the hard disks of new computers and allowing users to try it before they buy it. Users purchase over 25,000 shareware disks every day and at least a half-dozen shareware publishers sell over $1,000,000 of software a year. Shareware, with roots in thousands of companies started around kitchen tables, has become big business. But it remains one of the few businesses you can still start around a kitchen table.

This book shows you how to become a successful shareware author. If you are just starting out and have no business or marketing skills, you will learn everything you need to know to get started. If you are already running a successful shareware business, you will find tips and suggestions to help you improve your business.

This is the only book that includes everything you need to know to market software using the shareware method. You will learn what shareware is, why it works, and how to develop marketable software ideas. On the business side, you will learn how to price your software, get free publicity, run a home business, handle legal concerns, and get the equipment and supplies you need. You will find software reviews that may help you select programs useful for running your business. You will also read the comments and suggestions of shareware authors, disk distributors, and magazine editors. Their experiences reveal proven ways to effectively promote your software using the shareware method.

In every chapter of this book you will find practical information and real-life examples. This is not a book filled with theory. This book shows you how to combine your programming skills with solid business practices and proven marketing techniques to run a successful software publishing company. It is a step-by-step guide to success.

How this book is organized

This book has sixteen chapters plus an appendix. The first three chapters cover the shareware marketing concept and how you can use shareware to sell your software. They include a brief history of shareware, a description of how shareware works, and some suggestions to help you develop ideas for new software. You will also find out how to set a price for your software and how to encourage users to pay the registration fee.

The next four chapters are about promoting your software. You will learn that the primary method of promoting shareware is through shareware disk distributors and BBSs. Chapter 4 provides guidelines for sending your software to distributors and BBSs. You will also learn about advertising, free publicity, and trade shows.

Chapters 8 through 10 provide help with running a home business. These chapters cover everything from postage machines to writing a business plan. You will learn how to copyright your software and how to protect your trademarks.

The next two chapters examine techniques for writing good software. You will find out what users most want in software and determine whether your software is what users want. These chapters provide recommendations for testing your software and for designing your distribution disk. You will also learn how to write good documentation.

The final four chapters cover a variety of topics that will help you become a successful shareware author. Chapter 13 lists the software most often used by shareware authors and describes, in detail, some programs you may find helpful in running your shareware business. An important tool to ensure your success is to be part of a network of shareware authors that can provide support and guidance. The Association of Shareware Professionals provides this network and is discussed in chapter 14. Chapter 15 presents the results of several surveys on which parts of this book are based and chapter 16 provides a directory of suppliers and services.

Becoming a successful shareware author is what this book is about. I hope you enjoy it and I wish you good luck in running your business!

1
Introduction to shareware

When I told my family I was leaving a high paying job as a senior client manager for a major international multibillion dollar corporation to run a computer software company, they looked proud. Then I explained I would give my software away to anyone who wanted a copy and rely on their honesty to pay for it. My family clearly thought I was crazy. They did not say anything, but the looks on their faces said, "The crazy fool is putting our grandchildren's future in jeopardy by trusting people to send him money."

What shareware is

What shareware is all about is letting people try your software before they pay for it and trusting that they will pay for it if they use it.

Shareware is not a type of software, it is a marketing method, a way to let people know about your software. The idea originated with the late Andrew Fluegelman, the founding editor of *PC World* and the creator of PC-Talk software. As a user, you obtain a copy of a program from a shareware dealer for a small copying or handling fee, usually around $5. Or you might get a copy from a friend, a user group, or an electronic bulletin board. The software you get is fully functional, allowing you to try it, see how well it works, and decide whether it is useful to you. If you continue to use it, you are required to purchase the software by paying a registration fee. Registration fees can be anywhere from a few dollars to several hundred dollars. When you register the software, you usually receive a disk with the most recent version, a printed manual, access to telephone support, and information about future updates. You also might receive discounts on other software published by the same author or additional data files for use with the software. This procedure varies with the author and depends on the type of program, purchase price, and other factors.

Shareware is a great deal! I have an eight-foot shelf full of commercial software I purchased in retail stores, half of which did not work correctly, or was not what I needed, and I now do not use. For less money than you would spend on gas to drive to a software store, you can "test drive" software programs you think might be useful. You only pay for them if you continue to use them.

Before I go too far, let me define two terms. Software that has a user license that prohibits copying and sharing of the software is called *retail software*. This terminology is not entirely accurate, as the word "retail" means the sale of goods directly to the ultimate user. However, because most of this type of software is sold through retail stores or mail order houses, the term retail will do for our purposes. *Shareware* refers to copyrighted software that can be freely shared among users. Other important aspects of shareware further define it, and I discuss those shortly.

Several other types of software are sometimes distributed along with shareware and sometimes confused with shareware.

Public domain   Some software has been released into the public domain. This means it is not copyrighted and is available for anyone to use without obligation or limits. As an author, if you release software into the public domain, you lose all rights to that software. To release a program to the public domain, include a statement in your documentation that says, "I donate this program to the public domain" and do not include a copyright notice. If you want to give away your software for free, but have any thoughts about possibly converting your software to shareware or retail software in the future, then you should release it as freeware.

Freeware   Freeware programs are copyrighted programs you may use without compensating the author. Like public domain software, freeware has no registration requirements. However, by copyrighting freeware, the author retains all rights to the program. This allows the author to control distribution to some degree and to release new versions in the future that might require a registration payment or even be released as retail software. With freeware, the author generally does not provide support or help.

There used to be significant confusion with the terms shareware, freeware, and public domain software. For a time some "shareware" dealers mixed shareware, freeware, and public domain software in their libraries and implied users could "buy" complete programs for $3–6. This problem has almost been eliminated (it still exists in many foreign countries) as a result of user complaints and the efforts of the Association of Shareware Professionals (for more about ASP, see chapter 14).

Demoware   Some shareware dealers and BBSs (Bulletin Board Systems) carry programs that have been written to show the features of a retail software package. These types of programs demonstrate a program without letting you try it yourself. They also might include advertising and are really nothing more than disk-based advertising for software.

Crippleware   This is software with one or more major functions disabled, or software with incomplete documentation. Based on a survey I did of shareware authors, more than 25% of them had crippled their shareware version in some way. This is usually done as an incentive to encourage users to register and get a fully functional program. These authors feel they will get more registrations this way. Experience has shown the opposite to be true. I discuss this in detail in the chapter on marketing strategy.

Olderware   Another approach to shareware has been to release older versions of a program and call them shareware. This is not shareware. Shareware should be the most current and fully documented version of the software. You want users to see how good you are, not how good you were.

Shareware   Unlike public domain software, shareware is copyrighted, and the author retains ownership of that copyright. Anyone who continues to use shareware is obligated to purchase the program by paying the registration fee. Remember, shareware is just a marketing method that makes people aware of your software and gives them the opportunity to try it before they buy.

Some better-known programs marketed using the shareware method include Automenu (Marshall Magee), PC-Write: (Bob Wallace) and PC-File (Jim Button).

Does shareware work

According to a November 1988 *Forbes* magazine article, Bob Wallace of Quicksoft had $2 million in sales and a 5% before-tax profit. Yes, I would say shareware works. Is Bob Wallace an exception? No!

> *Our business has enjoyed a tremendous amount of growth over the last year. As a matter of fact, our business sells products other than shareware. For example, we're very heavily involved in commercial software distribution. But I see the shareware as, by far, the highest growth products we have in our line.*
>
> —Roger Jones, president of Shareware To-Go

Take a look at the results of the shareware author survey in chapter 14. Survey responses from 18 authors showed sales in excess of $50,000 per year. Yes, shareware works. The example I know the most about is my experience as a shareware author. I am a full-time shareware author. I have no other job. Next week's groceries and my children's college education depend on shareware working for me. And it does!

> *I think shareware is in an excellent position. More people are standing up and taking notice. If you look in the general PC press you'll see more and more mentions of shareware as people*

*realize how professional the shareware market is. I think share-
ware is going to take off.*
—Marilyn Young, editor of *Shareware Magazine*

Look at this from the other side. Maybe these shareware successes happened because the authors were lucky. They were in the right place at the right time. Maybe Bob Wallace made it big because he came out with PC-Write: before anyone else had a shareware word processing program.

I have heard these arguments many times in many different industries. The answer is always the same: Luck has nothing to do with it. You make your own luck. Being in the right place at the right time is nothing more than watching for, and being prepared to take advantage of, opportunities as they present themselves. Luck has nothing to do with being successful. Preparation, hard work, and learning everything you can about your industry and target market are the ingredients of success. Add to that the initiative and courage required to start your own business, and you are on the way to the top.

Yes, shareware works, but just like any other business it takes years of hard work. In almost any industry, you will find that "overnight successes" are actually built on a lot of work, past failures, and a strong background of knowledge.

As I first looked over the shareware author surveys, one characteristic was immediately apparent. The shareware authors getting the most registrations seem to be doing business in a professional manner. On the other hand, many of those getting few registrations seemed to have poor business skills. This is not a quantifiable result of the survey because it was not designed to measure business skills. I only offer this as a personal observation. The distinction was clearly seen in how the survey questions were answered and in the letters, brochures, and shareware disks some authors included with their survey responses. This book is designed to solve this problem by providing a complete shareware publishing guide in a single volume.

Yes, shareware works, but an important point to remember is that shareware is not a way to get rich off trivial or unprofessional software. Your software must be as good or better than retail software. People will not pay a registration fee because you put a lot of work into your software or because you are a nice person. Your software must be useful and provide value to the user. You do not buy a new car because GM spent a lot of time designing it and would really like you to buy it so they can make some money. You buy a car because you feel it provides you with something (transportation, image, or whatever) that has value equal to or greater than what you pay for that car. It is no different for software, but it is tougher for shareware authors than for car dealers or retail software publishers.

I say it is tougher for shareware authors because potential customers get to see and use what they are buying before they pay for it. The software has to be good. Much of retail software is sold based on advertising claims and packaging. Only after you purchase the software do you find out about limits on certain functions, incompatibilities with other hardware and software, and other disappointments. As I have already mentioned, I have a shelf of retail software and use less than half because of these reasons. That is a lot of wasted money.

Yes, shareware works. It can provide you with the reward you wish to achieve, if you are willing to put the necessary effort into your software and into your business. Many shareware authors run their business as a hobby and do not expect big returns. That is fine and that person is a great success if he or she receives 10 registrations a year. Success lies in achieving the goals you have set for yourself, not in how much money you make.

"Love, not money, drives the industry." This quotation is from an article called "Cheap Software" in the September 1989 issue of *Compute!* magazine. If you write software and market it using shareware just for pure enjoyment—go ahead, have fun! Enjoy yourself. If you want a good income from shareware, expect to put in a lot of hard work. Yes, some programs are so well written and so useful that they sell with little marketing effort. These are exceptions. Do not count on this happening with your software.

Why publish your software as shareware

What are the advantages of shareware for a small software publisher/author? Shareware is not a small industry. Over 85,000 shareware programs are in circulation, and more are released every day. We have over 1100 authors on our mailing list. They range from corporations with 20–25 employees to people working by themselves in an upstairs bedroom. Most shareware is written and published by individuals working alone in their homes part time. They have no advertising budget, marketing staff, or fancy packaging. For these authors, shareware is the only option they have for selling their software. They might have a good product, but the cost of selling it through traditional retail channels is prohibitive.

To understand why costs can be prohibitive, look at what is involved in selling retail software. It has to have packaging that looks sharp to catch a shopper's eye and a distributor's interest. Retail software needs advertising to make dealers and users aware it is available. Retail software needs to get onto dealer's shelves and be accepted by distributors. All of this is called *marketing*, and it is very expensive. With advertising costs running over $10,000 per page in some cases, even a limited marketing effort can cost a lot. Plus, distributors do not want to touch a product unless it already has a large demand and is backed by a strong advertising campaign.

The first shareware advantage   Shareware can cost as little or as much to market as you wish to spend. Some authors just upload their program to 1 or 2 bulletin board services (BBSs) or send copies to 5 or 6 mail-order shareware dealers. The total marketing cost is $7 or $8. This is a marketing budget anyone can afford. If you are serious about making a profit, I do not recommend such a limited marketing effort, but with shareware you can get started by spending almost nothing.

The second shareware advantage Shareware is the perfect way to sell specialized, hard-to-find products. Many shareware programs have a very limited market. My shareware is a good example of this. I offer a specialized database for cataloging antique documents. Not many people collect antique documents, and there is no way a retail store can carry a program like this. However, in a shareware catalog, this program might take just one additional line to list it, allowing shareware dealers to carry it and make a profit selling it.

The third shareware advantage You have control of your product. No one else can tell you to make changes. No banks or investors (who usually supply the marketing money) are putting conditions on your product. You make your software as you like it, package it the way you like and take orders from no one. Of course, if you wish to be successful and make shareware more than a hobby, you had better listen to your customers and your market. They will always be your boss and will ultimately determine the extent of your success.

The fourth shareware advantage Shareware makes life easier. I first started writing and selling software in the days of CP/M machines. I did not know about shareware, and I sold my software through small ads in magazines. My software received good reviews, and I sold enough to pay for my computer, which was the extent of my goals at that time. But I was always worried about people making unauthorized copies of my software. I knew it was happening because I would get calls from users whose names I did not recognize. (I knew nearly all my users by name back then.) They were stealing my software and I felt victimized.

Releasing your software as shareware immediately eliminates that problem. Anyone can get a copy essentially for free. No one can steal something from you that you are willing to give them. It is great, no more worries about piracy! Of course, if you need something to worry about, you can worry about all those people using your shareware who have not paid the registration fee.

Some people will use software without paying for it. I even know of a minister who is unintentionally using pirated copies of retail software. They "borrow" it from friends or get it from dealers that put "free" copies on a hard disk when they sell a computer. If someone is going to use software without paying for it, either intentionally or because they do not know they should be buying their own copy, there is nothing you can do to stop them. However, most people are honest and want to do the right thing. By most people, I mean well over 99%. If you provide software with value and make the user aware that your software is shareware that must be paid for, eventually they will pay for it.

The fifth shareware advantage With any type of product there are good sales and bad sales. A good sale is one made to a customer who buys, likes, and uses your product. It is what they need, and if they are pleased they will spread the good word.

A bad sale is when you sell something to a customer who does not fit your application. If they buy your product, you might have to take it back or else they will be unhappy and will tell other people. It is like fitting a square peg in a round hole.

Bad sales can waste a lot of your time. You can spend time on product support trying to help a user get your software to do something it was not designed to do. You can spend time answering questions, maybe doing some custom programming to try to keep them happy. Sometimes the user will call or write and verbally abuse you. (I have been through it all.) You do not need bad sales. No software is perfect for everyone, and with shareware you eliminate users who are not a good fit for your product before you get mired in problems and complaints.

Yes, shareware has many advantages over retail software—so many advantages that many retail software publishers are starting to market their software using shareware. One of the leading DOS shells, *XTree*, is now marketed as shareware. *VP-Info*, which has sold over 50,000 copies worldwide as retail software, has been upgraded and released as shareware. Some authors have become millionaires marketing their software as shareware. I know shareware authors who have used their shareware profits to pay for a beach house—with cash. Yes, shareware works, and there is no better way for you to get started as a software publisher.

2
Making money with shareware

What does it take to be successful with shareware? First you have to define what you mean by successful. What are your goals? Do you want to get rich? Do you want to write programs and play with your computer? Do you want to help people? Do you just want enough extra money to buy a new computer or maybe a big-screen TV? Do you want to learn more about computers? Do you want to learn more about business? Do you want recognition? Do you want to run your own business? Or possibly you are not sure what your goals are. All of these are acceptable answers, and I am sure there are many more. All of them can be achieved using the shareware method of marketing software. But first, you have to decide what you want and the direction you want your shareware business to go.

What type of business do you want

Some shareware authors feel they have a good idea and they put all they have into it. They quit their job, buy advertising, and design a great looking four-color package. They blanket BBSs, user groups, and distributors with copies of their program. They travel the country visiting magazine editors, talking at user group meetings, and attending trade shows. Several shareware companies have started this way, but it is a tough way to start.

Other authors, taking a more conservative approach, write a good program in their spare time and upload it to one or two electronic bulletin boards. They might have photocopied manuals, but they do not provide telephone support. About a year ago, I read a review in *PC Magazine* that highly recommended a shareware utility program. It also mentioned that this shareware program's author did not take phone calls or answer mail.

He shipped registered copies of his software only once a month. If you wanted to buy a copy, you had to be patient. How you run your business depends only on what you want to get out of it.

If you are going to approach writing software as a hobby, be sure you release only quality software. Even though you might not be trying to make money, your reputation will be based on the quality of your software and documentation. Releasing a poor quality program does nothing to help users, and only hurts you. In the end, all that you accomplish is to ruin your future as a software author. Although this book is for authors that want to make money marketing their software as shareware, you—the beginner—should follow the same guidelines for producing quality, non-trivial, and thoroughly tested software.

Marketing versus programming

The more financially successful you want to be, the more time, effort, and money you will have to put into marketing. Shareware is one of the few businesses that allow you to put your time into whatever aspect of your business you want. You can put as much or as little effort into it as you like. However, do not expect big dollar returns for a little effort.

Goals

A common approach is to start with only a few goals in mind. Most books on business say you must have clear goals in your mind and a business plan in your hand. This is great and is the theoretical ideal. However, most people do not know what they want, or what goals to set until they have gained some experience. With shareware, you can start small and build your business along the direction you would like it to take.

I am not saying you should start with no goals in mind. What I am saying is that your first goal can be to just get your business started. I have met many people who have had great ideas that someone else turned into a money-making venture. These people never got started.

The best way to learn how to run a software company is to do it.
—Bob Wallace

One possible sequence of goals and actions for a shareware company might be as follows.

Step 1 Write a quality, useful program that is not trivial. (This is your first goal.) For your first program, this could be something for your own personal use. Some people start writing software with no intent of publishing. Others start with the intention of eventually selling copies of their software and making money from it. By starting with a program you need, you are writing software in which you have some background and it is software you can use every day. If you do not get user registrations, you still have a useful program for yourself.

Step 2 Now that you have a program, your next goal is to have people with different perspectives use your program and give you feedback. Show the program to some friends who also need this type of software or upload it to a few local BBSs and ask for people's opinions. Change the program to take into account a wider range of requirements. Fix bugs, make the program easier to use, and add useful features you did not originally think of.

At step three, there are two possible directions you could choose. One is to write software as a hobby. The other is to run a business and make money with the software you have written.

Step 3a Write software for fun. Your goal is to enjoy using your computer and to write software. This goal requires no further marketing efforts to distribute your software. Just enjoy using and refining it, and if you receive any registration payments, that is an added bonus. (Note: regardless of the amount of time you put into your shareware, you should always acknowledge registration payments. It is rude not to send, at least, a thank-you note.)

Step 3b Test-market your software. Find out whether or not people will pay money for your program. You do this by further improving your program and sending copies to a few shareware distributors and user groups. You should continue to work to identify bugs and make improvements before your program is widely distributed.

After step 3b, there are again two possible directions you could take. One direction is a casual approach to marketing software that involves essentially no marketing efforts. The other direction is to run a serious business and work to make a profit from your software.

Step 4a Make no further marketing efforts and enjoy a small part-time income. Continue to improve your software (the improvement process never stops). Your goal is to supplement your regular income with a few dollars each year without interfering with your family life or Monday night football.

Step 4b Improve your program and send copies to as many shareware distributors and bulletin boards as you can find. Start writing a second program. Your goal is to start building a revenue stream that can be used to fund further expansion.

Figure 2-1 summarizes the four steps. As you can see, your business can go in the direction you wish, moving one small step at a time. You can change your goals as you progress. At each step you will learn more about the direction toward which you are moving and whether or not you will want to continue or get out of the software business.

Success requires marketing

If you are working toward expanding your business, increasing your sales (registrations), and increasing your income, you will find that most of your

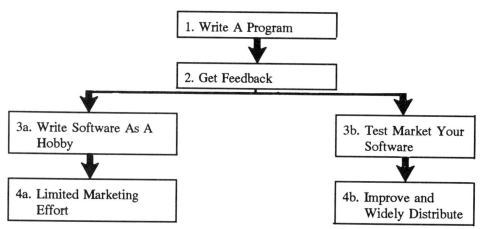

2-1 Shareware can develop into a hobby or a professional business, depending on the direction you want it to take.

efforts go into marketing. As the author of 22 shareware programs I have written a lot of code, yet I spend only about 10% of my time writing program code. I spend the rest of my time on marketing. This includes writing press releases, designing promotional material, taking orders, answering technical questions, and updating mailing lists. An interview with *Shooting Industry Magazine* (about my software called *For Gun Collectors*) was conducted in the middle of writing this paragraph. (More marketing.)

If you want a successful shareware business and you like writing code, but have little interest in the marketing side, you might form a partnership with someone who knows marketing. However, be sure you put together a written agreement stating what each party will contribute and how earnings will be split. Even between friends, a business relationship should always be established in writing. It has nothing to do with trust. It is the professional way to work and a good business practice. At a minimum, the agreement should cover how profits and losses will be split; what happens if one partner leaves the business; and what each partner will contribute (i.e., program code, writing a manual, graphic design, advertising, etc.). Although most people do not want to spend the money, if you are serious about your business, you should have a lawyer write the agreement.

Using distributors

Another approach is to find a distributor that will do the marketing for you. For example, some shareware distributors will handle the selling of registered copies for you. If you feel you will have enough volume to support it, you can even hire an outside service to handle printing and packaging, allowing you to also avoid this aspect of marketing. However, paying other people to handle marketing for you will cut your profits significantly. For example, a shareware distributor may require a 60% or higher discount off the selling price of your software. If this is what you want, it will free you to do what you enjoy—programming.

At this point, you might think you could just sell your program to one of the major retail software publishers and sit back and watch the royalty payments come in. They will handle the publishing and marketing. All you have to do is write the code! I'm sorry, but that is just a dream. It does not happen. Most software released by major publishers is written by their in-house staff. If a software publisher buys a program from the outside, it will either be an established product from another publisher or a successful shareware program that already has a proven sales record.

Time

The four steps I previously outlined, as a possible way to get started in shareware, take time. The length of time depends on how much effort you put into each step.

Step one is getting your program and documentation written. How long this step takes depends on the size of your program and how fast you write code.

For step two, testing and getting feedback, you could spend six months to a year from when you first issue your software until you work out all the bugs. On a small or no-budget basis, it also takes six months to a year to evaluate the market, get feedback on your software, and make changes in response to that feedback.

Steps three and four depend on the direction you set for your business. You might spend anywhere from a few days to several years working at steps three and four.

The difference between shareware and retail software

I briefly discussed the retail channel for selling software in the previous chapter. In this section I will go into more detail about marketing software through the retail channel and how it compares to shareware as a primary marketing tool.

The retail channel introduces several steps between you and the final user. For example, you might sell your software to a distributor. The distributor sells it to a retailer. The retailer sells it to the end user. Each person in this chain needs to make a profit, so each one has to add a markup sufficient to pay their costs and generate a profit. Few businesses can operate with markups less than 40%, and markups of 100% or more are common. Although a section in the next chapter is on pricing let us quickly look at an example.

Dealer/distributor discounts

Assume you have a program you sell at a list price of $100. A typical dealer discount would be 40%. Thus, you would sell this program to a dealer for $60. The dealer sells the software for $100, which is a 67% markup on the $60 price paid to you (the dealer's $40 markup divided by the $60 dealer cost). If you sell your software through a distributor, you need to discount it further to allow the distributor to make a profit. A 60% to 80% discount is typical. You might sell your software to the distributor for $30. The distributor sells it to the dealer for $60, a 100% markup. The dealer then gets a 67% markup when the software sells to the end user for $100.

Please note, discount percentages will vary depending on such factors as type of software, price, and volume. The point is your returns are much lower because of the middlemen. The benefits of middlemen are that you can have dramatically greater sales with less effort.

Regardless of how you distribute your software, you have to find a way to make potential users aware of it. If they do not know about your software, they cannot buy it. With shareware, awareness is achieved by sharing copies of your software. With retail software, you have to advertise.

Advertising

Advertising is very expensive. You can spend a lot of money quickly. Even the small ads in the back of a computer magazine can cost $400 to $500 per column inch. Small ads are usually measured in column inches. A column inch is a space the width of one column that is one inch high. To be effective, you need to run an ad for at least three consecutive months. With most magazine's two-inch minimum size requirement, you are looking at spending at least $2400 to $3000. This is the lowest cost for you to get started using a display ad in a major computer publication. Using the shareware approach, you can start with any level of financial commitment. For the cost of running one small ad for one month, you can send your disk to over 250 shareware dealers.

Inventory

Another big disadvantage of the retail software method is that you must manufacture and deliver a significant quantity of software to distributors before you get paid. You still might not get paid until they sell it. You could find yourself making several thousand copies of your software and having it sit on distributor's shelves. And the scenario can get worse—you might find a major bug. Now you have several thousand copies of your software somewhere in the retail channel, all with a bug that will create bad feelings among your users and tie up your phone with product support calls.

With shareware, you can produce what you need as you need it. If you want to start on a small scale, you can photocopy your manual as you receive registration payments. It is the ideal system of just-in-time inventory management. Shareware also has another advantage. It allows you to be much more responsive to the market.

Other advantages of shareware

With shareware, you can identify niche markets or market trends and respond to them faster than retail software companies. Big retail companies take time to make decisions, both on what to do and how to do it. With the large dollar commitment they must make to advertising, inventory and other marketing costs, a mistake would be expensive. As a shareware author, your risk is less and you can move faster. For example, I can come up with an idea to improve my software this morning, write the code by 10 A.M., test and debug it by 1 P.M., write an addendum to the manual, and have the upgraded version ready for my 3:30 P.M. UPS pickup.

Some people have identified Windows and OS/2 as big potential markets into which shareware can explode. These are areas in which there are still few applications, leaving the field open for new software. A good example of a niche market shareware authors recently filled is virus checkers. Virus checkers first came out as shareware, with several achieving significant financial success. Now, as viruses have gained widespread publicity, the demand for virus checkers is growing. As the market grows, it attracts the attention of retail software publishers. In this case, shareware publishers are already established with both brand name recognition and a quality reputation. A rule of business that Lotus, Microsoft, WordPerfect, and their competitors all know is that it is almost impossible to dislodge a company that has the top position. Thus, if you can find a niche, establish yourself, and gain significant market share, you have a tremendous advantage.

Niche markets

Shareware is ideal for niche markets that are too small to attract the attention of retail companies. Retailers can only offer software that sells in volume. The typical examples are word processing, spreadsheets, utilities, and games. To stay profitable they must turn over their inventory, meaning they cannot have software sitting on the shelf—it must sell and be replaced by new inventory. For example, the software I market as shareware is specialized database software for cataloging collections. There are not enough serious collectors, in any one area, to provide a large enough volume to make it worthwhile for a dealer to stock my software (although I do get a lot of special orders from dealers).

Dealers cannot afford to carry a program that is not well known and already a big seller. You might write the best word processing program that has even been written. But you do not have a recognizable brand name. No one knows who you are, so dealers will not touch your program. Shareware provides an opportunity for good programs to sell without having big marketing budgets behind them. It gives you the opportunity to build your brand name recognition, and a reputation for quality and service.

Marketing your software using the shareware method does not mean you should avoid the retail channel. As shareware becomes more successful, some programs, such as Automenu, have made it onto retail shelves. Other companies, such as Datastorm Technology (ProComm) and Hooper International, Inc. (Finance Manager II), have begun to court the retail channel aggressively. On the other hand, XTree is one of the companies that includes shareware as a part of their marketing mix, in addition to retail.

Shareware profitability

My personal opinion is that about 85% of U.S. users won't register.

—Jim Hood,
author of PC-LEARN and The $hareware Marketing $ystem

Probably only 1 in 10 people using the software will register it.
—shareware author survey response

I have read magazine articles that state some shareware authors estimate more than 80% of the people using their programs have not paid the registration fee. Some responses from my shareware author survey also state the same thing. Unfortunately, there is no way to test the validity of these statements.

My survey of users showed that everyone that uses shareware *eventually* pays for it. However, the users that responded to my survey might not be typical. My user mailing list was based on user group memberships, people that responded to my ads in magazines such as *PC Computing* and *PC World*, and a list of names purchased from a shareware dealer. All of these users are shareware customers that have already registered at least one shareware program. I wonder whether or not someone would respond to a survey and say, "Yes, I use shareware all the time and I don't pay for it."

An interesting result of my user survey is that some users reported it might take up to two years from when they obtained the shareware until they paid the registration fee. Many people pick up shareware disks that appear interesting and then let the disks sit until they have time to look at them. With disks selling for as low as $0.99 from some shareware distributors, users feel it is worth a few bucks to buy disks that look interesting.

My opinion on user registrations

My personal opinion, and the opinion of many other successful shareware authors, is that users do pay the registration fee. My experience with shareware is that users do pay. Let us look at an example of a program marketed as shareware that might be expected to get few registrations. My surveys show that shareware dealers and authors feel that business programs get the most registrations and games the fewest. I publish a disk of games for very young children (Play 'n' Learn). Based on conventional wisdom, I should expect few people to purchase this software, yet I receive registration payments daily. People do pay for software they use. One of the biggest shareware authors publishes games exclusively and is very successful ($300,000+ in sales).

> *I see why most people don't make money from games. They don't put the effort into marketing or into making a quality game.*
>
> —Scott Miller,
> president of Apogee Software and a successful game author

> *Make sure you have a good, solid, USEFUL program.*
> —shareware author survey response

Users will pay for quality software that is useful and provides value to them. Keep in mind that what you feel provides value and what you think is useful might not be valuable and useful for most people. Do not overestimate the value and quality of your software. Another possibility is that your shareware might not reach the right people, or there might not be as many people as you think in need of the software you write. Do not overestimate the number of potential users.

As a consultant, I have talked with many authors that have overestimated the quality of their software and the number of potential users. For example, here is a quote from a shareware author that has this problem, *"I've seen my software on BBSs all over the country, but I've gotten only 18 registrations."* If you find yourself in this situation, take some time to find out why you aren't receiving registrations. Check with the BBS operators (or disk distributors) to find out how often your software is downloaded. This will give you a feel for the potential market. If your software is being downloaded frequently, then work to improve it and add features users need.

> *Writing a program that meets the needs of a significant number of computer users is not easy.*
> —shareware author survey response

Users do pay, but they do not want to buy a dead end. It is important to continue to improve. Do not wait to fix bugs. Add new features as users tell you about their needs. One question people frequently ask when they call to buy my software is, "Do you issue upgrades, and how do you let users know about upgrades?" Users want software that is kept current, that takes advantage of the features of current hardware, and that grows with them as their needs grow.

Users do pay if they understand how shareware works. Although the problem is decreasing, some users mistakenly feel they purchased the software when they purchased a shareware copy. Do not get mad at these people. Do your best to help them. Explain how shareware works. You can also help eliminate this problem by joining the Association of Shareware Professionals (ASP). ASP has been very effective in publicizing the shareware concept and in making users aware of how shareware works. (Information in joining ASP is available in chapter 13.)

Two key factors that will affect the number of registrations you receive are your professionalism and your trust in the user. When I talk with other ASP members, they often say that the most important thing they have learned is how to be professional. Being professional means having a quality product; having someone available to answer the phone (or at least having an answering machine); answering your mail in a timely manner; using printed stationery; and never sending out anything printed on a dot-matrix printer.

Trusting your users is important. People like dealing with others who they feel they can trust. If you feel someone does not trust you, then you tend not to trust that person. The entire shareware concept is based on trusting users to pay a registration fee. When you cripple or limit your software, you demonstrate that you do not trust users. Your users will then tend to not trust you and you will get fewer registrations.

Some people will use your software without paying for it. There is nothing you can do about it. Adding code to restrict your software will only hurt the majority, the ones that pay for software they use. Do not hurt the majority of users in an attempt to block a small minority.

Perseverance! It takes years to become known and for your product to spread.
—shareware author survey response

Don't expect much during the first 9 months to 1 year.
—shareware author survey response

Typically, the two biggest problems authors have concerning registration payments are a lack of patience and a lack of marketing. Shareware takes patience. It can take a year for a program to get into circulation. While some distributors will add your program to their catalog as soon as they receive it, others might take 6 to 8 months to evaluate it. Once users have your program, they might take anywhere from a week to two years before they look at it. I know it is difficult to hear shareware distributors say they are selling lots of your software when you are not getting registrations. Give it time. Three years ago I would get reports from PC-SIG showing they were selling 600+ copies of my Book Minder software every quarter. Yet, I was only getting one or two registrations a week and only a few of those were from PC-SIG customers. Now, new registrations come in daily and quite a few are from PC-SIG customers.

Marketing is as important as having a good product.
—shareware author survey response

Not working at marketing is the other major difficulty shareware authors have. My guess is that because there have been no resources available, except for the ASP, to show shareware authors the importance of marketing and how to do it, most have not realized how important it is. And, without marketing, the success of any program will be limited. In this book I provide you with the information you need to successfully market your software using the shareware method and make a profit. The key marketing point to remember from this chapter is that if you are serious about making a profit, you will need to put a lot of time into getting your program exposed. Get it reviewed by magazines. Talk about it in front of user groups. Most importantly, get feedback so you can continue to improve it. This is marketing and it is what this book is about.

3
Shareware design

I have used the term marketing many times and have provided a brief definition in the introductory section called About This Book. Marketing encompasses a range of functions, including determining what product you want to produce, promoting that product, getting customer feedback, etc. Marketing is essential to your software's success.

Programming is only 25%, marketing is the other 75%!
—Survey response from a shareware author who
expects to make over $300,000 in the next year.

Developing ideas for new software

To start you need a product—a software program you want to market and sell using shareware as one of your marketing tools. There are several ways to come up with ideas for good, marketable programs. These range from intuition to extensive market research. Although intuition works for some people, it is a poor basis for developing a program you might spend several hundred hours and many late nights working on. If you are going to put that kind of effort into a program, you might want to see whether or not there is a market for it before you start.

Although there are many approaches for identifying good potential products, for shareware authors two stand out. The first approach is one I suggested earlier. Write a program you need or want for yourself. The second approach is to conduct market research to find out what type of software and features other people need.

Approach one—write software you need

> *Write what you need—make it a labor of love—but listen to users and exchange ideas.*
>
> —shareware author survey response

Write software you need and want. To be successful it also should be a program with unique features not already available in other software. If you need simple word processing software, do not write it yourself. Unless you value your time at about $0.10 an hour, you are better off buying an existing word processing package. Unless, of course, you enjoy programming as a hobby. However, if you need a word processing feature not available in any other software, write the program! This is called market positioning.

> *Before entering the market make sure you have a good solid USEFUL program.*
>
> —Survey response from a shareware author with $50,000 in sales in 1989.

Market positioning

Positioning is what makes your product unique or creates its special "personality." It is the reason people will buy your software instead of another program. You could position your product based on its unique features. You could position your software as the low price alternative in a market that is served only by high-priced software. Your software might be the only one available in a niche market. A market position I often use is to publish programs that are the only programs of their type available as shareware. (Competition exists for these programs in the retail channel.)

Your software is not limited to one position. Look for new opportunities to extend the market for your software, find new niches, take advantage of pricing opportunities, and add new features. Also do this for software published by others. You can create add-on utilities that provide additional functions or make other publisher's software easier to use.

Here are some responses from my survey of shareware dealers in response to the question, "What new software would you like to see available as shareware?" A complete list of all responses to this question is provided in chapter 14.

> *More educational software—especially for in-school use.*
> —shareware dealer who sells 250 disks per month

> *Desktop publishing and more LAN*
> *(Local Area Network) software.*
> —shareware dealer who sells 4000 disks per month
> This was the most common response to this question.

GUI (Graphical User Interface) application.
—Australian dealer who sells 200 disks per month
Many dealers said Windows applications are needed.

Point-of-sale inventory programs.
—shareware dealer who sells over 10,000 disks per month

Approach two—market research

You could hire a market research firm to do the market research for you. Expect the cost to be $30,000 to $50,000. For most shareware companies, a more modest, do-it-yourself approach is needed. Actually, you are probably conducting market research continuously and might not know it. It mostly involves paying attention to what other people do and say. Here is how you do market research.

Researching your market

Market research involves answering five essential questions:

1. Who/what is your market?
2. How big is the potential market?
3. Is the market computerized and to what degree?
4. How many competitors are already in the market?
5. How does the competition measure up in price/performance?

I will cover these market research questions one at a time. Typically, you will get answers to many of them simultaneously. This is not a step-by-step process.

Your market

First identify and describe the market you want to serve. For example, lawyers need to deal with large amounts of information, so a possible new software program might be a database for cataloging case histories and law references. Because, in this example, the author is attending law school and would like to earn a little extra money, this is a good market for him to work in. It is also a good market because it is one with which he is somewhat familiar.

This brings up another important guideline. Do not start by getting into a market you know nothing about. It is not that you cannot be successful. The problem is that you will spend a lot of time learning about the market, learning the language of the market, and learning the needs and requirements of the market. Start with a market in which you have some experience.

A good way to identify a target market is to talk with people you know. For example, pay attention to what is going on around you at work and in any groups you are a part of. Talk to as many people as you can, but do more listening than talking. This includes BBSs, as well as face-to-face conversations. Go to user group meetings. Attend COMDEX or other computer shows to see what other products are available and identify areas other software publishers are missing. (See the chapter on trade shows.) Read a variety of magazines, not just computer magazines. Read newspapers, the *Wall Street Journal*, *U.S. News*, *Business Week*, trade industry publications, and anything that discusses what people and business are doing.

Look at the industry where you now work. What software would help people where you work? What problems do they have with the software they currently use? Problems are opportunities. Find areas in which people have a problem and solve that problem. This is how the legal student in our example probably became aware of the need for case note software.

Sizing the potential market

Once you have identified a market, find out how big that market is. You need to know the market size to decide if it is big enough to support your software and to help determine the price you will charge. Again, a good way to start is to talk to people. For example, ask them about the size of their user group or *special interest group* (SIG). Check the circulation figures of specialty magazines that serve the market you are targeting. Talk to representatives from industry trade associations. Do not be afraid to call trade associations (or any other group) and ask the person who answers the phone for help. Tell them what you are doing and what type of information you need. In nearly every case, they will be happy to help you.

Continuing with the legal software example, the first step would be to find out how many lawyers there are. An excellent research tool is the *Yellow Pages*. How many lawyers are listed versus the population covered by that phone book? Then extrapolate from the local numbers to determine the size of the national market. The same approach works for plumbers, real estate offices, restaurants, or any other industry.

Computerized markets

For business software you can find out how computerized your target market is by reading computer publications directed at business users. They sometimes publish statistical information on how many people in a specific industry have computers and how they use them. For a specific industry use the phone to talk to editors of industry-specific publications or send them a survey. Not only will it help you research the market, you will make contacts that might be useful in publicizing your software in the future.

Talk directly with people in your target market or with other companies that serve it. For example, before I wrote my software For Baseball Card Collectors, I stopped in to visit about half a dozen baseball card shops. I talked with both the owners and customers and learned a lot about what they needed. If you want to talk to professional people such as managers, make an appointment. You also can use a written survey and send it to all managers of specific companies in your area. How do you find their names? Call and ask the person who answers the phone for the name of the manager in charge of the area you are targeting.

For software aimed at the home market, talk to people in organizations you participate in such as church, Elks Club, and especially users groups. Ask people whether or not they find your idea useful. Do not be worried about giving away your ideas. Most people do not have the interest, initiative, or skills to do anything with it. If you are concerned that someone might take your idea, ask them to sign a nondisclosure agreement. A nondisclosure agreement is a contract that prevents the signer from using your idea or discussing it with others. Do not expect people with whom you have casual conversations to sign a nondisclosure agreement. It is generally only used with people you have a formal business relationship with, such as a marketing consultant or beta testers.

Competitors

Next, learn about your competitors. How many are there? This is fairly easy to determine. Check retail software stores. Look through shareware dealer catalogs. Read directories such as Bowker's *Software Encyclopedia* and *Dr. File Finders Guide To Shareware*. Read computer industry publications.

Competitor's price and performance

Find out how your competition measures up in price and performance. To do this, talk to people who use your competitor's software. Ask about it on BBSs and CompuServe or GEnie. If you find someone using a competitor's program, ask them how they like it; what good features it has; what problems they have had in trying to use it; what they do not like about it; and what they would like to change.

> *I advise new sharcware authors to be very modest in their expectations. Check the competition and market need before beginning.*
> —shareware author survey comment

Market research summary

When you are finished asking all of these questions and have the answers, comments, and whatever else people have to say, you should have a good idea of what your market is, what the needs of the market are, and whether or not this is a good market for your software. Pay attention to what people say and you will learn a lot more about the market than just the answers to the questions I have outlined. People like to talk about themselves and what they do. Just give them a chance. Get them started with a few questions and you will soon be an expert on your targeted market.

Other marketing questions

Based on your market research you can now design and write your software. As you are doing this there are additional marketing questions to be answered. What price should you charge? How do you promote your software? Do you want to restrict sales to one country or sell it internationally? The answers to these questions affect how you design your software.

While writing your software, keep in mind that you should leave open opportunities for multiple marketing approaches to your market. Do not limit yourself just to shareware. Even if you do not intend to use other marketing methods now, leave your options open for the future. For example, many people are reluctant to put an unknown new disk into their computer. Especially among novice users, there is a fear that the disk will somehow interfere with the data or programs that are already on their computer. Some dealers actively recommend that their customers not use shareware because of the virus scare.

Plus, there is a large group of people who do not know shareware exists. Do not eliminate these people as potential users by limiting your marketing efforts to shareware only.

The early promotion of your software starts with the five marketing questions—even before you decide what your market is and what software you want to publish. I do not mean you should buy ads or send out press releases before you know what your product is. The process of answering the five marketing questions begins to develop name recognition for yourself and a demand for your software. Anytime you talk about your software, you promote it.

> *Create the first version of a product yourself before starting the business, distribution, or financing. Then grow the product, business, and distribution.*
>
> —Bob Wallace, author of PC-Write:

Once you have a product and are ready to offer it for sale to the public, you need to decide what price to set.

Pricing your software

> *Shareware authors can increase registrations by offering quality software at low prices.*
>
> —shareware dealer

There's a large market out there. Low price encourages volume.
—survey response from a shareware author

Shareware dealers want shareware registration prices to be low. Magazines tout shareware as a way to get low-cost software. Some authors say you have to have a low price to get registrations. Does this mean you should price your software at as low a price as possible? No!

These people have different perspectives and reasons for wanting registration fees to be low. Low prices get people's attention. Disk distributors and magazines like to see low registration prices because it helps sell more disks and magazines. But why does an author say that low registration prices are the way to go?

A truism many people believe is that the lower they price something, the more of it they will sell and the more money they will make. In fact, many times the opposite is true for software. Sometimes the sales volume goes up when you increase your price. Yet, if you set too high a price, you could see your sales go to zero. Finding the right price is one of the most difficult problems facing anyone who has a product to sell.

Don't underprice.
—common survey response from successful shareware authors

The price you set depends on the type of software, who your market is, the quantity you expect to sell, your product's reputation and image, and the competition. The price you set also depends on how you want to run your business. Is it a hobby or does it need to make enough to pay the mortgage? Notice that I did not include product manufacturing cost as a component in developing the price. The correct price for your software has nothing to do with what it costs you to make it. Users do not buy software based on the costs to make the software, they buy software based on the value it provides them.

Before you start to think about what price you would like to sell your software for, keep one important rule in mind: It is easier to introduce a program at a higher price, then come down if necessary, than to start at a low price and move up. If you introduce a product at a low price and later increase the price with no change in features, people will think you are taking advantage of them. If you introduce a product at a high price, then reduce it, people feel like they are getting a bargain. How do you feel about being able to buy Quattro Pro for $99? (The best mail-order price used to be about $250.) What if Quattro Pro originally sold for $99 and Borland increased the price to $450?

If you feel you must have a low price to enter the market, identify the price as introductory and available for a limited time. The time period can be anywhere from a few months to a year. For shareware, because it takes a long time to get to users, I would recommend a year. At the end of the year you can reevaluate your price and make changes without damage to your product's image.

Look at prices of other software

Some authors purposely underprice their applications in an effort to lure customers away from established competitors. It doesn't always work. Knowledgable users may notice the small registration fee and dismiss your program without first testing it. My advice for pricing a shareware program:

if your product performs BETTER THAN the competition, consider charging two-thirds of the general retail list price;

if it performs AS WELL AS its rivals, you probably want to offer it at half the going rate;

if SLIGHTLY LESS POWERFUL, consider charging a third of the retail price for similar applications.

—Rob Rosenberger, Barn Owl Software

To set a price for your software, first look at your market and the pricing of other software in that market. If you are publishing business software, a price in the $80+ range is reasonable. Business software priced under $25 will typically be ignored as too cheap to be useful in business. It has nothing to do with quality of your software. This image is created because business users are used to paying $80 or more to get software that provides the functions and power they need. In a different market, such as educational games, $35 might be the top price you can get, and $15–$25 is a good average price range.

How do you determine the price range your target market finds acceptable? First, look at the prices of other software that your targeted market purchases. Browse the shelves of retail software stores. Read catalogs and mail-order advertisements in magazines. Check the registration prices of other shareware. Join ASP and talk with other authors who publish software for the same market. You want to determine both their registration prices and whether or not they are getting any registrations. Do not price your software based on programs that are not selling! (For more information on pricing, see chapter 14.)

When discussing your software, ask questions of ASP members and other software publishers. Be honest about what you are doing and the type of software you are publishing. If you are planning to publish a spelling checker, do not go to authors of other spelling checkers and tell them you are writing a word processor. When you are eventually found out, your access to feedback and help will be cut off as your reputation in the industry drops below sea level. Be honest and complete in the description of your software. Give other authors and publishers the option of deciding for themselves whether or not they wish to help you, especially if you are a direct competitor. Try to find software authors that serve the same market that you are targeting, but who have different products.

Estimate annual sales

Once you know the price range that is typical for your target market, estimate the volume you expect to sell in your first year. This can be tough to determine. Most people overestimate sales for the first year. Base the estimate on your market research, as discussed earlier. As an example, my first big-selling program was software for cataloging record collections (LPs, CDs, cassettes, etc.). I looked at the subscriber base of the largest publication for collectors at the time, *Goldmine Magazine*, and came up with 7000 record collectors as a starting number. At the time, 10% of the homes in the U.S. had computers, so this gave me an estimated starting base of 700 record collectors with computers. I also added to my figures 7000 radio stations with record libraries, about half of which were computerized. Having talked with many collectors at record conventions, I estimated that about 10% of the record collectors with computers would be interested in my software. This gave me an estimated first year sales of seventy programs, plus whatever I could sell to radio stations.

At the time, the only way you could get software comparable to what I offered was to buy dBASE, or a similar program, for about $400 and write it yourself. There was no established software serving this market that I could use for comparison. Figuring I needed about $7000 in sales the first year, I set my original price at $129.95.

After I sold a few copies and talked with more potential users, I discovered I had defined my market incorrectly. My market was the home user. Software costing more than $100 was too expensive for general home use. The $30–$70 range was typical for home-use software. Within three months I reduced the price to $59.95, where it remained for four years. To be fair to the users who had purchased the software for $129.95, I gave refunds for the $70 difference. At the end of the year, I had total sales of over $16,000—exceeding my $7000 goal by $9000.

Leave yourself a way out

The example illustrates several important points about pricing. First, do not make fixed pricing or marketing decisions. Remain flexible and make adjustments as you learn more about your market. Second, in many cases, setting a price is based on trial and error. Always leave yourself a way out of a pricing decision. You can always justify a price reduction by saying a higher-than-expected volume allowed you to decrease the price. It is almost impossible to increase your price without releasing a completely new version of your software.

Notice that, in the earlier example, I set my price at the higher end of the home market price range. If you think there is a chance you might want to sell your software through dealers and distributors, remember that they require discounts of 40–60%, and sometimes higher. If you price your software too low, neither you nor the dealer can make enough money from this software for it to be worthwhile to sell through the retail channel. You will be passing up the high-volume benefits of this marketing channel.

Look at software prices in your market

You should base your pricing structure on the type of software you are selling, as well as the type of market to which you are selling. You cannot sell a small utility for $100 nor a spreadsheet for $10. Both will be ignored. Conduct a pricing survey. Check retail stores, catalogs, advertisements, and other shareware to determine the price range of your software. There should be an overlap between the price range determined from your market survey and the price range based on the type of software you are selling. If there is not an overlap, you have found a marketing opportunity, or are trying to sell software in the wrong market.

Reputation has value

Another factor that effects price is reputation and brand-name recognition. WordPerfect Corporation can charge a high price for a software product because of their reputation for quality support. In most cases, brand-name recognition will not be a factor in the pricing of shareware, except for the larger shareware publishers.

Competition

If no competition exists, you can charge a higher price. Having no competition allowed me to go to the upper-half of the home software price range for my record collecting software. At the time, I effectively had no competition.

Can you make a profit?

You now should have a rough idea of the price range your market supports. Can you make a profit at this price? Look at your costs. If you are publishing a small utility that sells for $20 and you had planned for a $22 package, you will soon be out of business. How much profit do you need to make? That depends on your goals. Here is a typical breakdown of software publishing costs:

Product manufacturing costs	5–15%
(disk copying, manuals, etc.)	
Advertising & promotion	25–50%
Overhead and product development	10–20%
(office supplies, phone, electricity, etc.)	

Product support	5 – 15%
Cost of sales	5 – 20%
Profit	5 – 25%

Some of the items listed are direct cash expenses, such as product manufacturing costs and advertising. Others, such as product support and possibly cost of sales, require no cash, but use your time. What is your time worth? How much time are you willing to spend on the phone explaining your software to a potential customer? If you charge $10 for your software you might not want to spend much time with potential customers. If you charge $500, a couple of hours on the phone per sale is not too bad. Estimate both your direct cash expenses and the amount of time you need to put into your software. Then determine whether or not the price range, the market, and type of software will provide you with an acceptable profit.

Many people expect shareware to be inexpensive. It is true that if you market your software from your home solely using the shareware method, your overhead costs will be less than a retail software publisher's. You will not have big marketing expenses or the costs of maintaining an office. However, 87% of shareware authors sell less than $20,000 of software per year. On such a low volume, production and support costs per unit are very high. Do not be fooled into thinking that using shareware for marketing means you must charge a low price. By the time you run down to the quick print shop to photocopy your manual, copy disks one at time on your computer, and then hand package and ship each program, it might cost you more per unit for a small utility than it costs Lotus to ship 1-2-3.

The main advantage of shareware's low overhead is that it allows you to start without a lot of cash. If you have a computer, you can start a serious shareware business with less than $1000. Thus, your financial risk in starting a shareware business is very low.

How do other shareware authors price their software?

My survey of shareware authors asked about the registration fees they charged for their software. TABLE 3-1 provides a summary of the results. I have divided these results into five sections based on the annual sales reported by each author. Notice that the higher the registration fee, the more successful the author is. A few authors do sell several hundred thousand dollars of software per year charging less than $25 per program, but they are an exception.

Shipping and handling charges

You should charge extra for shipping and handling. It is considered a normal part of doing business by mail. Because nearly all mail-order purchases require an additional shipping and handling charge, people expect

Table 3-1

These results of a 1990 survey of shareware authors show the average registration fees shareware authors charged. Notice that the more successful authors tend to charge more for their software.

Annual sales category	# of authors responding	Avg. annual sales per author	Avg. registration fee per program
$50,000+	18	$447,920	$58.50
$10,000 – $49,999	19	$ 23,412	$57.50
$2000 – $9999	67	$ 4965	$40.50
$0 – $1999	56	$ 300	$26.20
Not reported	25	NA	$59.40

to pay it. When most people look at your price they will not include the cost of shipping and handling. Thus, a product that sells for $49.95 plus $5 shipping and handling will be seen as less expensive than one selling for $54.95.

When including shipping and handling charges in your documentation, keep it simple. For example, you might say the registration fee is "$49.95 plus $3.00 S&H, $8.00 for air mail outside the U.S." Your order form can then provide additional details such as the costs for expedited next day air service or second day air delivery. You might also wish to have a lower cost for shipping to Canada and Mexico as air mail within North America is less expensive than shipping a package overseas. Some authors, including myself, also charge extra for shipment to post office boxes. I make an exception for APO and FPO addresses. Military personnel do not have the option of using UPS. Since they must use the U.S. Mail and an APO or FPO box, I do not feel they should be penalized by paying extra. For example, I charge $3 for UPS ground shipment and $5 for shipment to a post office box. The reason is that the post office does not automatically insure packages. If you want to, you can get insurance, but that usually involves waiting in line at the post office. It uses more of your time, and you should be compensated for your time. I do not like waiting in line, so I mail orders that must go via U.S. mail without buying the insurance and consider the extra $2 the cost of self-insuring these packages. Depending on the value of your software, this amount will vary. You might not even wish to charge extra for shipment to post office boxes.

Tiered pricing

Tiered pricing is when you offer the user several levels of registration. For example, you might charge a base price of $20 to register as a user. If the user wants a printed manual, there is an extra $15 charge ($35 total). If the user wants to become registered, get a printed manual, gain access to telephone support, and get the next two updates at no charge, it costs $45. This is three-level, or three-tiered, pricing.

Some authors use a tiered pricing approach because they assume users who might not be able to afford the cost of a manual will still pay the minimum registration fee. Experience has shown, however, that when an author switches from a tiered pricing approach to a single registration fee that includes a manual and support, registrations increase. To maximize your sales, you need to make registration as simple as possible. A tiered pricing approach is complex, and the result is that users procrastinate because they have to make a decision.

Updates and upgrades

What is the difference between an update and an upgrade? An *update* provides a minor modification to a program, generally to fix a bug or provide an enhancement that is necessary for the program to function. An *upgrade* provides major modifications such as new features, expanded capabilities, an improved user interface, or greater speed. The documentation for an upgrade often requires a new manual. Updates might require no documentation changes or might only be discussed in a READ.ME file.

Pricing updates and upgrades

Updates are usually provided free to users who recently purchased software. The definition of "recently" varies from three months to twelve months. (The ASP requires members to fix serious bugs at no charge during at least the first three months after a user pays the registration fee. I recommend having this policy for your software regardless of whether or not you are a member of the ASP.) My shareware author survey showed that most shareware authors price upgrades to just cover their costs. A good strategy is to price upgrades high enough to cover your costs plus a small markup, but low enough that the upgrades will be purchased by most of your users. You want most users to purchase the upgrade because it is a pain to support two software versions. You should have some markup in your upgrade price to cover the costs of supporting the installation of those upgrades. Upgrades always cause a surge of product support calls. Whether or not you include a significant profit in your upgrade price depends on your objectives.

From my survey, it appears most shareware authors are working to build market share and user loyalty. A minimum or no markup on upgrades is appropriate in this situation. The survey also showed that those authors that sold upgrades priced them at about one-third of the full registration fee.

Site licenses

Your software should always include a license that permits the use of your software on only one computer at a time. (I cover user licenses in the legal section of this book.) A *site license* grants permission to use your software on more than one computer or on a network. With the growing number of networked computers, site licenses are becoming more important. The price of a site license usually varies depending on the number of computers the software will be used on and the terms of the license.

Site license sales are good for you because they bring a high volume of sales with little effort. Site licenses are good for the purchaser because they provide a means to use software on many machines without worrying about copyright infringement. It is also to your benefit to offer a reduced price per copy to encourage users to purchase site licenses and not use your software on multiple machines without your permission.

You can structure a site license so that the purchaser does all disk and manual duplication and provides support. This would be appropriate for an unlimited site license in which the purchaser can use your software on as many computers as desired. Another approach is to sell the purchaser a copy of your manual for each computer on which your software is used. In this case, the purchaser does all disk duplication and product support. A third approach would be to provide a complete registered copy of your software at a reduced price for each computer. Each approach requires a different price structure in which you balance your cost-of-sales with your time requirements.

Site license pricing

Pricing site licenses can be difficult because there are many different types of contracts that can be set up. Some of the responses to the site license question on the shareware author survey included:

I usually charge about $20 per computer.
—author who publishes a utility with a registration price of $35

$500 per site which can be applied as a credit toward other goods and services we offer. Mostly we sell manuals.
—author with a $130 program

Site licenses are 50% off per user.
—author of business software with a registration price of $50

Same as regular user.
—author of a $25 utility with $50 of sales in 1989

Site license fees vary depending on the negotiated contract.
—this was the most common survey response

A suggestion I can offer as a starting point for site license negotiations is a sliding scale. Start by offering software at your dealer price for the first few copies (1 – 10 machines); your distributor price for 10 – 20 additional computers; then reduce the cost per copy incrementally until you reach 500 copies. Above 500 copies, you might wish to charge a flat fee of $3000 or $4000. There are no hard rules for site license pricing. It will vary depending on the type of software, the market, and how badly the customer wants to use your software.

In a competitive bidding situation, you can lose a site license sale if you are priced too high or too low (a price that is too low makes it look like you do not know what you are doing). If you do not know what a good price for a site license should be, go for a higher price. If customers like your software, but do not want to pay the price you have set, they will generally negotiate with you. If a customer tells you that pricing was the reason for not purchasing your site license, while in some cases that might be true, most likely they preferred to purchase another program based on the qualities of that program.

Most of us want to believe that price is the key ingredient in making a sale. In reality, price is secondary. From the buyer's perspective, telling a vendor that they lost the sale because of price is the easy way out for everyone. It is also easier for the vendor to blame the loss of a sale on price (rather than having to face deficiencies or problems with the software). Sometimes sales are lost strictly due to high price, but in most cases, businesses buy what they want, not what is cheapest.

Site license pricing example

Here is an example of site licensing pricing:

Program list price	$100		
1 copy	$100	total price =	$100
2 – 10 copies	$70	total price =	$730
11 – 20 copies	$60	total price =	$1330
21 – 50 copies	$50	total price =	$2830
51 – 200 copies	$40	total price =	$8830
201 – 500 copies	$20	total price =	$14,830
501 + copies	$4000 one-time fee	total price =	$18,830 +

Based on this example, the "total price" column of the site license fees is calculated by totaling the number of copies ordered and filling up each cost "level." Thus, if someone ordered 12 copies of your program the first copy would be priced at $100 (level 1), the next 9 copies (copies 2 – 10) would be priced at $70 (level 2), and the last 2 copies (falling in the 11 – 20 copies range) would be priced at $60 (level 3). The total cost of a site license fee for 12 copies of your program would be $850.

1	copy at $100 level (level 1, 1 copy)	= $100
9	copies at $70 each (level 2, 2 – 10 copies)	= $630
2	copies at $60 each (level 3, 11 – 20 copies)	= $120
12	copies	= $850

The total site license cost for 501 copies would be $18,830.

1	copy at $100 (level 1, 1 copy)	=	$100
9	copies at $70 each (level 2, 2 – 10 copies)	=	$630
10	copies at $60 each (level 3, 11 – 20 copies)	=	$600
30	copies at $50 each (level 4, 21 – 50 copies)	=	$1500
150	copies at $40 each (level 5, 51 – 200 copies)	=	$6000
300	copies at $20 each (level 6, 201 – 500 copies)	=	$6000
1	copy at $4000 (level 7, 501 + copies)	=	$4000
501	copies	=	$18,830

Depending on the type of software you sell, the market, the competition, the type of customer, your objectives, and the general economic conditions, the numbers stated in the previous examples can dramatically change. I have shown them only as a typical example. As you gain experience, apply what you learn to improve your pricing of site licenses.

Even a lost sale can be valuable, if you learn from it. The most important factor is that you price your software at a level you feel comfortable with. Do not underprice your software to make a sale—you might find that you are unhappy with the sale at a lower price.

Whether or not you provide support for software sold under a site license is a key negotiating point. For example, you do not want to sell an unlimited site license for $500 and then have 2000 people call you for support. Your initial site license offer should include a contract in which you provide support only for one key contact at the site. That person then supports all the users at the site. (See chapter 9 for a sample site license agreement.) If a customer demands that you support individual users, I suggest you propose an hourly rate for that support.

OEM pricing

The final pricing topic I want to cover is OEM pricing. OEM is an abbreviation for Original Equipment Manufacturer. These are computer manufacturers, many of which bundle software with their computers. Typically, the computer manufacturer provides disk duplication and manuals and pays a small royalty to the publisher. The manufacturer might even write their own manual to go with the software they bundle with their computers. The royalty payment will typically be about 0.5% to 2% of the list price of the software. For you, it is a good deal (pure profit with no effort), but watch out for one hidden danger—product support. Can you afford to support your $50 software package on a $2 royalty payment? Be sure your OEM agreement spells out who is responsible for support. If you are, make your royalty payment sufficient to cover support costs.

Encouraging users to register

Shareware authors should not put threatening messages on disks regarding registration obligations of the user. Don't insult and alienate your customers.

—Survey response from a shareware dealer who sells 1500 disks per month.

Don't expect registration dollars unless you limit your program. You won't hear from users unless your program has a bug or is limited.

—Survey response from a shareware author with $800 in sales for 1989.

An an author, I know the feeling of having people use my software and not pay for it. I know they are using it because they call for help. I know how it feels when it appears that distributors are getting rich selling my software while I do not make a cent. As an author I know these feelings. I want to do something to stop unregistered users from using my software. I would like to teach them a lesson!

I have known many authors who have expressed feelings similar to these statements. I hope, with the help of this book, you can avoid these types of feelings—they have no basis in fact and they only result in setting up an adversarial relationship with the people who can best make your software a success. These are thoughts that lead authors to cripple their shareware, and you will find that none of the most successful shareware authors use any form of crippling or limitations.

One of the best ways to learn about methods that encourage users to register is to try using shareware programs written by other authors. That is what I had to do to put together the reviews section of this book. I found out how frustrating these methods can be sometimes. For example, here is how I reacted to the following situations.

Programs with delay screens that could not be bypassed got tossed in the trash after a few uses.

Programs with limited features or limited documentation did not get tested. I do not have time to figure out what worked and what did not. Besides, many other programs do the same things, so why spend time fiddling with limited software?

Programs with poor error message reporting created frustration and were usually quickly eliminated, especially if the author did not provide a phone number I could call to get the problem resolved.

Programs that immediately ran smoothly and had a simple installation procedure were used and tested.

Test a few shareware programs you might find useful. Pay attention to how you feel as you use or try to use them. What programs do you quickly throw out and why? What programs do you take the time to look at in more detail and why? In the end you will learn how you feel about various registration encouragements, and you might find a few good programs you can use.

Have you seen the shareware fonts that leave out the vowels? Talk about a useless package! Even worse are the ones that work only in obscure sizes in landscape orientation.
—a comment by a user

The best way to design a program is to make it so good that you will not need a registration screen to get people to register. However, most authors responding to my survey reported that they included something to encourage users to register. The following are methods for encouraging users to register.

Delay screens

The most common encouragement is a delay screen—the purpose is to make daily use of a program annoying. There are several ways to do this, some better than others.

You can put up a shareware message screen that will not go away until a preset amount of time has passed. This approach often is too annoying and users stop using the software before doing a complete evaluation. A variation utilizes a timer that counts down the time remaining until the main program runs. This is slightly better because it gives the user something that tells how long the delay is, but it is still too annoying to be effective.

You can use an introductory delay screen that can be bypassed by pushing any key. This is a good approach as it allows the user to get to the program quickly, yet still notifies them that they are using shareware. Some shareware authors do not like this approach because they feel it is too easy to bypass the shareware notice screen. However, must users will read all screens the first time they boot a program and the main purpose of this screen is just to make them aware they are using shareware (see below).

Display a delay screen that can be bypassed by entering a random number included in the screen display. This forces people to read the screen because they need to look for the random number.

Display the delay screen only a few times, such as once every twenty times the software is booted. If you want to use a delay screen, this approach creates the least interference to the user running the software, but it also provides the fewest reminders that this is shareware.

Use a delay screen that comes up only for the first 10 or 15 times the software is used. The problem with this approach is that if one person tries

SHAREWARE MAILING LIST

Distributed by:
HomeCraft Software
P.O. Box 974
Tualatin, OR 97062

```
THE SHAREWARE MAILING LIST MANAGER
Copyright 1988,1989,1990,1991 by
       HCP Services, Inc.
     All Rights Reserved
Portions Copyright 1982-1987 by
       Microsoft, Inc.
Version 1.02
```

3-1 Introductory screens, such as this one for *The Shareware Mailing List Manager*, are the most common method of encouraging users to register.

your software then passes the disk on to someone else, the second person might never know they are using shareware.

Use a combination of the previous examples. A possible combination would be an introductory screen that can easily be bypassed, and a delay screen that cannot be bypassed that comes up every thirty to forty times the software is booted. Note that standards established by the Association of Shareware Professionals state that a shareware program can have only one promotional screen. This screen can appear just once for each time the program is booted.

Other types of promotional screens

Instead of having a delay screen at the beginning, another approach is to leave a message on the screen when the user exits the software. The message provides a reminder that this is shareware and encourages the user to register.

An excellent way to remind users that they are using shareware is to include a small message in the border of every screen. For example, you could put "unregistered" or "shareware evaluation copy" at the bottom of each screen. This reminds users they are using shareware, yet in no way interferes with their use of the software. This is my preferred method.

Evaluation periods

Some shareware includes a built-in evaluation period. Each time the software boots a message is displayed stating, ''This is the __ day of a 30-day evaluation period.'' At the end of the evaluation period a delay screen requesting registration is displayed each time the software is booted.

Hogware

A negative approach for encouraging registration is to create memory-resident software that uses a lot of memory. The ASP calls this *hogware*. When users register they get a version that uses a much smaller amount of memory. The general result is that users delete the hogware.

Whatever negative approach you can think of has probably already been tried. Look at the results. Authors that cripple their software are obscure or no longer marketing their software as shareware. Successful authors use positive incentives to achieve success.

Limited (crippled) software

My survey of shareware authors found that over 20% provide a limited program or omit part of the documentation. As an incentive to register, the user gets the complete program and/or documentation when they register. It is tempting to do this. Why should people who did not pay for the program get all of it free? Experience has shown it is not an effective way to encourage registrations. Let us look at examples from both the user's side and the author's side.

Limited software—the user's viewpoint   As a user I have needed educational games for my young children. I wrote one program, Play 'n' Learn, but needed more. I noticed an alphabet game that was consistently on shareware best seller lists, so I bought a copy. When I tried to use it I found that only about a dozen letters worked. I needed to register to make all the letters functional. My kids never used it because it did not do much. On the other hand, I also got a shareware copy of Amy's First Primer. It was fully functional, and when I saw my kids having a great time with it, I bought a copy by sending the author the registration fee.

Limited software—the author's viewpoint   As an author I spent several years experimenting with different registration incentives. I would put several different registration incentives in different versions of the same program and send copies to various distributors. All of my shareware is marked with the dealer's name, so I can keep track of which dealer sold the program when I get the registration form. I tried fully functional programs, versions with limited features, delay screens that could not be bypassed, delay screens that could be bypassed, limited documentation, and several other incentives. I found that although the crippled versions created frantic calls from people that desperately needed to use the software, the greatest number of registrations came from software versions that were unlimited and easy to use. I got the fewest registration payments from crippled software.

Using positive incentives

One author responding to my survey wrote:

> *To encourage registrations I do the following: include a message that comes up each time the program is run which describes good reasons for the user to register. These are:*
> 1) *Latest revision without annoying message.*
> 2) *Manual / documentation.*
> 3) *Next major version is sent automatically when it becomes available.*
> 4) *The "retail" price is $79, but shareware users can get it for half price, $39.50.*

This author publishes utilities. Notice there are no threats and no messages about crippled software, only positive incentives to register. Negative tactics might ensure a higher ratio of paid users, but they also cut down on the total number of users. Do not worry about people stealing your software. If they are going to do it, they will do it, or else they will steal another program that does work all the time.

Surveys have shown that one of the biggest reasons users register is to get printed manuals and updates. The author just quoted offers both of those and is very successful.

Timers and counters

In my survey of shareware dealers, several suggested including a user timer. One dealer wrote, "I think the opening screen should show how many days the program has been used." Using a counter is fine, but do not put anything in your software that causes the software to stop after a specified time period. Some users will try your software for the first time then set it aside for a few months before they try it again.

More positive incentives

The best approach for encouraging registrations is to offer positive incentives. The following positive incentives have worked for other authors.

1. Paying registered users a "distribution" royalty. To do this the shareware version and the registered version must be the same. When registering, a user receives a disk with a serial number that appears on the first screen. This user can then share that disk with other users. When new users register, will the serial number identify where the disk came from so you can pay the appropriate royalty.

2. Offer an additional program or utility free when a user registers. This works very well. Many of the users calling to register my software ask me to be sure I include the free hard disk menu program I offer. They have noticed it and want to get it.
3. Offer a free premium bundled with the registered version of your software. A book related to your target market is an excellent premium.
4. Customize the registered version to include the user's name on the opening screen. Users love this. Having their name appear as a part of the title screen makes them feel important and increases their ownership feelings.
5. Offer free support for a specified amount of time. (Usually a year, but sometimes as short as sixty days.) This is very important because users need to feel they can get help when they need it. One of the advantages for users of shareware is the ability to call the author directly for help. This can be a powerful incentive.

   My author survey showed that nearly all authors provide free support either by phone or by mail. In addition, most authors provide support for users who are not registered. Although you have no obligation to do this, it is one of the best ways to sell your software. Users will not register software they cannot use. My experience has been that over half the unregistered users calling for help became registered users at the end of the phone call.

   Free support does not mean installing an 800 number and paying for the phone call. Free support means you do not charge for the time spent answering questions and helping users.
6. Some of the reasons users register have nothing to do with the direct incentives you offer. Some people will like your software and want to support your software company. Others feel a personal obligation to follow the rules or want to feel honorable about paying for software. Possibly the number one reason users register is because they like the author. You should do all you can to encourage these positive feelings and make your users feel good about registering your software. Even if you do not offer a printed manual, each registration you receive should be acknowledged. For example, I do not provide a printed manual for my Play 'n' Learn software (which sells for $10). Each registered user receives a new disk with the current version, even if it is the same as the shareware version, and a thank-you note. Figure 3-2 shows the thank-you note I send with Play 'n' Learn.

For additional information about incentives to encourage registration, see chapter 13, in which I have reprinted the ASP guidelines on crippling shareware. In addition, the program mentioned in this book has an example of the way I set up my disks to encourage registration.

```
                    HomeCraft Software
                       P.O. Box 974
                    Tualatin, OR  97062
                      (503) 692-3732


Dear Play 'n' Learn user:

Thank you for becoming a registered user of Play 'n' Learn.  I
hope your children are enjoying this software as much as mine
did.  I very much appreciate your support of my software and
shareware.  People such as yourself are what make user
supported software work.  Your registration will help us to
continue to improve Play 'n' Learn and develop new software for
very young children.

Enclosed is a disk with the latest version of Play 'n' Learn.
The files on this disk will directly replace those you
currently have without altering the award settings for Amanda's
Letter Lotto.


THANK YOU!



Steve Hudgik
President, H.C.P. Services, Inc.
HomeCraft Software
```

3-2 The best approach for encouraging users to register is to use positive incentives such as this thank-you note.

Be patient

I have mentioned it before, but it bears repeating. Be patient. Here is a quote from a letter I received in today's mail:

> *We are very interested in your software program "Book Minder" and have a shareware copy of version 1.4. Before sending the registration fee I have a question. . . .*

Version 1.4 of my Book Minder software was discontinued two-and-a-half years ago. It took awhile for this person to get a copy and try it. Be patient, sometimes it takes awhile for your program to reach people and for them to look at it.

> *Be patient and persistent. In the beginning keep trying. If it looks like it won't go, improve your software and keep pushing it at anyone that will look at it.*
>> —Survey response from a shareware author with $100,000 in sales in 1989.

> *Don't give up. Spend time to build in quality.*

—Survey response from a shareware author with $30,000 in sales
in 1989.

Don't expect much during the first 9 months to a year.
—Survey response from a shareware author with $16,000 in sales
in 1989.

Stick with it and respond to every letter and call you get.
—Survey response from a shareware author with $5,000 in sales
in 1989 and $9000 in the first half of 1990.

Be patient.
—the most frequent comment on the shareware author survey

Old versions never die

The biggest drawback of shareware is that once you release a disk, it keeps
circulating forever. I first released my Home Insurance software in 1986. In
1987 I released a completely rewritten and expanded new version and
increased the registration fee from $25 to $60. I still get registrations for
the old version, but I no longer have manuals or copies of the software, and
I do not wish to continue supporting the old version. What can you do to
avoid this problem?

The solution I came up with is to have the main program file display a
message beginning two-and-a-half to three years after the date I released
the software. The message informs the user that the software is out of date
and they should contact me for a new copy. To accomplish this the software is designed to check the date in the computer's clock. If it is more
than three years from when I issued the software, the out-of-date message
is put on the lower half of the screen every time the main menu is displayed.

The date-related message states that the software is out of date and if
the user will send the disk plus postage, I will mail them the latest version.
This message is also printed on the registration form I build into my software. By doing this I inform users that both the software and registration
fee might have changed.

I identify the software as date limited in the READ.ME file with the following paragraph.

> *This version is valid through 1993. It will run in 1994 and later,
> but at that time the software will display a message stating that
> it is outdated. We want to be sure that only current versions are
> circulating. This allows us to be sure that you get the best, most
> current software. If you wish to have software without this mes-
> sage after 1993, please send us your disk and sufficient postage
> to pay for a two ounce package (stamps are OK). We'll return
> your disk with the latest shareware version of the software on it.*

In putting a dated message in the software, I do not do anything to destroy files or prevent program operation. The program functions fine with no limitations. The user also can run the program without the date-related message by resetting the date in their computer to a year that falls within the functioning range.

Another important part of putting a date-timed message in the software is to provide updates to all shareware dealers every year. These updates extend by one year the date on which the message appears. This has the additional benefit of discouraging unauthorized dealers from selling old versions of my software because their disks will go out of date.

The two-year time period is important because it might take up to a year for your software to work its way through the distribution channel and another year or two before a user tries the software.

Primarily, I use the dated-method approach with my software for cataloging collectibles. I do not use it on my educational games or home financial software. Although I continue to improve these programs I have no plans for major upgrades, thus I am not concerned about old versions that continue to circulate.

Do not do this

A negative approach that is similar is to put true date limitations in the software. Some authors limit their software to thirty days of use from when it is first booted. Others stop the software from running when a specified year arrives. Similarly, some programs limit their data files. For example, a check-writing program that only allows 100 checks to be written. Others limit features, for example, a label-printing program that allows you to design a label, but not save your design for future use. These all fall into the category of crippled software. Putting out crippled software is bad business and limits the potential of your software. Magazines and reviewers will ignore it, and few users will use it long enough to get interested in registering.

The best way to get the most registrations is to write quality software that is easy to use and has no limits or crippled functions.

4
Distribution channels

In marketing your programs as shareware, one of the prime objectives is to get copies of your disk to as many people as possible. Do this by sending disks to shareware distributors, user groups, BBSs and electronic information services, and giving away as many copies as you can.

I remember reading about a major shareware publisher several years ago. I cannot remember his name now, but the article talked about how he gave away copies of his shareware to anyone who asked—30,000 copies in a year. "How can I afford that?" I thought. I would go broke just giving out disks. You do not have to give out 30,000 free disks, but you should be generous in giving away free copies of the shareware version of your program. For example, in the previous section, I mentioned that my READ.ME file states I will send a new disk to anyone who sends me their old disk plus postage. Most people do not send the disk or postage but I still send them a free copy of the latest version. It is good business.

Send out as many disks as possible to dealers.
—shareware author survey response

Send it out to everyone. Put it on every board (BBS). Talk it up.
—shareware author survey response

Yes, it is good business and simple psychology. If you help someone they will want to help you and will feel better about purchasing your software.

Giving out disks one at a time is fine, but then you cannot reach large numbers of people. You need the help of organizations that distribute shareware.

Shareware disk distributors

Disk distributors have their roots in the user groups and public-domain software of the early 1980s. For example, I was the librarian for the Portland Epson Group (in the days of CP/M computers). When I took over the user group library, it was a mess. We only had about 250 disks, but it was almost an impossible task for one person to keep the library organized and up to date. Since that time, for-profit disk libraries have replaced user groups as the primary means of distributing public domain software and shareware. By charging a fee for their disks, the distributors are able to hire a professional staff whose full-time job is to maintain the disk library.

Disk distributors range in size from companies that sell 50,000 disks a week to small home businesses that sell 50 disks a week. The quality of service provided by disk distributors varies. Some small distributors provide excellent service to both authors and users, but some large distributors never return calls and sell crippled software. Send copies of your program to as many distributors as you can afford. The more distributors that sell your program, the greater the number of people that will see it, and the more registrations you will get.

Include two important things with each disk you send out. First, a form that grants the distributor the right to sell copies of your software and that states the terms under which they may sell it. Second, a cover letter with a short description of your program, the system requirements, the amount of the registration fee, and your name and address. If you decide to limit your software, do not forget to describe those limits.

The permission-to-distribute form

The form granting permission to dealers and distributors to copy your software at a minimum should include the following terms.

1. Place a limit on the fee distributors and dealers may charge for copies of your software. A typical limit is about $10, including shipping and other charges. I have seen some authors that allow fees as high as $20 and as low as $3. Many of the major dealers charge $5 to $6 for a disk, so setting limits lower than that might restrict the distribution of your disk. Lower limits also make it difficult for dealers that supply retail stores to carry your software. Typically, shareware sells for $9.95 in a retail store. A distributor sells it to the retailer for about half of that. If your limit is under $10 it is almost impossible for the retailer and distributor to make a profit. Thus, they will not bother with your program. You do not want to eliminate this channel of distribution. It is growing rapidly and reaches people that do not generally buy shareware. I now get more registrations from users that purchased their disks from a retailer than I get from those that purchased disks directly from distributors.

2. State that the software must be identified as shareware. The term shareware must be explained so that users know the software is copyrighted and that an additional fee must be paid if they use it. This explanation should be displayed so that all disk buyers have the opportunity to read it. Thus, it should be in all catalogs and on all retail packaging or point-of-purchase displays. In the past, some dealers created problems because they did not identify the disks they sold as shareware. Intentionally or not, they led people to believe they were buying the program when they purchased the shareware disk. Yesterday I got a call from a user who was upset because he thought he had purchased a copy of my $59.95 program For Baseball Cards for $3. I also have users complain because they think I get the money they paid to the dealer and they want a refund when they pay the registration fee. The extent of both of these problems has become much less recently, largely thanks to the efforts of the ASP. The ASP vendor requirements recognize distributors only if they meet certain standards.
3. The distributor must stop selling copies of your program upon written notification from you.
4. None of the files on your disk may be modified in any way. All the files must be distributed together, although other files may be added.
5. The dealer must correctly use and identify any trademarks you have. This is important to protect your trademarks. If you do not protect them, you can lose them.

The previous five items are musts in any distribution agreement. In addition, you might want to include one or more of the following.

6. The distributor must provide you with copies of any catalog listing your software. This allows you to check the description of your software to ensure that it is correct. It also lets you see whether or not the catalog properly identifies the software listed in it as shareware.
7. Describe any restrictions on distribution of your software. For example, you might not want it sold outside the U.S. in order to protect the rights you have given or sold to foreign distributors.
8. The distributor must refer any customer complaints or problems to you. This ensures that customers are not getting upset over problems you never hear about, and it is a good idea. You need to know what users are saying about your software and whether or not they are having problems with it.

What you should provide to disk distributors

Based on my shareware distributor survey, the two biggest complaints shareware distributors have are that authors do not provide descriptions when they send a disk and that authors do not keep distributors up to date with current shareware versions. If you do not provide a description of your software with your disks, distributors will have to write their own for their catalogs. No one knows your software better than you. You are the person best qualified to write a description that will help sell your program.

Here are some of the comments distributors wrote on my survey forms in response to a question that asked what shareware authors could do to help dealers.

> *Send better cover letters with programs; list registration fee, system requirements, if it replaces earlier version and include a short description.*
>
> —dealer that sells 2000 disks per month

> *Listen to feedback on how to improve their product. Include a user survey on each disk.*
>
> —new dealer just getting started

> *Send new programs/new versions as soon as available with no strings attached—i.e., if a distributor is willing to catalog, copy and distribute at his expense, then the author should not request payment in any form the distributor.*
>
> —distributor with 1500 disks in his catalog

> *Leave room on disks for dealers to put their menu program and logo.*
>
> —dealer that sells 350 disks per month

> *(1) Keep us updated. (2) Send complete descriptions of products.*
>
> —most common response

Tracking sales

If you want to find out which distributors reach the users most likely to register your software, you might find it helpful to put something on your disks that allows you to track who distributed it. I include the name and address of the distributor, BBS, information service, etc., in a file on the disk. When my software boots it reads the name and address from this file and displays them as a part of the introductory screen. When the user prints the registration form, the software puts the distributor's name on the form. Combined with my asking people that register by phone where they got their shareware disk, I can tell which distributors bring me the most sales. Two notes of caution:

1. It takes a lot of work but I put the distributor's name and address on a disk to help publicize the people distributing my disks. I feel it is worth the extra effort. A simpler approach is to code your disks with serial numbers and keep track of which number is assigned to which distributor.

2. Do not eliminate distributors because you do not get registrations that can be identified as coming from disks they sold. I have supplied disks to distributors for over two years before I received registrations coming from disks they sold. In one case, I had received no registrations that I could track to a specific distributor until that distributor began supplying disks to a retail chain. Now this same distributor is the leader in generating registrations for several of my programs.

BBSs, user groups, magazines

Besides shareware dealers, you should provide copies of your shareware to electronic data services. My survey shows that most authors upload their shareware to CompuServe. You also should consider other services such as GEnie and Delphi. They all have substantial subscriber bases. With these services, you generally must upload your shareware using a modem. Although they do not charge for connect time, you still have to pay phone charges and it ties up your computer. The IBM Database Manager at Delphi will accept disks mailed to him.

Uploading your software to BBSs is also an effective way of getting it to as many users as possible. However, if you are an occasional BBS user, this can produce some big phone bills. Many of the larger BBSs accept software mailed to them on disk. Addresses for some of these BBSs are included in the distributor mailing list. If you do not have a modem or do not want to spend time calling individual BBSs, Andrew Saucci, Jr., runs a service that will upload your program to a variety of BBSs and information services. You can contact him by writing to him at:

641 Koelbel Ct.
Baldwin, NY 11510-3915

To learn about BBSs and information services I recommend reading *Dr. File Finder's Guide To Shareware* by Mike Callahan and Nick Anis (Berkeley, California: Osborne/McGraw-Hill, Inc., 1990). This book not only includes the phone numbers for several hundred BBSs, but it also provides detailed instructions on using both BBSs and information services. It is also packed with other information about shareware. If you are going to be involved with shareware, you should have a copy of this book.

I also recommend you send a copy of your program to Dr. File Finder, Mike Callahan. His address is:

Dr. File Finder
c/o FF&P Enterprises
P.O. Box 591
Elizabeth, CO 80107

Dr. File Finder's BBS number is (901) 753-7213

User groups

Send your disks to as many large user groups as possible. Start with the larger groups such as HAL-PC and the Boston Computer Society. The best source of user group addresses and BBS numbers is *Computer Shopper*. They publish a comprehensive list of user group addresses on a regular basis. Even if it is not an issue with user group addresses, pick up a copy of this magazine. It is filled with useful information for shareware authors.

Why do I recommend sending disks just to large user groups? In general, smaller user groups are not good sources of registrations. No one seems to know the reason for this, but the general experience has been that few registrations result from disks distributed by the smaller user groups. Unless your software has a proven capability of drawing registrations from these user group members, you will do better to stick with the larger groups that distribute large numbers of disks.

Magazines

How you approach magazines depends on your budget and the amount of time you want to put into marketing. The general experience has been that sending shareware disks to magazines for review will probably not result in a review. However, I feel it is worth the cost of mailing 30 or 40 extra disks.

It is worth the extra effort because sending your shareware disks to editors does make them aware of your existence. Keep in mind that if you do not put your software in front of these editors, no one else will do it for you. I also suggest that you include a printed copy of your documentation with any disks you send to editors. These are busy people and they will tend to look at software that can quickly be installed and used. Forcing an editor to print the documentation puts a barrier between your software and the editor.

Do not expect much feedback from the disks you send to editors. Over 85,000 shareware programs are already in circulation and a flood of new shareware is being released (150+ disks per month according to George Pulido, librarian for PC-SIG). Plus, the volume of retail software released each month is even greater. It is very difficult for your software to get noticed.

> *Increase the frequency of contact—if a major new version is released, send out a press release. Also include the product along with your release—even interesting releases often go without follow up, but I'll always boot a disk.*
> —editor of a computer magazine with 100,000 readers

Watch out for bugs

Be sure that your software is bug-free before sending it out to a lot of BBSs and user groups. If you are still in the bug-fixing stage, keep it among friends, local user groups, and local BBSs. It is always best and cheapest to do things right the first time. You do not want to send out a lot of correction disks to fix a bug. Serious bugs give your software a bad reputation from which it might be difficult to recover. If you are trying to get feedback, be sure to identify the disk as a beta test version or early version. If you do not properly identify your disks you might end up having some very angry users and a reputation for producing buggy software. Plus, remember that old versions will circulate forever, so you do not want a version with bugs in it to be widely distributed.

Selling through retail stores

Going through retail channels is difficult and expensive. You need brand name recognition and a list price that allows dealers and others in the distribution channel to make a reasonable profit. Next time you are in a software store look for the lowest-priced software you can find. You are unlikely to see anything priced under $25, and most items will be priced well above that.

I have already discussed the retail channel in the previous chapter, but there are a few additional suggestions I can add. If you are determined to try retail stores, first contact a few local dealers. Usually they will not be interested. It is not worth their effort. But if you have a unique program you might find one that is willing to give your software a try. Your best opportunity might be to get to know someone that works in a software store. You might be able to get them to put out a few copies of your software on a consignment basis. Do not think that this will not cost them anything. Shelf space has a cost and is very valuable. Some of the fiercest battles in retail stores are fought over shelf space. By putting your software on his shelf, a dealer might lose sales from another, better-selling program.

If you really want to get into the retail channel work, create both a *push* and a *pull* for your software. Go on the road and push your software at trade shows and conventions. Talk to dealers and distributors. Show them how they will make more money carrying your software. Become a nonstop whirlwind of promotion for your software.

Create a pull for your software by referring users that want to register to retailers. These retailers will order your software for the user. You run the risk of the user not bothering to buy a copy of your software, but you will also show dealers that there is a demand for your programs.

Pushing your software into the retail channel is tough and the risk of failure is high—especially if you do not have big money backing you. However, even if you want to stick with just the shareware channel, you should not hide from the retail channel. Many users feel more comfortable buying from a dealer, and many dealers will special order software for users. Be sure that your software is listed in several directories that dealers use for locating names and addresses of software publishers. I will discuss directories and will provide you with the names and addresses of several.

If you would like to contact computer dealers directly, here are several directories that provide the names and addresses of dealers.

Chromatic Communication Enterprises, Inc.,
P.O. Box 30127
Walnut Creek, CA 94598-9878
The cost is $495 for a list of 5135 computer stores in the U.S. A second list of 1126 Canadian dealers is available at $425. Their phone number is (800) 782-DISK or (415) 945-1602 inside California

CSG Information Services
425 Park Ave.
New York, NY 10022
The cost is $289 for a directory of 2800 computer/software resellers. A list of 5000 VARs also is available for $289.

PC Computer Source Book
21684 Granda Ave.
Cupertino, CA 95014
They publish regional listings of computer distributors and dealers. Each book costs $14.95.

The NACD National Directory:
The Official Computer Yellow Pages
NACD
13103 FM 1960 W. #206
P.O. Box 690029
Houston, TX 77269
This is a compilation of names, addresses, and phone numbers for distributors, manufacturers, publishers, rental companies, retail stores, service companies, VARs, and used-computer dealers. The cost is $69.95.

Selling your software internationally

It is difficult to get recognition from U.S. shareware authors; our letters go unanswered. —a shareware distributor in England

Offering your software to users in other countries can be a significant source of sales. Many software companies report that 25% to 35% of their revenues come from sales outside the U.S. My experience is that about 25% of my registrations come from foreign users.

Selling your software outside the U.S. does involve some problems. The biggest problems have to do with U.S. shareware authors not responding to inquiries from users outside the U.S. and the difficulties U.S. authors have with banking and currency exchange.

Unfortunately, many U.S. shareware authors do not respond to letters from foreign dealers and users. This has led foreign users to be hesitant about registering shareware with U.S. authors. In many cases, these users pay the registration fee by purchasing a money order in U.S. dollars. If the author does not respond, or even if the author sends the money order back, the user cannot get a refund. The money is lost, and the user gets nothing in return.

If you are not going to accept registrations from outside the U.S., then say so in your documentation. If you wish to include Canada but exclude all other countries, state that you accept registrations from the U.S. and Canada only. If you do not do this, you might build a reputation for unresponsiveness to foreign users. This reputation could hurt your business should you wish to expand outside the U.S. in the future.

If you are going to accept registrations from other countries, handle all correspondence, letters, and software shipments just as you do for your U.S.-based customers—with the exception that you should use air mail for anything you send. Answer all letters the same day you receive them. Ship all registered versions of your software as soon as possible. To cover the higher shipping costs, you can charge two to three times more for shipping and handling than you do for U.S. orders. Do not get carried away, however. One of the sore points with users in other countries is the high shipping and handling fees some U.S. authors charge. You should charge more, but be reasonable.

In responding to foreign inquiries for information, if you do not want to pay the extra cost of air-mail postage, you can require that your users pay for it. Ask your users to purchase International Reply coupons and include them with any request for information. International Reply coupons can be exchanged for the minimum postage of an overseas letter. However, these are relatively expensive for your users to buy. For example, a coupon costs 60 pence ($1.20) in the U.K. I do not recommend this as a good way to encourage foreign users to register. The best advice is to treat foreign users the same as U.S. users. This means you pay the cost of air-mail postage. The same rule discussed earlier applies here—the easier you make it for users to register your software, the more registrations you will get.

Getting paid—credit cards

The easiest way for you to handle registration fees is to have your customers use VISA or MasterCard. To accept credit cards, you need to establish yourself as a VISA/MasterCard merchant. (I discuss how to get merchant status for credit cards in chapter 8.) The credit card company will handle the necessary currency conversion.

Do not expect all foreign users to have credit cards. For example, some countries do not allow their citizens to have VISA and MasterCards that are valid internationally. This was true in Argentina for quite a while. In other countries with differences in culture, very few people have credit cards. They are not an accepted way of doing business in that culture.

Getting paid—checks and money orders

An alternative is to require checks, or money orders in U.S. dollars, drawn on a U.S. bank. Be sure your documentation specifies that the check must be drawn on a U.S. bank. If you do not require the check or money order be drawn on a U.S. bank, you can get into some hefty bank fees when you try to cash it. This has happened to me only once. I received a $67 check in U.S. dollars drawn on an Italian bank. My bank charged me $20 to cash the check. The Italian bank added another $20 in fees. I ended up with $27 out of a $67 registration payment.

The ease of cashing a check or money order drawn on a foreign bank depends on the country from which the check comes. Most of my foreign registrations come from nine countries: Canada, Australia, New Zealand, England, Ireland, Germany, Sweden, Norway, and France. I have never had any problems with checks from these countries, regardless of whether or not they are in U.S. dollars or the local currency. To handle checks from foreign countries, you need to work with a bank with a foreign currency department. In addition, as with most other banking services, you need to establish a personal relationship with your banker. The manager of the branch you visit should know you personally and feel comfortable working with you. You know you have accomplished this when the branch manager says hello to you in a grocery store (or other non-banking location).

Getting paid in cash

Another alternative is to ask people to pay in cash. You can request U.S. dollars or accept foreign currency. You can then get the foreign currency converted at your local commercial bank. Do not add a hefty surcharge to cover the cost of currency conversion. In many cases, you can convert cash payments in foreign currency at about the same rate your bank charges to handle a credit card transaction.

Accepting registrations through foreign dealers

You can also work through a foreign shareware disk dealer who is set up to sell registered versions of software. This provides users with a local contact for purchasing your software. And, it eliminates the problems of currency conversion for you. If you are interested in finding out more about this type of arrangement, write to the foreign shareware distributors.

Encouraging foreign registrations

If you are going to pursue foreign registrations, make foreign users as comfortable as possible. Put a statement in your documentation or READ.ME file that welcomes foreign users. Let them know you will answer their letters ASAP and that you will return their phone calls (if you provide phone support). Overseas calls are not as expensive as you might think. If your software includes $ or anything else specific to the U.S., make a version that includes £ for the U.K. or eliminate the $ in foreign versions. Also keep in mind that most countries use a different format for the date. Instead of mm-dd-yy, most countries use dd-mm-yy.

To encourage foreign users to register, I even go as far as offering to accept personal checks in their local currency. My bank can handle most foreign checks, so this is not a big problem. In two years, I have received only a few personal checks in a foreign currency, but making this offer is a good marketing strategy that shows I am seriously interested in foreign registrations.

International support

You must support foreign users the same way you support U.S. users. Here is a comment I received from a user of my software in London:

> I wish U.K. suppliers of hardware and software were as efficient and helpful as you.

If you get letters with comments like that, then you are properly serving the foreign market. Just remember to treat everyone the same, provide them all with super service, and you will be going in the right direction.

Following are some helpful hints for doing business internationally.

There is a helpful booklet from the post office on international postal rates. Ask for Publication 51, International Postal Rates and Fees, at your local post office.

There is a helpful booklet from the post office on international postal rates. Ask for Publication 51, International Postal Rates and Fees, at your local post office.

When mailing catalogs, software, or other small packages to a foreign country use small packet air mail. It is significantly cheaper than regular air mail.

Include the words "All Rights Reserved" as part of your copyright notice on your disks and in your manuals. Some countries require these words to protect your copyright fully.

According to the Commerce Department, to provide complete protection for your copyright on an international basis, you should also mark any package containing software with the letters GTDR. This stands for General Technical Data Restricted.

5
"Free" publicity

I once saw a CompuServe message from a shareware author that contained the following listing:

Best response rates:
 Review in magazine (even negative review generates sales)
 Direct mail
 Large ad in major publication
 Small ad anywhere
 Trade show/convention
 Classified ads
 Listing in a directory

Reviews *are* the best means of increasing sales. A good review can provide the initial boost it takes to get started, and has done so for many shareware authors, including myself. How do you get a magazine to review your software? You must tell them about your software. Do not wait for them to find it in a shareware library. How do they find out how good your software is? You tell them.

Here is a key point: Announce all of your products with a press release. Even if your software has been out for a while, it is better late than never. If you have never sent out a press release, get ready to write one now.

Writing a press release

I've never seen a press release from a shareware author that I would classify as outstanding.
 —computer magazine editor

In my survey of magazine editors, almost all said they wanted press releases from shareware authors. However, the quality of the press releases they have received in the past from shareware authors was described as poor. Here is one magazine editor's response to a survey question about what shareware authors could do to improve their press releases.

> *Stop using DOT-MATRIX printers! Use laser printers with a proportional typeface; anything less looks unprofessional. Be sure to include capsule overviews of the product described, along with addresses, phone numbers, PRICES and requirements to run the program. This is obvious, but use a spelling checker (sometimes even PR writers forget to do this, it seems).*
>
> *Pay attention to grammar. Most importantly, lead with the most important information. If a press release rambles to its key information, it has likely lost its reader a few paragraphs back. Finally, don't over-jargon the reader and keep a humorous touch.*
>
> *I have to read a lot of press releases, and nothing turns me off faster than the things I mentioned. We receive hundreds of press releases a week. Frankly we look for excuses to pitch them in the trash (or else we'd have time for nothing but poring over press releases).*

Since only a few of the hundreds of releases can be printed, editors try to select those that are concise, well organized, and well written.

> *Make press releases more concise, easier to read. Include more facts and features (remember, everybody calls their program the best). What sets this program apart from others like it?*
>
> —survey response from a magazine editor

Remember, magazines are always constrained by time and space. Include a short version of your press release, possibly in a cover letter, and a longer, more detailed version. Make it easy for editors to reprint what you have written; it saves them time. They will tend to make a quick judgment of whether or not your product will interest their readers and how easily your press release can be edited down to the essential information. Concise writing and careful organization of the press release are crucial. If you have black-and-white photos, slides, or screen prints of your products in action, be sure to include them.

Write two versions of your press release

First, write the long version. Put it on company letterhead or have special letterhead printed. Then write a one-page version. If you provide two versions of your press release, you make it easier for the editor to find a space where it will fit. I always write a one-page cover letter on my company stationery that provides a short summary of the press release. The longer press release is typed on stationery with a big green "NEWS" banner across the top and is usually just under two pages long. Try not to write press releases longer than two pages. If editors need additional details, they will call you.

Since I am giving examples of how to write press releases, I should mention the success I have had with my press releases. During the past twelve months, my software has been reviewed or discussed in articles in national publications or syndicated newspaper columns at least once every month. During the past week, I have been interviewed twice for articles about my software and contacted by two publications that are reviewing my software. Of these four publications, only one is a computer publication (*PC Sources*); one is a new magazine (*Business Week*); and the other two are special-interest magazines.

Getting back to the guidelines for writing a press release, you should include only the necessary details in your press release. Do not use superlatives or make extravagant claims that cannot be verified. Editors have seen it all and extravagant claims and superlatives only detract from the chances of your press release getting published.

A step-by-step guide to writing press releases

The press release must tell us what it is about the product that sets it apart from the competition.
                                    —survey response from a magazine editor

Professionalism. I cannot emphasize that enough. Editors can get nervous if the company looks like it's fly-by-night. The product might look interesting, but if it looks like the company's going to fold—they don't have letterhead, it's printed on a dot matrix printer—we don't want our readers to call a company a few months later and find nobody answering the phone. It makes us look bad.
                                    —Marilyn Young, *Shareware Magazine*

Here is a step-by-step description of what a good press release looks like (see FIG. 5-1 for an illustration of a sample press release).

A Give a date when the information in the press release may be published. Some editors mentioned that they like to receive press releases two to three months before the product will be available to accommodate publishing lead times.

B Give the name of someone who can answer questions. This most likely will be you, but, if not, be sure it is someone who is knowledgeable and very familiar with your software. When I was talking with Marilyn Young, editor of *Shareware Magazine*, she mentioned she sees a lot of press releases that do not include a phone number. Do not forget to include your

5-1   This press release was written for an earlier version of this book. It illustrates the key
components of a good press release.

phone number. Even if you only have an answering machine, give your
phone number; if someone from a magazine calls, they will leave a message.

C Magazines like to keep their readers up to date with the latest information. They are looking for new software, new ideas, and anything that is on
the leading edge of the market. The word "new" will tend to catch an edi-

tor's eye. If your press release is announcing a new product, include the word "new" as one of the first words in the first paragraph.

D List the computer system(s) with which the software will work. This allows editors to immediately see whether or not your software runs on the systems their magazines cover. Incidentally, you should differentiate the magazines to which you mail press releases. It is a waste of time to send a release about a PC-only program to *MacUser*.

E Give a short summary of the advantages of your software. Highlight the key benefits and feature. Do not try to cover everything. Your press release needs to be focused. What are the unique benefits of your software and why would the magazine's readers be interested?

Describe each technical feature of your software and then explain the benefits of that feature. Do not just list features. Editors and potential users are interested in benefits. Ask yourself why someone would pay for your software. Why should a user put time into learning to use your program? If you already have people using your program, conduct a survey or ask about it when they call for help. Find out why your current users like your program and include that information in your press release.

When describing the benefits of your software, be specific. Terms such as faster, cheaper, and better are all open to debate. Everyone makes claims for their software. Document your claims and make them quantitative, such as 25% faster.

In describing the benefits of your software, the key question you are trying to answer is: Why should a user choose your software rather than similar programs?

As a salesman, I was once giving a presentation to a group of engineers at a utility company. I was working to sell a software package priced at $250,000. I was well prepared, with slides and demo programs, and I was rolling along feeling good about my presentation when one of the engineers stumped me with a simple question. "Why should we buy your software instead of someone else's?" I knew all about the features and benefits of the software, but I could not answer his question. I did not get the sale, but I always knew the answer to that question before starting another presentation. You should always know the answer to that question and put it in the first paragraph of your press release.

It is a good idea to write your press release so that the first paragraph and last paragraph will stand alone if the editor is really cramped for space. Typically, the first paragraph should describe what type of software yours is and the key benefits it provides. The final paragraph gives your phone number, address, and ordering details.

F Except for the rule about repeating the contact information in the final paragraph, always write press releases in an inverted pyramid, i.e., from most important to least important. Describe secondary, less important features later in the release. Descriptions of less important features might need to be edited out to fit the available space in the magazine. Try to write your press release so that it can be cut off at the end of any paragraph and still make sense. Newspaper stories are written in this manner. The writer gets all the key information into the first paragraph. The next few paragraphs discuss secondary information. Once all of the key information has been concisely presented, the writer will go back and discuss the story in detail from the beginning.

G The last paragraphs should describe other products such as add-on modules because this is the information most likely to be dropped. Many times, if you do offer add-on products, these can be discussed in a separate press release. A press release should be concise, short, and to the point. Discussion of add-on products might take the editor's attention away from your software's key benefits and features.

H At the end of your press release, give a complete description of the system requirements. These include the types of computers the software will run on, the earliest version of DOS the software will work with, memory requirements, hardware requirements, and any requirements for additional software.

To finish the press release, include list prices and purchasing information. Provide an address and phone number the magazine's readers can use to contact you.

Choosing target publications

First, identify the magazines your potential customers read. How do you do this? You can ask them. When you first release your shareware to a limited group of people, ask users who register about the magazines they read. If someone expresses interest in your software in a BBS message, ask them what magazines they read.

Sometimes, it might be obvious what publications your users read. If you have written a utility program, then computer magazines immediately come to mind. If you have written a specialized program, for example, software to track thoroughbred genealogy, then you should be aware of the special interest magazines that serve this market. One of the most effective approaches is to send press releases to publications and newsletters that focus on a special-interest area in which your software is useful. Sending press releases to noncomputer magazines generally gets more attention because computer software is unusual to them and their readers. For example, I send press releases for my record cataloging software to *CD Review, Audio, Stereo Review*, and about a dozen other publications related to music and record collecting.

If you need help finding publications that target the audience you are trying to reach, use a directory of magazines. A good directory is *The National Directory of Magazines*, which is published by Oxbridge Communications, Inc., at (800) 955-0231 or (212) 741-0231. Another excellent source is the *Standard Periodical Directory* also published by Oxbridge

Communications. You should be able to find these or other similar directories at a public or university library.

Most people are too stingy with their press releases. Be sure you cover all publications whose readers might be interested in your software. For example, this could include the *Wall Street Journal, Business Week,* and *U.S. News* for business software. Although they might not publish a news announcement based on your release, you will increase your name recognition. When they need to interview someone concerning shareware or your type of business software, they might remember your name and call you. I have been interviewed twice concerning software for home use on this basis.

Where to send press releases

If possible, a press release should be addressed to a specific person. It is alright to send releases to "News Editor" or "Software Review Editor," but if you can get it directly into the hands of the person interested in your type of software, you will be better off. It is important to find out who is interested in your type of software. Hardware editors are not interested in software press releases. Entertainment editors do not want to see sales management software.

How do you find out who the right person is?

First look at the masthead. If it's not evident from that, probably the person to call is the editorial assistant. Just ask for the name of the person who takes care of the software press releases. Or ask for the person who's in charge of software product listings. Or talk to the receptionist. When you call you might also double check editors' titles and the spelling of their names.

—Marilyn Young, editor of *Shareware Magazine*

Read the magazine and pay attention to who writes articles and reviews about your type of software.

—computer magazine contributing editor

Both of these are excellent suggestions. A third approach I have used is to ask one of the advertising salepeople. If you get a call from a magazine trying to sell you ad space, ask the caller to help you identify any editors who might be interested in your software. Salespeople are usually eager to please potential customers and generally will be glad to help.

How often should you send out press releases?

You should only send out a press release when you have news. Some companies send out a press release everytime someone in their company burps. Editors eventually start to recognize the return address as coming from a company that has nothing important to say. To get the most impact from your press releases, only send them when you have something to announce.

For example, always send out press releases when you announce a new product or update. If your company is doing something interesting related to an industry trend, you might also send out a press release. Do not send press releases to announce that you have hired someone, unless that person is a recognized name in the industry. Do not use press releases to announce minor changes in your software or an upgraded manual.

Local publications

Include local and regional newspapers and magazines on your press mailing list. It is often easier to get a feature story written about your software in a local publication than in a national magazine. These stories are excellent sources of quotes you can use to promote your software. Here is an example taken from a newspaper review of one of my programs.

> *I found data entry to be simple and the file saving process to be crisp and speedy.*
> —*Monterey Herald*, February 26, 1990, writing about HomeCraft's software *For Record Collectors*

You can use quotes such as this to build interest in your software and to demonstrate to larger publications that you have a worthwhile product that is getting attention. Quotes from reviews or articles are your most effective means of selling your software to both end users and the press.

Should you include copies of your shareware with your press release? Some editors in our survey said they would like copies of shareware with press releases. Be careful with this technique. Do not send out an incomplete version or, if you must, be sure to identify it as an *alpha* or *beta* version. Be aware that a magazine's testing of a beta version can result in negative comments.

If you send copies of your shareware to reviewers, include a printed copy of the documentation. Reviewers are generally working to meet tight deadlines. Not only will they appreciate having the documentation immediately available, if they are running out of time (as is typical), the program with the preprinted documentation is more likely to be reviewed.

Usually, it is not worthwhile to send your complete software package (registered version) to editors unsolicited. I have tried it several times and it has never prompted a review or article. Sometimes the magazine returned my package with a statement saying in effect, "Don't call us, we'll call you if we want your software." And they will call. If something happens that makes your software interesting, the magazine will call. If it is important, they will give you their Federal Express number so you can ship them a copy as soon as possible. Unless there is something unique about the way your software is packaged, or what you have included in your package, a press release is probably more effective.

Giving out review copies of your software

When someone requests a review copy of your software, do not be stingy. Give out free copies of your complete registered version to anyone who asks, even if their name or publication is not familiar. You never know what will come of it. Reviews that catapult your software into six-figure sales can come from unexpected places.

When you send copies of your software for review, never expect to get them back and never ask for them back. It makes you sound cheap and unprofessional. Even if reviewers offer to return your software, tell them they can keep it or donate it to a nonprofit organization, if they wish. Usually, once they no longer have use for it, magazines destroy software they have received for review. They do this because they do not want to be seen as a source of software that is sold in a gray market. This happens in many other industries such as the music business (i.e., you can buy promo copies of records and CDs).

Other ways to get free publicity

A multipronged approach to getting free publicity is often the best. If sending press releases and review copies of your software does not get a response, try some different techniques.

Writing articles

A good approach for getting free publicity is to write magazine articles yourself. These should be related to your product or be articles about your users. (To do this, interview users. It is a good way to get both feedback and an article.) The best place to submit these articles is to noncomputer publications. Often, these publications do not have anyone qualified to write about computer-related topics and you might find your article is happily accepted.

Using directory listings

Directories are books that list available software. Some just contain listings of program and publisher names, others include descriptions of software. Nearly all sell enhancements to listings that make your software more noticable. If you would like to see what a directory looks like, you can usually find them in major book stores such as B. Dalton and Waldenbooks.

You will not get many sales from a listing in a directory and any leads will generally be of poor quality. However, most directories list your software for free. Purchasing the listing enhancements, such as additional headlines or bold type, generally is not worthwhile. The main advantage of being listed in the top directories is that a dealer can then look up your name and address should a customer request your software be special ordered.

The following directories will list your software at no charge.

Software Encyclopedia
R.R. Bowker
245 W. 17th St.
New York, NY 10011
(212) 645-9700
(fax) (212) 242-6987

TPS Software Directory
Technical Processing Services
Montague Publishing Co.
P.O. Box 3159
Gardena, CA 90247-1359
(213) 770-6929
This company is also interested in receiving press
releases and provides software testing services.

Business Software Database
Information Sources, Inc.
P.O. Box 7848
Berkeley, CA 94707

Microleads
Chromatic Communications Enterprises, Inc.
P.O. Box 30127
Walnut Creek, CA 94598

To be included in the directories listed, write to them and request the required forms for a listing in their publication.

There are also industry-specific publications that specialize in computer news and publish yearly buyer's guides. You should make it your business to be aware of all publications that target markets related to your software. Do not hesitate to purchase a magazine that might target a market related to your software or area of interest.

Give away your software

One of the best ways to build a user base is to give away copies of the registered version of your software. Give it away to any group that is interested and from whom you might get free publicity. For example, be very liberal in giving away copies to user groups. A user group can use your software as a prize in a raffle or as a door prize at a meeting. You get publicity because your software will be announced as "the prize" during the meeting.

One of ASPs members, Herb Kraft, has made an excellent suggestion that provides another approach to giving away software. He has an idea that helps authors get publicity for their software and, at the same time, helps small BBSs to continue to operate. He suggests authors donate copies of their software to BBSs to give away as a part of a fund-raiser. This might be a great idea. By posting the name of your software "prize" as an announcement on a BBS, your software gets free publicity. You might try contacting some of the BBSs you would like to support and see if they would be interested.

Keep your mind open and watch for opportunities. I have donated copies of my software to my children's elementary school for prizes at their annual carnival. I have given software to church fund raisers, charity auctions, and other fund raisers run by nonprofit groups. It takes time, but each copy is another small step in the process of building the reputation and name recognition of your software.

6
Paid advertising

The best form of advertising is a quality product. If you do not have a quality product (software), then do not use shareware as one of your marketing tools. You will only reach a market unwilling to pay for your product and you will only damage your reputation as a software author.

> *Advertising does a good job of reaching a specific target market.*
> —shareware author survey response

Many shareware authors do not consider advertising. In my survey of shareware authors, only 77 authors out of the 210 that responded (36%) reported having tried advertising. Do not rule out advertising without considering your market objectives. Shareware reaches a certain group of people who might be only a small percentage of your potential users. Advertising will help you reach more.

Of the 77 authors who said they had tried advertising, 40% said it had some value, 60% said it was a waste of money. From these results we might conclude that advertising is not worthwhile. This is not a valid conclusion. Although these authors did not have good experiences with advertising, it is possible they were not approaching it correctly. Two important ingredients are needed for achieving good results from advertising. For it to be effective, it has to be directed at the correct target audience and the ad itself must achieve the objectives you set. Notice that I did not say the ad must sell a lot of software.

Advertising basics

Discard the notion that readers of magazines with the largest circulations are your ideal buyers. Start by finding out what your current users read.

Also, find out where other software companies—selling the same or similar products as you—have advertised on a regular basis (for more than six months).

To get a feel for what types of ads work and what types do not, look through the direct marketing section of any major computer magazine. Take notice of the ads that catch your eye and the ads that you actually read. To gain an understanding of how they work, pay attention to those techniques that make you want to respond to the ad. Try to apply the same techniques in your ads.

When people respond to your ad, follow up fast. The longer you take to get information to someone, the less likely they are to buy (or they might have already purchased software from someone else). A good policy is to respond to all requests for information the same day you receive them.

Choosing a publication

In choosing a specific publication, know your potential users. Determine the demographic characteristics that distinguish your likely customers. (*Demographics* are statistics that characterize a group of people. This information might include age group, personal interests, education, and job experience.) Then look at the advertising in the magazine to find out who its readers are and match their characteristics with your existing customers. For example, are they business or home software users? What types of things do they buy? How much time do they spend with the computer? Do they buy or plan to buy products similar to yours? The quality of your target audience is of prime importance.

Magazines can give you survey results that provide a profile of their readers. Read these magazines (you might already be a subscriber to the appropriate publications). If you have written software to meet a need you had, then people that read the same magazines as you might have the same need.

Publications can also tell you how their readers use their PCs. They can tell you whether or not their readers make recommendations on product selections and whether or not they actually make buying decisions. (It is important to reach the decision-maker, especially when selling software to businesses.) Publications can also tell you what their readers do with the magazine. Whether or not they read and discard it or keep it as a reference has a big impact on the durability of an ad. A magazine that is retained is the first place a buyer will go when making a buying decision.

You should be aware, though, that the information you obtain might not be completely reliable. For example, every publication I have talked to claims to reach decision-makers. They are not lying. This is what their surveys tell them. But, in 10 years as a salesman, I found many people that like to say that they are the decision-maker, but few who really are. There is no way for you to tell whether or not you are reaching a decision-maker other than by trial and error.

Finding out how well a magazine's audience will respond to your software is also a trial-and-error process—in most cases. About the only way to get a feel for how well a magazine will work for your software is to gauge the response you get after the magazine publishes your product announcement or does a review of your software.

Choosing specific media

Up to this point, I have been talking about magazine advertising. However, a variety of media is available and the same advertising principles apply to all of them. The different types of media you could advertise with include the following.

- Radio/TV
- Newspapers (national and local)
- General-interest magazines—*Newsweek*, *People*, etc.
- Computer magazines—*PC Magazine*, *Byte*, *PC World*, etc.
- Special-interest magazines—hobby magazines, industry journals
- All advertising magazines—for example, *Computer Bargain Line*
- Card decks
- On-line services—for example, *Prodigy*
- Disk advertising

The closer you match an audience to your typical user, the better response you will receive. Radio and TV are very general media. Products that everyone uses, such as soap and breakfast cereal, do well, but you almost never see software advertising on TV. Newspapers are also general in nature, but some have targeted audiences. You will see some advertising, though, by the major software companies in newspapers such as the *Wall Street Journal* and *USA Today* because both have many business readers. General-interest magazines also have broad audiences.

You pay for advertising based on a dollar rate per thousand readers (or viewers). The more people your ad reaches, the higher the rate you can expect to pay. If you advertise in any of these more general media, you pay for a lot of readers who are not potential users.

Computer magazines

Most shareware authors' first inclination is to advertise in the big computer magazines. After all, they are selling computer software and the readers of these publications are all computer users. But, that is only true if they have a software product that all computer users need. Think very carefully about your market. If you publish a hard-disk utility, then the general computer publications might be right for your product. If you publish C libraries, then maybe *Byte* or *Dr. Dobbs Journal* are the right publications.

Special-interest magazines

Special-interest publications target very specific audiences. If their audience coincides with your typical user, then this is probably the most effective place in which you can advertise. If, for example, you have written a word processor designed for fiction writers, advertise in magazines that fiction writers read, such as *The Writer* or *Writer's Market*. Your target market is not computer users. Your target market is fiction writers, whether or not they currently use a computer.

All my software is specialized. I have found that advertising in publications targeted at specific audiences is very effective. For example, I advertise my software for cataloging record collections in publications such as *CD Review* and *DISCoveries*, both of which are publications record and CD collectors read. My stamp-cataloging software is advertised in *Scott Stamp Monthly*. Find the publications that your users read; that is the place to advertise.

When purchasing advertising, look at what the ad will cost you per thousand readers in your targeted group. An ad in a computer magazine might draw a lot of responses. But, if that magazine targets Amiga, Commodore, Apple, and IBM users, and your software only runs on IBM and compatibles, most of your responses might be from people that have computers on which your software will not run. The result is that you have wasted a lot of money on an ad and a lot of effort responding to people who cannot use your software.

All-ad magazines

Several magazines publish just advertising, with little or no editorial content. Before purchasing an ad in a publication such as this, look at an issue for the types of things that are being advertised. Most of the ads I have seen have been for hardware, components, chips, etc. If this is the case, the audience the publication is reaching is a hardware-buying audience. Unless that is the market at which your software is directed, an ad in this type of publication will not be very effective. If you would like to take a look at an all-ad publication, write to:

Computer Bargain Line
P.O. Box 1662
Ft. Dodge, IA 50501
(800) 654-3129
(515) 955-7231 in Iowa
(fax) (515) 955-8235

Card decks

Card decks are those stacks of post cards you receive with a single ad on each post card. If you can find a card deck that targets the specific audience you want to reach, then they can be very effective. Typically, specialized software sells better in a card deck than general applications.

Card decks have proven to be a very effective means of generating leads for some shareware authors. I discuss card decks and direct marketing in more detail later in this chapter.

Electronic media and disk advertising

Electronic media such as *Prodigy* are just starting and it is too soon to evaluate them. This approach reaches a broad, general market of computer users. It might be good media for advertising software that all computer users can utilize. Your software should have a unique feature that can be described quickly in a line or two that will catch the user's eye.

At one time, several companies were promoting advertising on floppy disks as the media of the future. You could purchase several screens on a floppy disk to describe or demonstrate your software. Other than disk-based magazines, disk advertising seems to have died. However, with the arrival of hypertext and the growing popularity of CD-ROM disks, this media might make a comeback. For example, Ziff-Davis is putting together a CD-ROM containing software demos and advertising.

Defining your advertising objectives

The first step is to find the best publications for your ads. Step two is to determine the objective of your advertising. Are you building an image for your software? Are you announcing a new product or upgrade? Are you trying to sell your software directly? Are you trying to expand your mailing list? One of the main reasons advertising does not work for some authors is that they do not have an ad designed to meet their objectives.

There are four types of objectives advertising can achieve. Advertising can produce sales by calling attention to your software. This is the objective most people have in mind when they buy an ad. To do this, the ad must be clear, simple, and it must get and hold the reader's attention.

Second, advertising can get people that might be interested in your software to request additional information. These are called literature ads. The most effective ads use this as their objective, although they also might list a price and provide purchasing information. Instead of trying to sell software directly, the ad offers a free catalog or brochure. If you have good, strong promotional material, such as copies of reviews, articles about your software, outstanding references, etc., then this is a good way to identify potential users for a subsequent direct-mail campaign.

Advertising can also create a positive image of your software in the reader's mind, or it can increase your brand-name recognition. This is called *image advertising*. You should realize that most readers are not making a buying decision when they see your ad. Therefore, the ad should, as at least a second objective, produce a lingering, positive image in the reader's mind. When the reader becomes interested in buying software, this image will predispose them toward purchasing your software. Many of the full-page ads you see in computer magazines are solely image ads. For example, Microsoft generally does not advertise to sell their software directly to you, it advertises to create a positive image of its products.

There is another reason for using image ads. After the reader buys your software, an image ad reinforces the buyer's decision. They help the buyer to continue to feel good about purchasing your software.

Finally, advertising can help establish you as a serious business. By advertising, you are announcing to the world that you are in business and you are paying your bills. Magazines will not run your ad for long if you do not pay for it. I have found that having an ad in a major publication helped my business establish credit. One of the biggest problems you might face as a home business is having banks and suppliers take you seriously. An ad in a major magazine shows you are serious about being in business; it is not just a hobby that you will abandon on a whim.

The best advertising is either a literature ad or an ad that combines all four objectives. Your ad should be professionally typeset to produce a quality image. Do not run ads printed on a dot matrix printer—even if it is a 24-pin printer. A laser printer is an acceptable alternative if you have some experience with fonts and advertising design. Your ad should offer free literature, quote a price, and provide ordering instructions.

Designing your ad

Display ads are the most effective type of ad. If a magazine has a direct-marketing section, that will generally be the best place to run your ad. Unless you can afford a one-third-page or bigger ad, avoid the main body of a magazine. Small ads become lost among larger ads in the main body of a magazine.

Classified ads are usually the least expensive form of advertising. They work well for reaching those people that are looking for your product. They do not do especially well at selling your product. The most effective ad, in either the classified or direct-marketing section, is a display ad.

A display ad should include a headline, printed in larger type, that captures what your software does in two to five words. The heading should be designed to catch the reader's attention as they scan the page. For example, I use the heading ORGANIZE YOUR COLLECTION at the top of my ads.

The Crescent Software ad shown in FIG. 6-1 is a good example of a literature ad. It makes no attempt to directly sell software. The headline is eye-catching and will get the interest of anyone who programs using BASIC. The body of the ad gives you reasons why you want to learn more about Crescent Software. It sells Crescent Software as a company, it does not sell any specific product Crescent Software publishes.

Graphics also help to call attention to an ad. If you have a good logo or graphic art that will produce a quality image when it is reduced to a small size, include it in your ad.

If you are trying to sell software directly, the body of the ad should describe what you are selling and why the user should buy your software. Quotes from reviews or user comments are usually very effective sales tools. An ad I have run in several magazines, shown in FIG. 6-2, is a good example of this.

BASIC Programming Made Easy

Crescent Software publishes a wide variety of tools and enhancements for use with QuickBASIC. We offer more than a dozen packages, all complete with commented source code and extensive tutorials, and all very easy to use. Assembly routines, graphics, screen design with data entry, BASIC TSR programs, database, and much more. No royalties. Call or write for our free catalog.

Crescent Software, 32 Seventy Acres, West Redding, CT 06896
Orders/Catalogs: 800-35-BASIC   Technical Info.: 203-438-5300

6-1   This is a literature ad used by Crescent Software to make potential users aware of their programming tools.

6-2   This is one of my ads that has worked well. It is a good example of an ad designed to sell software. Ads that are designed to sell include a price, ordering information, and usually offer a money-back guarantee to help the customer feel comfortable making a purchase based on limited information.

Pricing ads

How much should you pay for an ad? There are no set guidelines. If a $10 ad has no response, then it is an expensive ad. If a $10,000 ad sells $1,000,000 of software, then that ad is cheap.

Getting a discount

When purchasing an ad, you should try to get several discounts off of the published rates. Ask for a 15% discount for camera-ready art. This means you supply your ad typeset and ready to be inserted in a magazine. It is cheaper for you to have the typesetting done locally than it is to pay 15% extra for your ad. For example, a two-inch display ad can cost $500 per month. Fifteen percent of this is $75. Having the ad typeset locally might cost $30 to $40. You save at least $35 the first time you run the ad and $75 each time after that. Sometimes this discount is listed as an agency discount. Ask for it and most publications will give it to you as long as you have camera-ready art. If they will not give you the agency discount, form your own advertising agency. All you need is printed letterhead. You can typically get letterhead and business cards for under $100, an investment that can easily be recouped in one or two ads!

Discounts for multiple insertions

Magazines also offer discounts for multiple insertions. The more times you run an ad, the less it costs per issue. To be effective, you need to run your ad in at least three consecutive issues, preferably six. Ads generally do not get noticed the first time they are run. It takes about three issues before you will start to get a good response. If the ad is not paying for itself after six issues, you should evaluate both the publication and whether or not your ad is written correctly.

Prepayment discount

You also might be able to get a discount of up to 15% for prepayment. If you have the cash available, this can save you some money. However, with smaller publications, judge the value of this against the durability of the magazine. Will the magazine be around awhile or fold and take your money with it? If a major magazine stops publication, they will usually arrange for another magazine to carry your ad for the duration of your contract. *PC Resource* did this when they stopped publishing in August 1990. Small publications can just disappear and take your money with them.

Typical ad costs

The cost of an ad is normally measured in dollars per thousand readers. TABLE 6-1 shows the rates four magazines were charging in 1990.

You should also ask magazines what they mean by prepay. Do you have to prepay the entire contract, or can you prepay each ad on a month-by-month basis? If you do not have the cash to prepay your ad, you can still get a discount if the magazine bills on a "2-10 net 30" basis. This means you get a 2% discount if you pay your invoice within 10 days, otherwise the balance is due in 30 days. Depending on the magazine's prepayment discount, you can sometimes save money working on a 2-10 net 30 basis.

Large software companies spend up to 50% of their revenues on advertising. For a small company, it is usually the largest singly budgeted item. It is also an item where it is difficult to start small and work up. If you are going to advertise in the major computer magazines, plan on spending at least $2000 to $3000 to start.

Table 6-1

Typical advertising costs in 1990. Actual cost per issue for a 2″ ad in the mail-order/direct-marketing section of magazines before discounts, at the 6X rate.

	2″ ad cost	Cost per 1000
Small circulation computer magazine (40,000 readers)	$132	$3.30
Large circulation computer magazine (362,000 readers)	$600	$1.66
Small circulation specialty magazine (10,000 readers)	$23	$2.30
Large circulation specialty magazine (102,000 readers)	$72	$0.70

Selling by direct mail

Another effective advertising method for shareware authors is direct marketing. As a shareware author, direct marketing is your primary method of selling software. Using shareware to market your software is a form of direct marketing. You are promoting your software directly to the end user. But that is not the type of direct marketing I am talking about. The traditional way people define direct marketing is to say it is direct mail or telemarketing. *Telemarketing* is the use of the telephone to call your prospects directly. An example of telemarketing would be those phone calls you get, usually at dinner time, selling carpet cleaning, insurance, and investment opportunities. The aspect of direct marketing other shareware authors have found to be the most useful is direct mail.

There is no way around it. As a shareware author, you will be using direct mail to promote your software. If you send out a newsletter, that is direct mail. If you mail upgrade announcements, you are using direct mail. This section will help you understand and use direct mail more effectively.

Direct-mail uses

The following examples give uses for direct mail.

Direct mail can be used to sell your software. When we think of direct mail we usually think of "junk" mail—third-class mail used to sell something. Although this term has a negative image, direct mail is a very effective way to sell software.

Upgrade announcements are usually sent using direct mail. One of the reasons people register shareware is to get access to upgrades. Upgrades are important to users and most users look forward to getting upgrade announcements—as long as they do not come too frequently. Whether you send out post cards or color brochures, direct mail is the most effective means of letting your users know about upgrades.

Direct mail announces new products. How do you let the world know about your new software? One of the best ways is to put a product announcement in front of prospective users. Use their mail box with direct mail.

Direct mail helps you maintain contact with users. You should stay in contact with your registered users. They are a source of feedback that will help improve your software; help identify bugs; help spot market trends; help develop ideas for new products; and they will help spread the word about your software. Some authors publish newsletters. Others send marketing surveys to selected users. Regardless of the method you use, staying in touch with your users provides a valuable source of feedback.

Direct mail is excellent for getting names of prospects and building your mailing list. Shareware disks reach only a limited number of the millions of computer users. Most computer users are not familiar with shareware. Direct mail is one way of reaching them. Use direct mail to build a mailing list of prospective customers. Then, use direct mail again to tell these prospects about your software.

Use direct mail to build your image. People follow the companies and products they consider leaders in a product category. If you can build an image of leadership and stability, people will feel more comfortable buying your software. Regular direct mailings to users, for example a bi-annual newsletter, is a good way to build your image.

Direct mail can create a demand for your products. Once you achieve success and dealers across the country carry your software, direct mail is an effective way to tell people about it and encourage them to buy your software from their local dealer.

Why direct mail works

Whether you are announcing a new release or prospecting for new sales, if done correctly, direct mail works. Here are some statistics that demonstrate why direct mail works.

Direct marketing is big business. People like to buy through the mail. The Direct Marketing Association reports that over 98 million people shop by mail every year. This is a 72% increase over the past seven years.

One of the reasons direct mail is successful is that it has little competition within the medium. For example, according to the Radio Advertising Bureau, each day we hear 42 commercials on the radio. The Newspaper Advertising Bureau says the average newspaper reader sees over 180 newspaper ads every day. Almost 60 billion inserts are included in newspapers every year. An average adult watches 3.6 hours of television and is exposed to 95 TV commercials every day. The March 22, 1991, edition of the *Wall Street Journal* reported that every day the average American is exposed to about 300 ad messages.

On the other hand, a U.S. Post Office study has shown that U.S. households receive an average of 10 pieces of third-class mail per week. That is only slightly more than three advertising messages every two days. Businesses receive an average of 25 pieces of third-class mail per week, a number that is still much less than any other media. The point is that direct mail puts your message in front of a potential user without a lot of competition from other messages.

A recent U.S. Post Office study done by the University of Minnesota showed that the term "junk mail" is a misnomer. People do not consider direct mail as junk mail. Seventy-one percent of all Third-Class Mail is immediately opened and read. Fifteen percent is set aside for later reading and 91% is eventually read. People like to receive mail, especially if it is about a subject that interests them. This is why direct mail works.

Characteristics of direct mail

Direct mail has some unique characteristics that can work to your advantage. For example, it is personal—your message can be designed for specific types of readers. In fact, that is a key ingredient of direct mail. Your mailing must be about a subject that interests the recipient. If you mail information about Pascal utilities to people interested in gardening, you are wasting your money. However, if you send it to Pascal programmers, you are directly reaching people with a personal interest in what you have to say.

A good use of direct mail, that adds a personal touch to your software and your company, is a newsletter. Users like to hear from you. They want to know what is going on. They want to know about updates and upgrades. A newsletter is a great way to stay in touch with your users, and if you use it to announce new products and upgrades, you should be able to get it to pay for itself.

Direct mail is flexible. With direct mail, you can adapt your message to the needs of the recipient. Unlike other forms of advertising in which the same message goes to everyone, you are not limited in what you can say in a direct mail piece. You can change the contents of your mailing to adapt it to different types of people. If you have the time or are selling high-priced software, you can even write a personal letter to each potential user. And you have as much room as you need. If your message takes six pages, that is not a problem. (Try paying for six pages of advertising in a magazine. That bill would put most of us out of business.)

Direct mail is measurable. You can evaluate the results from direct mail and run tests to find what brings the best response. You can send a mailing to a group of potential users and measure its effectiveness by counting the number of people that respond. Of course, you have to know what you are measuring, meaning you need to know the objective of your mailing. I cover direct mail objectives in the next topic.

Direct mail is selective—you can send your offer to the people most likely to be interested in your software. This provides the same advantage as advertising in specialty magazines—you do not pay to reach a lot of people that are not interested in your software.

Direct mail has the reader's full attention. Generally, you look at one piece of mail at a time and at a convenient time. Unlike magazine advertising, where competing software might be advertised on the same page as your software, direct mail does not have your competition's message present to distract your potential customer.

With all the good aspects of direct mail, why did I bother talking about advertising in the first part of this chapter? The answer is that they both have their place in a good marketing plan. For example, you cannot use direct mail until you have a mailing list of interested prospects. Magazine advertising can be used to identify prospects, and then direct mail can be used to contact those prospects. In fact, this is where many people make a mistake. They place an ad in a magazine and expect sales to soar. When nothing happens, they declare magazine advertising a waste of money. The problem, in many cases, is not that the ad did not work, the problem is that the advertising objectives were not correct. With an advertising objective aimed at building a mailing list, a combination of advertising and direct mail can be very effective.

Getting started with direct mail

By now, you might be getting tired of my telling you the first step is to identify your objectives. But, if you do not know where you want to go, you might never get there. In direct mail, as with anything else, the first step is to set your objectives. I have given you a list of ways direct mail can be used. Now, you need to determine what you want to accomplish. Do you need to inform your users of an upgrade? Are you trying to sell more software? The design of your direct-mail package will depend on what you are trying to do. For example, if you are announcing an upgrade, you can do it with a post card. However, if you want to announce an upgrade and a new product, you will be better off mailing a newsletter.

When determining your objectives, keep in mind that it will take several mailings to sell your software by direct mail. Experience has shown that people generally need to be contacted five times before they buy. Table 6-2 shows a typical response to a direct-mail campaign.

Table 6-2

This table shows that the typical qualified prospect generally does not make a purchase until he has been contacted five times.

# of times a prospect is contacted	% of prospects who buy
1	6.0%
2	2.5%
3	3.5%
4	9.0%
5	79.0%

To help you identify your direct-mail objectives, here are some questions you should answer before you mail anything.

1. Is your mailing a bug-fix that needs to get out as soon as possible, or a regularly scheduled newsletter? Are you trying to coordinate your mailing with the release of a new shareware disk to distributors?
2. What is your budget for this mailing? Can you afford to send a four-color brochure to 30,000 people or just a photocopied letter to 50 people?
3. Who is your target audience? Do you want to reach your registered users or find people who do not currently use your software?
4. What is the message you want to get across? What do you want to tell the recipient and what action do you want him or her to take?

Once you have put your objectives in writing and answered these questions, you are ready to start designing your direct-mail package.

Direct-mail package design

To be successful, direct mail must do certain things. It does not matter whether you are mailing a post card or a two-pound box of brochures. The following things must be incorporated into your direct-mail package.

1. Your direct-mail package must attract attention If the prospect throws away your mailing without reading it, you have wasted your money. Getting the prospective customer to open the envelope is the first key step. Once the envelope is open, you then must hold their attention.

Studies have shown that the best way to get a recipient to open an envelope is to do nothing. Use a plain white envelope with only your return address printed on it. Do not include advertising copy on the envelope. Of course, there are exceptions to this rule, as there are exceptions to everything I have talked about. However, in general, a plain white envelope with no advertising copy will generate a better response than an envelope with advertising.

Although special classes of mail and services such as Federal Express can be attention-getting, do not use them for direct marketing. Special-delivery services will decrease the response to your mailing because people will feel deceived. With direct mail, always do what people expect. People expect Federal Express deliveries to contain important and necessary information. They do not expect a sales pitch.

When reading a piece of direct mail, most people glance at, more often than read, what you present to them. Your package must be designed to catch and hold their attention as they scan it. A good approach is to use bold headlines and bulleted points that provide the key information.

2. Include a direct-mail letter   When selling something, whether it is a new product or an upgrade, always include a letter. (An exception to this rule is when you are sending out a newsletter. Newsletters do not need an accompanying cover letter, although you may include one if you wish.) A letter is the first thing people will read. The copy style should be informal and written to a single reader. Write the letter as if you are writing to a friend. You do not have to follow the formal rules of grammar as if it was a business letter. In addition, the title of the person signing the letter is very important. One of the first areas people check is the signature block. Be sure the letter is signed and that your title is included. A letter from the president or owner of a company is much more impressive and effective than one from an unknown name or a lower-level person.

Always include a P.S. as a part of your letter. The P.S. is the most often-read section of a direct-mail letter. Use the P.S. to summarize your offer and the action you want the prospect to take.

In designing your letter, do not try to be creative. As I have already stated, do what people expect. The most effective letters use black ink on white paper. Although purple ink on yellow paper might be eye catching, it is not an effective way to get people to read your letter. When selecting a typeface for a letter, always use a standard typeface. Do not use small or fancy print—do not try to be creative. Again, the key point is to do what people expect; a letter should look like a letter.

The layout of your letter impacts on its readability. Use short sentences and bulleted (or numbered) points. Sentences should be no longer than 25 syllables. Use as many pages as you need to explain your offer and tell the reader what you want them to do. Long letters get as good a response as short letters. The content should be based on the proven rule of thumb that you need to first tell people what you are going to tell them, then tell them, and finish by summarizing what you told them.

3. Include a variety of materials in your direct-mail package   Your direct-mail package should include several different types of materials, such as a letter, brochure, catalog, coupon, and reminder note. Plus, you should not have all the pieces in your package matching in style, color, paper stock, and typeface. Design variety into your direct-mail package. With each piece handled separately, providing a variety of styles results in a better chance of having the recipient read each piece's message. Also keep in mind that people are different and different people will be attracted to different parts of your package.

4. Include a message that is of interest to the prospect   For a direct-mail piece to hold someone's attention, it must relate to that person's interests. The key to doing this is to use the correct mailing list. As I said before, do not mail information about Pascal programming utilities to people interested in gardening.

A good way to get and hold people's interest is to use real-life testimonials. In fact, testimonials are the best and most effective means of communicating your message. They are better than anything the best copywriter can write.

Another way to catch people's interest is to include pictures. People like to look at pictures. For example, when scanning through a brochure, people will first look at the pictures and read the captions before they read the rest of the brochure. Do not write off picture captions as being unimportant. Picture captions are one of the best ways to deliver your message. The best brochure includes a photo story. Include photos, if you can, and use screen shots to illustrate the key benefits of your software.

When a brochure is about computer software, how do you include photos? What else can you show other than a computer screen? Some software easily brings photographic possibilities to mind. For example, a brochure for genealogy software might include a family photo that has three generations of family members. For my Play 'n' Learn software, I used a photograph of a baby in a highchair using a computer. A brochure for word processing software can contain pictures of people using the software in an office setting. But what do you do if, for example, you publish programming utilities? Falk Data Systems (publishers of shareware such as the Programmer's Productivity Pack) came up with an excellent and creative approach. Its brochure shows recreational activities you could enjoy as a result of the time you save using Falk Data's *ProPak 2.0*. The photographs are attention-getting and they deliver a message that says you will save time if you use this software.

5. The direct-mail package must suggest a course of action   Do not assume the reader knows what you want them to do. Explain everything fully and in detail and then ask the reader to perform a specific action. Do not assume anything is obvious to the reader or that the reader will know what to do.

Also, keep in mind that people always have questions about the next step. People want to know both what they need to do and what you will do in return. For example, when they order your software, will they have to wait four to six weeks or do you ship the same day you receive the order?

Another fact of direct mail is that most people procrastinate over making decisions. Twenty-nine percent of direct-mail sales are impulse sales, meaning the prospect reads your material, likes what you are offering, and orders it immediately. The remaining sales come from people who put off responding to your offer. In addition to procrastinating, people tend to only keep the return vehicle (e.g., a coupon, business reply card, order form) and throw out the rest of your materials. Be sure to include a reply vehicle with a complete recap of your offer and specific directions telling the prospect what to do. You might also include a testimonial or a captioned screen shot on the coupon or order form.

6. Your direct-mail package must encourage a positive response   Do not forget to ask for an order. Tell people what you want them to do and tell them to say "Yes!" If you want people to buy your software you might say, "Call (555) 555-5555 today for immediate shipment of your new software." This tells people you want them to say yes, and it specifically tells them what they need to do.

If you want people to give you their name and address for your mailing list, you could say, "Mail the enclosed coupon today for a free shareware copy of the QuickPay Accounting System."

Here is another approach for selling: "The QuickPay Accounting System is so easy to use that we know you'll want to get started right away. Check the YES box on the enclosed coupon, mail it to us, and we'll ship your copy of the QuickPay Accounting System via Federal Express at no extra charge."

Notice that all of these encourage the prospect to say yes. They also tell the prospect what they need to do and encourage the prospect to take action now instead of procrastinating.

Sometimes, asking for an order seems difficult. But, people want you to pursue them. When you ask for the order, you make people feel that you care and that their business is important to you. If you do not ask for an order, you give the impression that you do not care whether the prospect orders your software or not. If you do not care, why should the prospect care about ordering your software?

The list

The key factor in the success or failure of a direct-mail campaign is the quality of the mailing list. Your mailing must reach your target market. There are two types of mailing lists. Those you generate internally and lists you purchase from outside vendors. With a list you have put together, for example a list of your registered users, you know the people to whom you are mailing. If you send an upgrade announcement to your registered users, you know you are reaching the right audience.

When you prospect for new users, you most likely will buy or barter for a list from an outside source. The only way to know whether or not you will get a good response from this list is to test it. Never do a large mailing using a list from outside sources until you have tested the mailing list and the material you are including in your mailing.

List testing

Statistically, to have a valid test you need to get at least 56 replies. This will provide you with an 85% confidence level that the results from a repeat mailing will not decline more than 12.5%.

Unfortunately, no rule of thumb gives a percentage response rate for direct mail. Responses can vary from a fraction of a percent to 30 or 40%. Until you have done some testing, you have to guess at what your response rate will be (a classic catch-22). However, as an example, if you anticipate a 2% response rate, you must mail 2800 pieces to get a valid test. But, if you think you will get a 10% response rate, you need to mail to only 560 people.

Testing is critical for companies with big direct-mail programs. Companies that mail hundreds of thousands or even millions of pieces of mail do not want to make mistakes that render their mailings ineffective. However, if you are a small, one-person company with a limited budget, how can you run a test involving 2800 pieces of mail when your budget only supports a total mailing of 500 pieces?

One nice thing about direct mail is that if your budget will not support a mailing to several thousand people, you can still effectively use direct mail. To take advantage of bulk mail rates, you only need to mail 200 pieces at a time. For many years, I routinely built my mailing list by trading names with other authors and adding them to the names of people who responded to my advertising. Each time I collected 200 names I would do a bulk mailing. Sometimes, I would get a good response. Other times, my mailings generated no response. I did not have the resources to test my mailing lists. But, unlike mailings involving possibly millions of pieces of mail, when you mail just a few hundred pieces and do not get a good response, you will not have lost a fortune. The risk is very low.

Getting no response to a mailing does not mean the mailing was a failure. At a minimum, you are building brand recognition and your company image. You are letting people know you exist. That is an important part of building your business.

Building a mailing list

There are companies that rent or sell mailing lists, but it might not be necessary for you to purchase a list. If you are a member of the ASP, you can use the mailing lists the ASP has generated from their trade-show booths. Some authors have reported outstanding success using the ASP mailing lists.

If your software serves a niche market, you might be able to purchase the subscriber list of a magazine serving that market. Give the magazine a call and ask.

Another source of lists are professional association directories. You might be able to find these directories in your library or you might be able to purchase a copy from the professional association. Some libraries also have industry directories that can be used for compiling a mailing list.

If you sell software to businesses, you can compile a list of prospective customers by looking at the ads in trade magazines and publications. If, for example, you publish software for cataloging software disk libraries, check computer magazines for the addresses of shareware disk distributors. (Of course, you can always use the mailing list included with this book.)

Anytime someone calls you with questions or a request for information about your software, be sure to get their name and address. This is your most valuable source of names. People who take the time to call are interested in your software and are the best prospects for becoming registered users. This list becomes one of your most valuable resources.

We get a lot of technical support calls from copies of our disks sold by other vendors. Of course, we give them technical support, but I'll tell you something—we try not to let that customer hang up without giving us their name and address so we can send them a catalog of ours and make them our customer.

—Roger Jones, president of Software To-Go

A good way to build a mailing list is through a booth at a trade show. For example, COMDEX is a great place to collect all sorts of toys and trinkets. Last fall, I came back with hula hoops, a slinky, a globe, sunglasses, and all sorts of buttons, badges, and letter openers. Why do COMDEX exhibitors give away all that stuff? They want to attract people to their booths so they can build their mailing lists.

Some magazines can be good sources of names. For example, *Computer Shopper* publishes a list of user groups, providing you with a current list of user group names and addresses. Some trade magazines publish industry directories that can also serve as a good basis for a mailing list.

If you know of someone who targets the same market as you do, consider swapping names with that person. It is an inexpensive way to build a great mailing list of prospects already identified as being in your target market.

Finally, you can purchase lists from list brokers. There are several brokers listed in chapter 16.

Renting/buying a mailing list

When you "buy" a list, you are usually renting the right to use it for a specified number of times. The list broker will send you a set of mailing labels, and you may use each label one time. When can you add names you receive from a list broker to your permanent mailing list? As a general guideline, after you have contacted someone, and that person has responded to your offer, the name is yours.

The cost to rent a mailing list is typically in the range of $40 to $150 per thousand names, and, in many cases, there is a 5000-name minimum. Some premium mailing lists will be priced higher than $150. The average list cost is in the $90–$100 range per 1000 names. In a few cases, you can buy the mailing outright and make it a part of your permanent list. Typically, expect the cost to be anywhere from 3 to 10 times the rental rate.

Keep in mind that when you rent a list, that list is the customer file belonging to some other company. Most companies do not want to jeopardize their relationships with their customers. In some cases, you will be asked about the product you are selling and there might be a request for a copy of the material you will be mailing. If you have a competitive offer, you might not be able to rent the list. For example, I do not think *PC Magazine* would rent its subscriber list to *PC World*.

Producing your direct-mail material

Here are a few guidelines for the actual production of your direct-mail material.

- Study the direct-mail packages you receive. What catches your eye? What do you like about them? Which ones do you throw in the trash and why? Model your package on the ones you think are most effective.
- When you start, talk to your printer early in the design process. Discuss what you are planning to do and find out what you can do to minimize costs. For example, if you are including a multiple-page flyer, find out from the printer what would be the optimum number of pages. Many times the printing process results in catalogs/flyers of eight pages (or multiples of eight) as the most cost effective to print. Be careful that you do not design a flyer that is hard to print.
- To save money, you can do as much of the work as possible yourself. If you have a laser printer and good font software, you can handle the typesetting. Folding and envelope stuffing are simple jobs that you can do, but because many printers have automated equipment, sometimes the money you save is not worth the extra time you would have to put into it. Weigh the value of your time and your ability to produce quality material against the cost of paying someone else to do the work.

- Before bringing your material to the printer, make a dummy of your package with everything cut and folded as it will be in the actual package. This will give you a chance to see if your package is within the post office's weight limits and whether or not the materials will fit in the envelope you are using. There is nothing worse than designing a super package, printing 5000 copies, and then finding it will not fit in the envelope.
- Where possible, use standard materials. It might be exciting to use odd-shaped envelopes or inserts, but it will cost more. Also, you should avoid special inks. Some printers have a regular schedule of when they run certain standard colors. If you can build enough time into your schedule, you might be able to save the extra costs of special print runs for additional colors. Also, if you specify a color background, some printers will print the background. If you are thinking that you want your flyer printed on colored paper, be sure to tell the printer to specifically use colored paper.
- When working with vendors, put everything in writing. For phone calls, always send a follow-up letter to confirm your understanding of the conversation.

Using card decks

A card deck is a package of post cards sent to a targeted group of people. Each post card contains an advertising message. To respond to the ad, you can generally put a stamp on the card, write in your name and address, and drop it in the mail.

Card decks are effective in two ways:

1. They are good for selling inexpensive impulse products. For example, some shareware distributors have found card decks to be very effective in selling disks priced at $3 or $4 each.
2. Card decks are excellent at generating leads in highly specific target markets. Advertising in a card deck can be excellent for generating leads at a low cost. What is a lead? A lead is the name and address of someone who is interested in your software. It is the first step in selling your software. Lead generation is the most effective use of a card deck for a software publisher.

Before you advertise in a card deck, know your objectives. What do you want to get for the money you are spending on card-deck advertising? Do you want to generate leads? Are you trying to sell copies of the shareware version of your software?

Next, be sure the card deck is targeted at a group of people who need your product. For example, if you sell programing utilities, the *Byte* magazine card deck would be an appropriate place to advertise. However, it would be better to advertise software for cataloging book collections in a card deck going to Book-Of-The-Month-Club members.

One of the big advantages of card decks is that it costs a lot less to use than it does to mail a letter to everyone receiving the card deck. A typical cost might be $0.04 to $0.05 per prospect.

What type of response can you typically expect from a card deck? As with direct mail, the response will vary with different card decks and products. A typical response might be in the 2% range for requests for additional information and an additional 0.05% for immediate purchase of your software. With card decks you can expect to receive 50% of the responses within three weeks of the mailing date and 90% within eight weeks.

The design of your card is important for achieving a good return rate. The elements of a good card-deck design follow.

The headline and visual are the most important elements. They must work to stop the prospect at your card as they scan through the stack of cards. Include a bold headline that concisely summarizes the major benefit of your software. Then, include a graphic that supports the headline. Once your card has been set aside for further consideration, the battle is half won.

The copy on your card must be clear and concise. With the limited space provided by a post card, every word counts. Get to the point quickly, state your proposition, and ask readers to take action.

It is important that you close the sale. You do this by telling buyers how to order or request additional information. Should they mail the card back to you or can they fax it? Do they get something, such as a discount, if they respond within a specified time period? Tell readers what you want them to do and what they will get in return.

Get a commitment. Leave room on the card for name, address, phone number, and credit card information. Take a look at some of the cards you receive. (If you do not receive any card decks, then you are not subscribing to business publications that can help you run your business. Take a look at the list of publications in chapter 16.) Notice that some ask you to tape your business card to the post card. This provides a way to identify your title and weed out non-business responses. Notice that some cards have you write your name and address in the space where a return address typically goes. This saves space and leaves more room for copy.

Do not forget to include your phone number (many people do). Also, include a fax number if you have one. Fax machines are increasingly used to order merchandise by ''mail.''

In looking through card decks, you might notice that many cards are business reply cards. The respondent does not need to put a stamp on it. Making your card a postage-paid, business reply card will help generate more responses. The easier you make it for someone to respond, the more responses you will get. However, providing a postage-paid card is not a necessity when selling a product that costs more than $10 or $20. Before buying into a card deck, you might want to look at a few past decks to see what others have done.

7

Trade shows and conventions

You can attend a trade show as an exhibitor or as a spectator. First, we will look at attending trade shows at which you'll want to have a booth. Many trade shows and conventions, other than COMDEX, can help boost your business. Without some previous experience, COMDEX can be a difficult first step. Many chambers of commerce run local trade shows. You might try user group meetings, industry-specific conventions, and government-sponsored trade shows that highlight local products. There are many meetings and conventions where you can put trade-show skills to work to promote your software.

Exhibiting

In general, trade shows are not effective for directly generating sales. But, usually, that should not be your objective in exhibiting at a trade show. As with everything else I have discussed, you first must determine your objectives.

General trade-show objectives might include the following.

- Getting sales leads.
- Increasing name recognition in the marketplace.
- Selling your software.
- Meeting magazine editors.
- Exposing your software to dealers.

You also need to set specific objectives for a trade show. Specific objectives might be to contact 80 dealers, 5 distributors, or 10 magazine editors, or to meet 12 other shareware authors. After determining your objectives, you should determine how you are going to get the attention of your targeted group.

Notice that I used the word "or" in the listing of possible objectives. If you try to achieve all of those objectives, you will usually not achieve any of them. You need to focus on one specific objective, although you may have some secondary objectives. Of course, if an opportunity presents itself, take advantage of it even if it is not part of one of your original objectives. Conventions and trade shows are exciting, dynamic events. You might unexpectedly meet someone who can help you. That is how this book got published.

Overall, however, you need to maintain your focus on your identified objective. If you want to talk with distributors, you will not have time to sell software to individual users. If you want to generate leads, you will be so busy collecting people's names and handing out copies of your shareware, that you will not be able to meet distributors. If you want to sell software, you will end up talking about its features and benefits with users or dealers and have many potential leads pass by your booth.

Once you have identified your objectives, you next need to put together a plan for achieving them. What type of booth will you need? What equipment will you need to bring? Will you need to rent computers? Be sure to tell the show organizers that you need power if you will be running a computer. How many people will you need to staff your booth? What handouts do you need? Are you going to give away copies of your shareware? All the details must be planned months before the show's date. Simply setting up a booth and standing around to see what happens will result in an unsuccessful exhibit.

Planning your booth

Before a show, call or send a mailing to the people whom you are targeting and have them meet or talk with you at the show. If you are trying to contact dealers, use a direct-mail campaign to let them know about your booth. If you are trying to sell to users, go through your mailing list and send invitations to anyone who has expressed interest in your software. When inviting users to a local trade show, you might limit the mailing to people who live within 200 miles of the show.

When sending out a mailing to announce your show booth, offer a show special to get people to come to your booth or to make their first purchase at the show. If your objective is to get sales leads, you might offer a small, low-cost gift. If you are trying to make sales, offer a special show price or include a coupon with your invitation. Another incentive is to ask people to bring in problems that your software can solve. It is a great way to qualify prospective customers and it provides you with an opportunity to demonstrate your software. (To qualify a customer means that you determine whether or not that person has a need for your software, and whether or not that person has the authority, or inclination, to specify, purchase, or recommend your software.)

Most business people will have their time at a show fully scheduled in advance. If you want to meet with people such as distributors or editors, call them before the show and make an appointment. You should have a good reason for wanting to talk with them. For example, you might want to meet with an editor if you have a new product that might particularly interest that editor. If you plan to talk with distributors or dealers, know what you want to talk about, and what you are willing to offer them, before you meet with them.

When sending out press releases before the show, include a cover letter that mentions your booth. If your objective is to get exposure with the press, prepare a press kit you can leave in the press room at the show. Here is what Marilyn Young, editor of *Shareware Magazine* has to say about press kits:

> *Include short press releases on the news you have. For instance, if you have a new product or an update, include that information. Answer the question: What is your product? So many times, we get a press release and it sounds like a neat product, but we can't quite figure out what it is. It sounds fun. Is it a game, or is it a database, or a contact manager? You have to spell out clearly exactly what it is. Also, state the advantage your product has over other products. And include other basic information about your product's capabilities. Include the price, system requirements, and where we can go for additional information.*
>
> *The press kit should also include information about your company background. Are you a new company? Have you had a name change or major staff change? Just a little background. Nothing in-depth, but enough to help the editor remember where they heard about your company before.*
>
> *You might include a longer press release as well, offering more in-depth information about your key product.*
>
> *Photos are helpful. Usually, magazines can use black-and-white glossies or color slides. You might want to have a product shot as well as a screen shot.*
>
> *Include basic information about how to look you up. How can the editor contact you at the show? And don't forget to include your company's phone number and address.*

In putting together your press kit, make it look professional. Use good-quality paper, a laser printer, and put it all in a nice binder. Do not make it too thick, because most people already have more stuff to carry around than they want.

In addition to everything else, you should also be sure to mention the show in any of your ads.

Assuming you can afford it, the size of your staff and the design of your booth must be tailored to the show and your objectives. For example, if you are trying to sell site licenses to corporate customers, your booth should be designed to accommodate as many 10-minute "quickie" demonstrations as possible. A hotel room or suite is then set up for in-depth demonstrations to qualified prospects. This same approach might also be used for distributors, except that your presentation should be oriented around showing the benefits distributors would have in carrying your software.

At a large show, your booth should be staffed by people that can give a quick overview of your product. If the prospect is qualified and wants more information, you then schedule a follow-up appointment or invite them to your hotel suite for a demonstration. The objective of the booth is to qualify prospects and either schedule a follow-up meeting or give them a brochure and send them on their way. It is easy to get tied up with prospects that have lots of questions. But, one prospect that ties up your time might cost you five others that walk by and find no one to help them. By the way, do not expect to meet more than four or five qualified prospects per day.

For large booths, you will need a staff of three or four people. They should pay attention to the people who walk by your booth, and talk to anyone who shows interest in your booth, to determine whether or not that person is a qualified prospect. There will be a few times when someone who appears to be a casual browser actually turns out to be a corporate buyer interested in your software. These are the people you are looking for. If someone does not stop them and ask a few questions, that person might pass by your booth and never realize that you were offering the solution to all their problems.

For smaller companies, the formula is the same, just on a smaller scale. If you are a one-person company, you might be the only person available to staff your booth, although you will be much better off if you can get a second person. Do not try to operate a booth alone during a multiple-day trade show. There is too much to do and you will become too tired to effectively demonstrate your software. Even with two people, a three-day show can be tough. My wife and I once tried manning a booth by ourselves for a three-day show. By the morning of the third day, we were exhausted. It took us a week to recover after the show.

How should you run your booth? If you are trying to sell site licenses or meet distributors, set it up for quick demonstrations. Invite qualified prospects to dinner or to a demonstration in your hotel room. With two people, one can qualify prospects while the other can give more detailed demonstrations.

To build a list of names of people interested in your software, but with whom you do not get a chance to talk, set out a bowl for business cards.

Run a contest giving away a copy of your software to a name drawn from the bowl. If you are the only person in your booth, having a bowl for business cards is a very important way to collect names.

What to say and do

In manning a booth, do not just stand around and wait for prospects to talk to you. Be a little aggressive. Stand up, look alert. If there is not much traffic, move around so that it does not look like you are guarding the entrance to the booth. Be aware of your body language. Do not stand around with your arms folded and a scowl on your face. Smile, keep your hands loose at your side, and move around.

When someone comes into your booth, be aware of his or her body language. For example, if a visitor glances at a watch, time is short. If the person leans toward you, totally engrossed in what you are saying, he or she is interested. By the way, do not spend all your time talking at prospective customers. Ask them questions. Find out what their needs and problems are and then fit your discussion to center on their needs.

What do you say to people who come by your booth? Try to avoid saying things like, "May I help you?" and "Are you familiar with our spreadsheet software?" (Replace spreadsheet with whatever type of software you publish.) While "May I help you?" might be appropriate in a store, at a trade show it is too easily answered by a simple "No." Openings such as, "How are you doing?" are not good either because they do not move the conversation toward determining the visitor's qualifications or interest in your software. A good opening line might be, "Thanks for stopping by. What made you interested in our software?" The objective is to get customers to talk with you and tell you about their needs. Then, follow up with questions about their business or about problems your software can solve.

Another, less-direct opening could be, "How are you enjoying the show? What are you here to see?" The topic of conversation is directed toward what is happening at the show and the visitor's interests and needs. A more direct approach that I use frequently is, "Welcome to my booth. May I give you an overivew of what this software can do?"

Following up contacts

Follow up trade-show contacts fast, especially with potential customers. Send a letter that reminds them of the show, of the circumstances under which you met, and include your literature and possibly a copy of your shareware disk—even if you gave them one at the show. Important contacts should be followed up with a phone call. Figure 7-1 shows a sample follow-up letter.

```
                    HomeCraft Software
                       P.O. Box 974
                    Tualatin, OR 97062
                       (503)-692-3732

XYZ Stamp Company
555 Main Street
Anywhere, ST  99999

ATT: Mr. John Smith

April 25, 1991


Dear _____:

Thank you for attending our booth at the recent Portland
User Group Computer Trade Show.  Enclosed is our catalog
describing the software we currently publish.  Please note
that the dealer price for any of the software in this
catalog is 50% off list, plus shipping.

If you find that you have customers interested in software
for cataloging stamp collections, please give me a call.
We always have copies of For Stamp Collectors in stock
ready to ship to you or directly to your customer.

If I can be of any further help, or if you have any
questions, please feel free to call me.


Sincerely,


STEVEN C. HUDGIK
President
HCP Services, Inc.
HomeCraft Software
```

7-1 Always follow up the contacts you have made at trade shows and conventions with a letter. Most people are so busy during the show that they need a reminder in order to remember you and any discussions you might have had.

Attending trade shows

The most important trade show is COMDEX. You should attend COMDEX to meet people and build a network of contacts. At COMDEX, everything is secondary to making contacts and meeting people. You want to make contacts with the press, with people in distribution companies, with other shareware authors, and with dealers. Talk with everyone. Several times, I have spent time talking with someone I thought was not important to me, only to have them call three or four months later to place a big order or hire me as a consultant.

How important are contacts? When I started my sales career, one of the managers who interviewed me described the company's sales strategy by telling me they would hire me, and keep me employed as a salesman, for possibly 10 years before I made my first sale. What was I supposed to be doing during those ten years? Making contacts! This company was willing to invest 10 years of an employee's time just to have the right contacts in place when the time came to make a big sale.

Unlike working in a booth, where you want to qualify the people you meet, when attending COMDEX, the people you meet do not have to be direct business contacts. Make as many contacts as you can with anyone. Maybe you won't meet the president of a company, but if you've gotten to know a product manager, you have a contact—a way in.

The importance of contacts

When I was first introducing my software for cataloging collections, I wanted to meet magazine editors for the opportunity to demonstrate my software. They are busy people and it can be tough for a small, part-time software publisher to get an appointment. What I did was to call the salesperson who handled my advertising at each magazine. This was the contact I needed to get in. In each case, the salesperson gave me the names of the right people to see and set up an appointment for me. Once, the salesperson bought me lunch after I spent all morning talking with the editors.

If someone does you a favor by arranging a meeting or making an introduction, be sure to thank them. At a minimum, send a thank-you note. If you can, include a small gift. In my case, I usually send a small package of dried Northwest Salmon. It symbolizes the region in which I am located and it is something most people like.

COMDEX parties

Press contacts are important because the press reports on people they know of, people they have heard of, or people they know personally. At COMDEX, to meet and know the people of the press, you not only have to attend the show, but you have to go to the parties. Calling them parties is not accurate. They are more like informal meetings. You are not going to meet any reporters walking around on the show floor. On the show floor, there is not enough time to talk to one particular person—especially when thousands of others want to talk to that same person.

When attending a COMDEX party, introduce yourself to people, particularly the press. In many cases, I have noticed people from the press standing around by themselves or talking with other members of the press. They also are there to meet people. If you do not know what to say to someone from the press, come straight out and tell them so and ask them to tell you what they discuss with other software publishers. It is a way to get a conversation started and it works quite well.

Do not be disappointed if someone from the press is not interested in talking with you. We all have our special areas of interest. If your software does not interest someone, do not be upset when that person wanders off. Remember, most press people attend conventions to find things they can write about. Some of them are looking for you, but finding you is difficult—there are too many people. So, if someone is not interested in talking with you, move on and find someone else. The next contact might be the one that gets your software reviewed in a magazine.

Both vendors and magazines sponsor parties at COMDEX. The best way to find these parties is to ask about them. Ask the people manning booths about their company's or magazine's party. Join the ASP and you will automatically get information about the ASP party. Once you are at the ASP party, ask other authors which parties they recommend you attend. Or, try wandering near the ballrooms and meeting rooms of the hotels hosting COMDEX—you will surely spot some parties. Most of them are open parties and you can walk right in. Once you are in a party, ask people where they are going next. You will be able to build a schedule of four or five parties to attend each evening.

For shareware authors, the magazine parties are the most useful. At the magazine parties you get to meet the press—it is their party and they have to be there. And, you get to meet the people in the software industry who are interested in being visible. Recently, the magazine parties have become invitation-only parties. However, you can still get in. This is where the contacts you made earlier come in handy. When all else fails, my tactic for getting into invitation-only parties has been to wait outside the door, introduce myself to people leaving the party, and borrow their passes to get in.

Another method for getting into closed parties is to do what you normally should be doing—meeting people. For example, last November I wanted to go to the *PC Computing* party, but found I had arrived an hour early. While there, I met an interesting couple from England. We had a very enjoyable conversation, at the end of which they gave me their press pass for the *Computer Shopper* party. By the way, both are members of the press in the U.K., although I did not know that when we started talking (they were not wearing their press badges). Meeting people who can help you happens in the most unlikely places, so take a moment to say hello when you are standing in line or waiting for a cab.

There is one other way to get into closed magazine parties and that is to be invited. When I was buying advertising in computer magazines, I was invited to the closed COMDEX magazine parties. This, however, is the expensive way to get an invitation to a party.

You should also attend some of the smaller parties. At the bigger parties, you might get the opportunity to shake the hands of magazine editors. At smaller parties, you might have a chance to talk with them.

One objective in attending a party is to see how the press works. Watch how other people work with the press, how they answer questions. Listen to the types of questions being asked. Listen to how other people answer. Listening and paying attention will help you avoid being caught off guard when you are talking to the press.

Visiting booths

During the day, you can set up appointments at booths and spend a lot of time on the show floor. Exactly what you do depends on your objectives. One possible objective is to get to know the competition. Find out how people react to products similar to yours. Find out what other software publishers are doing so that you do not reinvent the wheel. Look for products from major publishers for which you might be able to make add-on utilities. Visit booths run by other shareware publishers and those run by shareware distributors. You also might take the opportunity to test your software on various machines. Most of the computer manufacturers are there. If you ask to try your software on their machine, they will generally say that it is okay and schedule a convenient time.

Plan ahead

Get the COMDEX guide before the show so you can look at the floor plans and building locations. Find the booths you want to see and plan your schedule to get to them all. It is a big show. You can see only 20–30% of it. Seeing everything you want will take some planning.

Plan the logistics of going to COMDEX well in advance. If you are coming from an area with a lot of computer companies, make your airline reservations early. Call the visitor's bureau in the host city and get a map of hotels around the convention center. Most times, you will be better off making your own hotel reservations instead of going through the Interface Group.

What to bring

It is a waste of time to give out software packages at COMDEX. You should not go loaded down with copies of your product and expect to hand them to people in booths. They are not interested in carrying stuff back to their office. Just take your literature and use it to show what your product can do. You might bring a supply of shareware disks, but do not bring the complete, registered version. If you do bring disks to hand out, expect people to lose your disks. You are better off mailing a disk to someone after the show.

What to wear

Wear business clothes. Dress as you would for a meeting with an important corporate client. Jeans and T-shirts are definitely not appropriate. The best approach is to dress conservatively. You never know who you will meet.

Get business cards from the people you meet. You can also hand out your business cards, but expect people to lose them. When you finish talking with someone, make a few notes about your discussion on the back of their business card. It is the only way to remember what you talked about. Follow up any important people you meet by sending them letters after the show. Include a copy of your software if you think it is appropriate.

Listening

While at COMDEX, you should be a good listener. Everyone wants to talk and push their product. Be a good listener and you will learn more. Get near the people you have seen quoted in print. See what they are like and listen to what they have to say.

Spring COMDEX

Up to this point, I have talked about attending fall COMDEX. Whether or not you should attend spring COMDEX depends on your market. Spring COMDEX is smaller and more oriented toward corporate buyers as opposed to dealers. If you are trying to sell to corporate buyers, and you can afford a booth, spring COMDEX might be worth attending. If you live in the Southeast (or have frequent-flyer miles to spend) and can afford the time, spring COMDEX is worth attending just to make press contacts.

For more information about COMDEX, and for an attendee preregistration form, write to:

The Interface Group
300 First Ave.
Needham, MA 02194

Other meetings—the ASP

The day before fall COMDEX starts, the ASP holds its annual meeting at the COMDEX meeting site. In addition to a business meeting, speakers are invited to talk about various aspects of shareware. For example, in 1990, Bill Machrone, editor of *PC Magazine*, spoke for two hours about registration incentives, how to get the attention of the press, GUIs, the home market, and strategies for increasing sales. In addition to Bill Machrone, several successful authors presented talks on techniques to improve documentation, how to handle viruses, and customer service.

If you can get to Las Vegas for fall COMDEX, the ASP meeting is an outstanding benefit of being an ASP member. You have the opportunity to meet and discuss shareware marketing with other authors in addition to learning from the various presentations.

Other meetings—Summer Shareware Seminar

In June 1991, Public Brand Software sponsored a "Summer Shareware Seminar" in Indianapolis. It looked like an event that all shareware authors should attend. Over 200 authors, disk distributors, bulletin board sysops, and user group officers signed up to attend. It was a three-day conference featuring panelists such as Bob Wallace, Marshall Magee, Paul Mayer, and Ross Greenberg, to list just a few of the better-known names. With such an excellent attendance, I expect this meeting will be repeated in future years.

Topics scheduled for the Summer Shareware Seminar included panel discussions on getting media attention, writing for ease of use, packaging, customer support, legal aspects of shareware, and the international marketplace. Sixteen panel discussions were scheduled. In addition to the panel discussions, this meeting was an excellent opportunity to get to know other shareware authors and meet members of the shareware press and the managers of some of the largest disk distribution companies. I think this meeting will become the "must-attend" meeting of the year for shareware authors.

Finding meetings

How do you find out about shareware-related meetings and seminars? If you have a modem, check the ASP forum on CompuServe. The library for Section 0 normally will contain information files announcing upcoming meetings (if any are scheduled). The best way to stay in touch is to join the ASP. The ASP newsletter, *ASPects*, includes announcements for upcoming meetings. You could also subscribe to shareware-related publications such as *Shareware Magazine* and *The Alternate Software Bulletin* (or *PC Shareware* in the U.K.). The directory in chapter 16 has the addresses for these publications.

8
Running a business

The purpose of this chapter is not to make you an expert in running a business—that would take a whole shelf of books. The purpose is to make you aware of some of the basic tools and principles used by successful business people. The best way to learn about running a successful business is to get started and run a business. Then, read as much as you can, take business courses (starting with marketing courses), and spend time with other people who have home businesses.

Running your own business is nice. You get to do what you want. You make the decisions and control what your business does. And you only have to work a half-day—you decide which 12 hours that will be. In running your own business, finding enough time to do everything can be your biggest problem. Learning more about running a business is the first thing that is pushed aside when time is short. I have found audio cassettes helpful in allowing me to continue learning about business while using my time productively. An excellent source is the Tape Rental Library, Inc. You pay a yearly fee and borrow all the tapes you want. For the cost of buying one or two audio programs, you can listen to a dozen or more. Contact them for a free catalog. Their address is:

Tape Rental Library, Inc.
One Cassette Center
Covesville, VA 22931

Start with the *How To Start and Succeed In Your Own Business* tapes (number 25184) by Brian Tracy. They are excellent. A key point that Tracy makes in his first tape is the difference between winners and losers in business—winners learn from their mistakes, pick themselves up, and try again. You have a choice. You can either make the same mistake again or learn from your mistake. When you learn from your mistakes, you gain judgment.

> *When I started with the first version of AutoMenu I didn't know much about running a business. I talked to friends of mine and they suggested I go to the school of business where they had a small business assistance program. After we talked, they wrote three pages of notes on things I wasn't doing right.*
> —Marshall Magee, president of Magee Enterprises, Inc.

Do not expect to be successful without making a lot of mistakes. When we look at successful people, we tend to see the trappings of their success: the profitable business, nice cars, big house, etc. We do not see the hard work and mistakes littering the path to that success. Expect to make mistakes and learn from them. That is why starting a business is the first and most important step in learning how to run a business. Start as soon as possible. Make your mistakes when you and your business are as young as possible. That is when mistakes have the smallest impact and you can most easily recover from the results. Since you will never be any younger than you are today, today is the day to begin.

> *The one thing I think is more important than anything else is to be a self-starter. You have to know when to work and when not to work. Especially when working at home.*
> —Martin Schiff, a shareware author

Targets and goals

Once you decide to start a business, the first step is to determine your targets and goals. A *target* is where you want to go. *Goals* are the intermediate steps you use to reach your target. If you do not know where you want to be or what your target is, you will not know when you get there or if you are getting any closer.

Of course, your goals will change over time. Do not put off thinking about where you want to be in one year, two years, or five years from now just because you know you will change direction as your business grows. Target where you want your business to be and then set goals to reach that target. If needed, you can modify them later.

Possible targets for your business include making a lot of money, building sales, gaining market share, getting a 25% return on your investment, or establishing a market position. You should note that these are business goals. I discussed personal goals in a previous chapter. For example, you might have a personal goal of learning about running a business. Based on that personal goal, a target you might shoot for would be to stay in business for the first year and have a 5% profit at the end of the second year.

Characteristics of targets and goals

Targets and goals must have several characteristics to be effective. They must be specific, measurable, and have a set time limit. In the examples I just gave, both targets meet these requirements. They are specific: stay in business and make a 5% profit. They are measurable: you will know if you are still in business and a 5% profit can be measured. They are time based: the first target covers one specific year and the second target a second specific year.

Nebulous or indefinite targets are not effective in building a successful business. For example, you could say your targets are to stay in business and make a profit. Does that mean that if you get a registration payment in the mail this afternoon and make a profit for the day, that you have reached your target? You did stay in business until this afternoon and you did make a profit. Exactly what do you mean when you say you want to stay in business and make a profit? If I asked ten people, I would get a variety of answers. To be effective, your targets and goals must be specific, measurable, and time based.

Once you have set your targets, then set the goals you need to achieve to reach each target. For example, to help achieve a target of having a 5% profit within two years, one of your goals could be to have 300 shareware dealers selling your shareware by the end of the first year. Now you have a direction and can focus your energy toward achieving your goals and reaching the target you have set.

Running your business

If your primary motivation is service to people and providing a superior product, you will make more money than if your primary motivation is just making money.
        —Bob Wallace, Quicksoft Inc. (maker of PC-Write:)

Here are 11 suggestions to help you run your business. When setting your targets and goals, keep these points in mind.

1. Be concerned about the customer at all times   That is what the quotation is about. Profits are the *result* of running a successful business, not the objective. If your objective is to make a lot of money, you will fail. To be successful, you must be service oriented. One of the most profitable and successful companies in the world, IBM, defines its business not as manufacturing computers, but as providing service. I recommend reading *Father Son & Co.* by Thomas J. Watson Jr. and Peter Petre. (New York, NY: Bantam Books, 1990) Be concerned for the customer at all times. Be concerned about complaints and problems. Treat customers as if they were important, because they are. Love your customers.

2. Do more than you are paid to do   Put a little extra effort into anything you do for your customers. Give a little extra. If you promise two free updates, give your users three under some circumstances. If you promise a printed manual, include a free quick-reference card. This is how to get happy customers.

For example, when someone calls with a problem, I help them, even if it is a hardware problem or a problem with not understanding DOS. I promise help only for registered users and only for problems with my software. But, I will help anyone who calls with any problem they have. As a result, many of the people I have spent an hour with on the phone buy two, three, and sometimes four additional programs. They recommend my software to friends and write nice letters to magazines. The letter section in the Sept./Oct. 1990 issue of *Shareware Magazine* has a letter one of my customers wrote about my Home Money Manager IIa software praising my customer support of unregistered users.

3. Write a business plan   Yes, it is difficult to do, it is tedious, and it takes a lot of time, but it is one of the most important things you can do. Why? Because, in learning how to put together a business plan, you will learn a lot about running a business. The ability to put together a good business plan demonstrates competence in business. It requires skills and knowledge that you will need to run your business. Having a business plan is the best way to show you are a competent manager. It tells the world you are ready to run a business.

4. Generate cash flow and conserve the cash you have   This means you must sell your software (get registrations) and have cash come into your business. Cash flow is the lifeblood of a business. You need cash flow to survive. Without a cash flow, you do not have the money to accomplish your other goals. If you have no cash flow, you either stop paying your bills or you go into debt.

There is more than one way for your business to go into debt. Bank loans or running up charges on a credit card come to mind immediately. But without a positive cash flow, you will not be able to get a loan. Banks only lend money to businesses that do not need it. Your business also has debt when you put money into it. Any money that you put into your business should be looked at as an investment and you should expect a return on that investment. In other words, plan for your business to pay back your investment with interest.

Shareware is unusual because you can start a shareware business with very little cash. However, this does not eliminate the need for cash flow; it just makes it easier for your business to survive on a lower sales volume.

It seems like a simple concept—you need to sell software to stay in business. It is so simple that many people forget how important it is. A lack of cash flow is one of the leading causes of business failure. How do you generate cash flow? Put most of your efforts into marketing. Marketing and sales are like a pump and water. If you stop pumping (marketing), the flow of water (sales) stops.

I also mentioned conserving cash. Many people starting a business go out and spend money on things they feel a business needs. They will rent an office, hire a secretary, buy all the "necessary" office equipment, etc. The cash starts flowing out, but there is little coming in. The business quickly bleeds to death as the owner runs out of cash.

5. Make market share a prime objective when your program is first released
Get as many people as possible to use it. Send out disks to as many dealers and user groups as you can afford to. Upload your program to Compu-Serve, GEnie, and the major BBSs. Give away copies to anyone who asks. Do everything you can to make your software the most widely used program of its type. Do not worry about registrations; work to get everyone using your software.

Market share gets your software noticed by the press. The quicker you build market share, the more difficult it is for your competition to get started. Once you have a significant market share, people, and particularly large businesses, will buy your software just because it is the program everyone else uses. Build a large user base and your business can be supported just by selling goods and services to your user base.

6. Plan to use lots of patience and hard work   If you are the only person running your business, expect to work long hours, seven days a week. Do not forget the "law of three"—for anything you want to do, take your most conservative estimate and multiply by three. Be patient, because things will take three times longer than you expect. Be ready to work hard, because getting a business started will take three times the effort you expect.

7. Join professional groups and associations related to your software's field of interest   Join your local chamber of commerce. When I discussed COMDEX, I talked about meeting people and making contacts. Your local chamber of commerce is a source of contacts that can help your business locally. For example, you can get to know bankers, who are essential to any business. You will also meet people that can help you find employees (when you need them) or used equipment, and help you evaluate services such as legal and accounting services.

Keep in mind that business "social" meetings are not really social gatherings. They are a means to meet and talk with people in a more relaxed atmosphere. Just as COMDEX parties are really ways to make industry contacts, chamber of commerce breakfasts (or whatever your local chamber sponsors) are a way to make contacts with people that might be able to help you. You are not there to eat. You are there to listen and to meet people.

You should also join the Association of Shareware Professionals. The ASP is where you can meet other shareware authors and make useful contacts that can help your shareware business. The ASP will be discussed in chapter 13. In addition, if there are any local or regional software associations in your area, join them. These groups are another important source of contacts.

ASP has been a source of professional contacts I would not have otherwise had. It's been a great source of education. I've learned how to conduct myself in a professional manner. Since joining ASP my sales have gone up over 300%. Being an ASP member has done more than anything to increase my registrations.
—shareware author telephone survey responses

8. Make a specific division of duties and responsibilities   If two or more people are involved in your business, you can divide tasks according to skills. A software business can typically be separated into three areas:

A. Product Manager—programming, product development, writing manuals, user support.
B. Marketing Manager—sales and marketing.
C. Operations Manager—production, fulfillment (order processing and shipping), finance.

If you took my advice from chapter 2 and found someone who is good at marketing, the two of you can divide the functions handled by the operations manager.

9. If you are running your business from your home, set aside a specific room or area exclusively for your business   Make it clear to your family that when you are in your business room, you are not to be disturbed. One of the most difficult aspects of running a home business is to get family and friends to recognize that you are working.

10. Do not expect to use venture capital to hire a staff and get your company started   To get venture capital, you must first have a track record showing previous successful experience starting another company. You also need an innovative product ready to be delivered to users and good experienced management.

11. Watch out for people who offer to make a lot of money for you   I regularly get calls from people who want me to give them the right to use my software in one manner or another. They have "great" ideas that cannot miss and will make me rich with little effort on my part. Look into these "opportunities," but be prepared to run. Just like in the AT&T ads, ask the caller to describe their proposal in writing. Never sign a contract until you get your lawyer's opinion or at least discuss it with other ASP authors.

These are just some basic guidelines. Running a business involves much more than I can include here. Please take the recommendation I made at the beginning of this chapter and read as much as you can and attend some courses in marketing and small business management. Start today by going to your library or bookstore and look for books on running a home business.

Services and equipment

The purpose of this section is to describe some of the services and equipment you might need and explain why you might need them. Although I am cheap and will pinch a penny until Lincoln screams, I have always found that it pays to have the right tools and to hire the right expert. I have also found that buying quality, not low price, is the best way to save money. I do not mean that when you are buying something that you should evaluate only high-priced services and equipment. Many times you can find the quality you need and still not spend much.

Keep in mind that your time is valuable. But, do not sacrifice your health or your family by running yourself into the ground so that you can build a big cash balance in your bank account. Buy the equipment and services you need to run your business properly. For example, do not spend all day copying disks when an outside service can do it for a few cents more per disk. Or, hire one of your neighbor's kids to do disk copying for you. Your time would be much more productively spent on marketing or improving your software. Evaluate expenses by asking yourself whether or not the money you spend will buy something that will bring in more profits. If buying a $10,000 desktop publishing setup will bring in an additional $12,000 in profit, then buy it. That is a 20% return on your investment.

Buying used equipment or buying from warehouse discount stores might allow you to get the equipment you need and still conserve cash. Among your contacts in local businesses, you might find people willing to give you equipment they no longer need—that is how I got my fax machine. Your contacts also can let you know about businesses that are closing or moving and selling off equipment. And do not forget warehouse discount stores such as Costco, Office Depot, Bizmart, and Office Club. Watch for sales and special prices on closeout items.

Now, I will discuss specific equipment useful to a business. I am not going to discuss computer equipment. I will assume that you have a computer and that you have the capability of reading all the disk sizes and formats that your customers use.

Answering machines

An answering machine is essential for a small business. It will answer your phone while you run to the post office or are in the shower (the most likely times that people call). Be sure to get a machine with remote message retrieval capability. This way you can pick up your messages when you are not at home. Expect to pay a minimum of $50 to $100.

Answering machines are becoming more accepted as greater numbers of people use them. Although a few people still do not like to leave messages on machines, you will get more orders if you have an answering machine. You can even have people leave their order on the message tape.

I have tried several outgoing messages and the most effective has been:

Hello. This is HomeCraft Software. I'm very sorry, but I can't get to the phone just now. If you will leave your name and number

I'll call you back as soon as I can. If you are calling to purchase one of my programs, please leave your name, address, phone number, the name of the program you are purchasing, and your VISA or MasterCard number. I will ship your software within 24 hours.

Notice that this message does not say whether I am there or not. Because I work out of my home I do not want to tell people that I am not home. The message is very generic, yet reassures the caller that if they leave a message, they will get a response. If they order software, it will be shipped within one day.

Telephones

A telephone with a hold button is another vital piece of equipment. It allows you to put the caller on hold while you switch to another phone, look up an error message, or confer with another person. This is especially important if you have kids. There is nothing more unprofessional-sounding than the background noise of kids yelling and dogs barking when you set down the phone. With phones costing so little, it is worthwhile to get a phone with a hold button.

Should you have a separate business phone line? Yes, once you start exceeding $30,000 to $40,000 in sales, or sooner if you can afford it. I ran my software business for four years using one personal phone. This worked fine. My wife and I always answered the phone as if it were a business call and our family and friends quickly got used to it. However, having a line dedicated to your business has several advantage. I converted my personal line to a business line when I started working on shareware full time. The first day the number was listed under my business name I got two calls from people who got my number from directory assistance. Both became registered users. A few months later, *Business Week Magazine* printed an article about my software, but did not include my phone number or mailing address. Fortunately, their readers could get my number from information and my phone was ringing constantly for two weeks.

A separate business line lets you take time off. If you use your personal phone, you feel like you must answer every call. You never know when it might be a family member trying to get in touch or a neighbor with an emergency. If you have a separate business line, you can stop taking calls in the evening and spend more time with your family.

800 numbers

Do you need an 800 number? A basic fact of business is that the easier you make it for customers to buy from you, the more sales you have. An 800 number makes it easier for users to call and register your software. However, my telephone survey of shareware authors showed mixed feelings.

Some authors said that 800 numbers made for larger phone bills, but no increase in sales. Others saw a dramatic increase in sales after installing an 800 number. Whether or not an 800 number will increase your profits will depend on your circumstances. For example, an 800 number should be used only for customer's orders, but this might require a separate line for the 800 number. A small business might not be able to justify paying for the second line. I will discuss more about 800 numbers in the section on telephone services.

Laser printers

For printing manuals, press releases, and business correspondence, a laser printer has become a "must-have" item. You can get by if you have a daisywheel printer. This is a good way to get started without spending much money. However, sending out a press release printed on a dot-matrix printer hurts the image of your software. It looks unprofessional, and generally is a waste of time because it will be ignored. The same applies to writing business correspondence. Letters printed on a dot-matrix printer are taken as a sign of a lack of professionalism.

Photocopier

A photocopier was one of the first major office machines I purchased. Now I would not give it up even if I closed down my software business. In many cases, having your own photocopier cannot be immediately cost-justified. However, it is a tremendous convenience and timesaver if you have a lot of small-quantity printing jobs such as duplicating press releases. Another use is for making brochures. I buy $8^1/2''$-×-$11''$ glossy paper and make my own brochures in small quantities. This allows me to include the latest quotes from magazine reviews and produce specialized brochures for each of the small niche markets I target.

If you get a copier, you should also get a service contract. Copiers are the only equipment for which I recommend buying service contracts. They are complicated machines that seem to need constant cleaning, tuning, and attention. Many of the parts that wear out are inexpensive, but the labor to replace them runs into many hours and big dollars. A service contract will save you money. The cost of a service contract will vary depending on the type of copier and the number of copies you expect to make.

Fax machine

A fax machine is another piece of equipment that comes to mind. If you need to quickly exchange documents with someone, a fax machine is the only way to do it. Fax machines are also starting to be increasingly used for placing orders. Customers like using a fax because they can place their order now and do it in writing.

I do not feel a fax machine is essential unless you publish business software or work on an international basis. However, they are convenient and handy. If you get a fax machine, also get a line switch that allows you to have the fax machine and your voice phone on the same line. Fax machine prices are dropping rapidly and will be going down more. Currently you can expect to pay between $500 and $1000 to get a fax and about $100 to $200 for the line switch.

Fax boards for your computer are also available. You can get a combination 2400 baud modem and 9600 baud fax for under $150. There is a disadvantage to using a fax board. You cannot send documents that are in paper form, for example, a contract your lawyer just wrote. There have also been times when I needed to fax a section of my user's manual. It is quicker and easier if you can photocopy a document and send it using a stand-alone fax machine.

Postage machine

A postage machine was one of the most important pieces of equipment I added to my business. The postage-machine manufacturers advertise their machines by telling about the money you save putting the correct postage on your mail. I did not have that problem. I kept a box containing a wide variety of stamps and could always put the correct postage on my mail. What a postage machine did for me was save time, and that was more valuable than saving a few cents.

You cannot buy a postage machine, you must rent one from a postage-machine company. Look in the Yellow Pages for a listing of the brands available in your area. Pitney-Bowes is the biggest supplier of postage machines and I have found its machines to be the best. However, it is also the most expensive, costing about $29 a month to rent. I have also found Pitney-Bowes' service to be terrible, but maybe the company can get away with that since it's the biggest.

Postalia is a brand that is cheaper to rent (about $24 a month), but its machine is technically not as good at a Pitney-Bowes. For example, to change the date on a Postalia, you need a flashlight. Even then, the numbers are still difficult to read. The Pitney-Bowes has easily accessible thumb wheels. The Pitney-Bowes includes a lock that prevents printing postage over $1 without pushing a second key. On the Postalia, you can easily enter $7.50 when you intend to enter $0.75 (I have done it).

Office supplies

Some basic office supplies are also necessary if you want to be taken seriously as a business. The most important are business cards and letterhead. Both should be professionally typeset and printed on quality paper.

If you have a laser printer and some good fonts, you can design your own letterhead and print it as a part of each letter. Otherwise, get it typeset and printed.

I have done something unique with my letterhead. The top portion is a standard, conservative business letterhead with my company name and address. In the lower right corner, I include a $1'' \times 3''$ ad that I ran in *PC Computing* and *PC World*. Since my software is unique, having the ad as a part of my letterhead immediately shows the reader what type of software I publish.

Producing your manuals

It is best to keep, as much as possible, the production of your registered versions directly within your control. This means you might want equipment such as bookbinding machines and shrink-wrapping machines. I list sources that supply this type of equipment in chapter 16. I have found a shrink-wrapping machine to be particularly useful. Shrink-wrapping your software makes it look more professional and helps your company appear more substantial and stable. The neat, professional look it gives to your package increases the value of your package significantly. You can purchase a shrink-wrapping machine for under $400.

Services

Now let us look at services your business might need. There are three essential services: a good lawyer, a good accountant, and a good printer.

Finding someone who is "good" is a major problem. Unlike a product you can examine and for which you can get a feel for the quality, it is difficult to determine the quality of a service until you try it. My experiences with referral services for lawyers and accountants suggest they are really no better than looking in the phone book. You also can ask a friend to refer you to someone. Sometimes this will work out well; other times, your friend's needs will be different from yours and the person he or she hired might not be the best person for you.

Joining the chamber of commerce or a regional software association is one way to find the services you need. It gives you a chance to meet professional people whose services you might need in the future. You can evaluate them and determine how well you communicate and work with them before you actually need their services.

Another method is to call the lawyers and accountants you have picked out of the phone book. Tell them what you are looking for and ask what they can do for you. Make this a short, ten-minute conversation. Some will ask you to come to their office and will charge $100 or more for this visit. I pass those by. In my conversations, I look for someone I feel comfortable talking with. The most crucial element in this type of relationship is the ability to communicate and understand each other. The person I feel comfortable with is the one I can communicate with.

You should also ask about rates. I can feel just as comfortable with $75-an-hour lawyers as with $200-an-hour lawyers, if I can easily work with them and they have the required knowledge and skills.

Establish a relationship

When do you need to hire a lawyer or an accountant? When you have a problem that needs to be resolved. In starting a shareware business, you are not in a position to hire a lawyer for every small question (remember, conserve cash). However, if you have a personal need, such as a will, use a lawyer who also can help with your business. Once you have hired a lawyer for one or two small jobs, you have established a relationship. It is then easier for you to call with small questions or for advice.

Legal services

Your business will require a lawyer when you form a corporation or partnership, or need to review contract documents. Do not try to do these on your own unless you have some experience; even then you might want to consult an expert. For example, I have extensive experience as the team leader in negotiating multimillion-dollar contracts. Yet, I would not sign a partnership agreement, for example, until my lawyer reviewed it.

You can reduce your costs by using standard forms and learning the key points to look for in some types of contracts. However, be sure the standard forms you are using are applicable to a software business and that you are not blindsided by a contract that has all your key provisions, but has an additional clause that you do not understand. For this reason, for reviewing contracts involving software, it is a good idea to hire an attorney who is familiar with shareware.

Accountants

A good way to find an accountant is to hire one to do your personal income taxes. An accountant is usually worth the cost and, again, you establish a relationship that is handy when you need more important services. It also allows you to evaluate how well you work with this person and the quality of the work.

I found it very useful to have had an accountant doing my taxes for several years before I formed a corporation. There were some tax implications based on the timing of when certain documents were signed. My lawyer called my accountant, they worked it out, and I just came in to sign the papers on the correct day. And, my accountant did not charge me! Because he was familiar with my financial situation, he could answer the questions in just a few minutes. If he were starting from scratch, it would have cost me $50 to $100 for the accounting advice.

Printing services

Why do print shops fit in the same category as lawyers and accountants? Having a good printer is essential to your business. You need a printer you can count on to do quality work, get it done right the first time, and to handle rush jobs. You can find printers that fit these requirements both in quick-print chains and local print shops. The only way to determine who is good and who is not, however, is to try them.

Almost all printers have the equipment to do the type of work you will need, although many quick-print shops cannot handle color printing on glossy paper. (Make this one of your criteria for qualifying printers; it is a service you might need in the future.) The service and quality you get depends on the people you deal with. The first good printer I found was part of a national chain. Everything was fine until the manager of the store I was dealing with left the company. I then went through five or six printers until I found the one that currently does all my work.

I am constantly approached by other printers offering lower prices and faster service, but there is no way I will change now. With my current printer, I know that I will get my printing when it is promised and that I will get quality work. Besides, they do exactly the type of graphic design I like.

When you find a good printer, treat them right. For example, when I exhibited at a local trade show recently, my exhibit included a poster of the front cover of my software package. This poster was made by the graphic artist at the print shop I use. I asked the artist to make up a little sign that stated the printer had designed the cover and that gave its address and phone number. I put this sign next to the poster. The printer appreciated this and it cost me nothing.

Getting VISA/MasterCard merchant status

We talked about VISA merchant status a month ago. You and a few others gave me some very good advice. I took it. I visited the branch manager of the bank I have had a checking account with for over 20 years and today I got my merchant account.
— shareware author John Bauernschub

When you decide to start operating as a business, one of the first things to do is to get a separate checking account and use it only for your business. Deposit all your receipts into this account and write checks from this account to pay all your expenses. You will immediately see whether or not you are making money and your bank statements will give you much of the information you need at tax time.

When you select a bank for your business checking account, you should also check to see whether or not they offer VISA/MasterCard merchant accounts. One of the biggest problems shareware authors have is obtaining VISA/MasterCard merchant status. Accepting credit cards brings you more business. It allows you to convert calls for help from unregistered users into immediate sales. If you cannot accept credit cards, your business appears smaller and less legitimate. In addition, the more home users you have, the more sales you will get from credit card users (most businesses and institutions pay by check or purchase order). If you are going to sell your software internationally, credit cards are essential. They eliminate all the problems with currency conversion, making registration of your software easier for both you and the user.

Here is the bad news: it is harder to get merchant status than it is to get a loan. Banks must meet the guidelines set by the credit card companies. However, these are just guidelines and banks can choose to grant merchant status to companies that do not meet all of them.

It is your job to help your bank decide to grant you merchant status by getting them to waive some of the requirements. Banks are in the business of making money. One of the ways they make money is by issuing credit card merchant accounts. They want your business. You just need to give them what they need to feel comfortable.

The best situation is to work with a bank that you have had personal accounts with for many years. If this is not possible, get to know the bankers in your community better. For example, join the chamber of commerce—many bankers are members. Or, go into a bank and ask to meet the manager. Tell him (or her) that you are starting a business and wish to learn more about the services a bank can provide. Do not be in a rush to establish a merchant account. Banks do not like to rush into things that require them to bend the rules. Project an image of someone who is thoughtfully and carefully investigating the right way to run a business.

When you visit a bank, be sure to dress like a banker. People feel more comfortable talking with others who are similar to themselves. Men should wear a gray or blue suit, or a sport jacket with matching pants. Women should wear solid-color suits or dark dresses. If you are not sure what to wear, pay attention to what the bank manager wears (not the tellers) the next time you visit your bank.

Applying for merchant status

The merchant status guideline that will cause you the most problems is the one requiring a store front. There is a good reason for this guideline. The credit card companies have often lost money to "boiler room" mail-order businesses that can quickly go out of business and leave town. To get around the store-front requirement, demonstrate your long-term stability. Have you lived in the same place for five or more years? Have you banked at the same bank, and do you have money in your account? Have you been in business for several years? Have you shown a commitment to the business—by advertising, for example? Answering "yes" to questions like these helps to demonstrate your stability.

Document the proof of your stability, and bring that proof along on your visit to the bank. Bring all the information you can put together that will make the bank feel comfortable with you. Be sure that any information you bring helps your cause. For example, leave out a personal balance sheet if it shows you are heavily in debt. The following is a list of possible documents that you could bring with you to the bank.

1. Bring your personal financial statements, including a balance sheet. These should show that you personally are financially stable and can back the financial obligations of your business.

2. Bring your last two or three year's tax returns. These should show that you have already had a steady income over the past few years. Again, you are showing that you personally are financially stable. It is even better if you have been in business for a few years and your tax returns show that your business has made a profit.

3. "Sell" your software to the banker. Bring copies of your registered version, if it looks like a quality package that could go on a retail shelf. Also bring copies of any magazine reviews, promotional material, and letters from satisfied customers. The shareware marketing method might not appear to be a reliable source of income to many bankers, so be prepared to discuss shareware in general. Take along information, such as magazine articles, that discuss successful shareware authors. Bring a copy of *Dr. File Finder's Guide To Shareware* (available in most major book stores).

4. If you have worked for the same company for more than five years, bring a copy of your resumé showing your work experience, educational background, and accomplishments. Continuous employment shows that you are less likely to relocate and helps the bank feel more comfortable about your staying around.

5. Bring a copy of your business plan, if you have one. If you do not have one, put together a one-page description of your market, your estimate of how much software you expect to sell, why you expect to sell that much, and a description of how you plan to market your software.

6. Bring a recent assessment of your home or, if one has not been done, bring a picture of your home and something that shows its value, such as property-tax bills. Also, bring a history of your previous addresses, if there have been few. This again is to show that you have assets and a commitment to staying in the community. Homeowners are less likely to relocate than renters.

The banker might tell you that none of this is needed; mine did—but he then took copies of it all and put it in my file.

Expect to get "no" for an answer. Some banks have a firm policy on accepting no mail-order businesses, while others will work with you. This can even vary from branch to branch for the same bank. I recently talked with four banks. Two said no way. The other two said no, but agreed to submit my package of information to the bank manager. If you are completely turned down, try again at another bank. Your first objective is to find a bank that will give you the application form. Once you have completed an application, your chances of being approved are much greater.

When you go to a bank to discuss merchant status, ask to talk to the manager. That is the only person who can waive the bank's rules and requirements. If you start at a lower level, it can be difficult to have your information forwarded to the manager. If you start with the manager, you are speaking with the decision maker. If the manager refers you to a lower level, the person at the lower level becomes aware that the manager is interested enough in what you have to say to ask another person to spend some time listening to you.

Rules for keeping merchant status

Once you gain merchant status, do not lose it. Be aware of the activities that can cause your business to lose its VISA/MasterCard merchant status. The following list describes the activities that will cause you to lose your merchant status.

- Entering a credit card transaction long before shipping the product.
- Not letting the customer cancel the purchase within three days.
- Chargebacks and credits totaling more than 10% of credit card transactions.
- Excessive complaints to the Better Business Bureau.

Alternatives

You might find that you cannot present a positive image to the bank if, for example, you work for a company that has relocated you several times or if you live in an apartment. You can sometimes still get a merchant account, if you establish a track record as a VISA/MasterCard merchant. It sounds like a catch-22 situation, but there is a solution. There are companies that will process your VISA/MasterCard orders for you. They work under a contract with a bank because merchants with VISA/MasterCard status cannot generally process charges for other companies. The advantage is that they are not prejudiced against mail-order companies. The disadvantage is that the cost is high. However, it is better to pay the cost than to lose an order because you cannot take credit cards. A company that provides this service is:

State Retail Service Association
Attn: Sharon McManis
110 Lavista Dr.
Easley, SC 29642
(803) 855-9764

You will need to reimburse the credit card processing company for the bank's application fee (about $50) and, most likely, there also will be a set-up fee (approximately $500). Plus, the per-transaction fee will be higher than the bank's normal fee, and might be as high as 4% to 5%.

Ad response companies

Some answering services will take your calls, handle your orders, and process your charges with their bank. These services are actually 800-number ad response companies (thus, they are also a way for you to have an 800 number). The problem is that they know nothing about your software. They are good at handling orders for simple consumer products, but many software users ask questions before placing an order. To find an ad response company, check the Yellow Pages under answering services.

Having disk distributors handle your orders

Some shareware dealers will handle credit card sales for you. The Public (software) Library (PsL), one of the largest, probably offers the least expensive service of this type for authors. PsL charges a small handling fee and passes on the fee its bank charges for each transaction. PsL can be reached at (713) 524-6394. Some of the larger shareware disk dealers also sell registered versions. This provides another alternative for users to order your software using a credit card (and access to an 800 number). Expect to sell your software to the shareware dealer at your distributor price of about 60% off list. One of the larger shareware dealers that offers this service is PC-SIG, which can be reached at (408) 730-9291.

National Association of Credit Card Merchants

Another organization you can turn to is the National Association of Credit Card Merchants. This group is a for-profit organization operated by a company called the Credit Card Bureau. This company is in the business of publishing books and supplying information to merchants who need VISA and MasterCard merchant status. It can help you get and keep your merchant status.

A yearly fee of $250 provides you with a free copy of the book *Getting And Keeping Your VISA/MasterCard Merchant Status* and provides access to help in getting merchant status. For example, the association maintains a list of over 200 banks located around the country that will work with home-based mail-order companies. The association claims that, with its help, nearly everyone who joins is able to get merchant status—if the member is a legitimate business. For more information about this company, call (407) 737-7500 or write to:

The National Association of Credit Card Merchants
217 N. Seacrest Blvd.
Box 400
Boynton Beach, FL 33425

Discover card

The Discover card is a fast-growing alternative that is more receptive to direct-market (mail-order) business. It operates on an all-electronic basis— you enter the transaction in a terminal and the money is electronically transferred to your checking account that same day. The disadvantages are that more people have VISA/MasterCard than Discover cards and the cost is slightly higher as a result of the need to purchase a terminal. However, if you already have a terminal for VISA/MasterCard, you can use that same terminal. For more information call (800) 347-6673.

American Express

If you are interested in accepting American Express, you can contact the company by calling (800) 528-5200, or (800) 528-4800 in Alaska and Hawaii. American Express does not have any problems with accepting mail-order businesses as merchants. The disadvantage is that you must mail your charge slips to American Express and it mails you a check. You usually can expect to wait two weeks to get your money.

The post office and UPS

Anyone running a mail-order business should know how the U.S. Postal System works. First, let us look at how mail is handled.

First-class mail First-class mail receives the highest priority. It includes personal mail, mail that must move quickly, and mail that includes checks and money orders. In 1989, 53% of all mail was sent first class.

Second-class mail This includes newspapers, magazines, and other periodicals. Second-class mail makes up 10.5% of all mail.

Third-class mail Third-class mail includes advertising and promotional mail, and parcels weighing less than a pound. It is handled only after first- and second-class mail are delivered and only when carriers have room in trucks and bags for it. This accounts for 38% of all mail.

Since you can send mail weighing up to three ounces for $0.198, third-class mail can save you a lot of money. For example, you can mail update disks for $0.198 each instead of $0.52 each for first-class mail. Third-class mail is ideal for mailing newsletters and promotional material. However, if you are just mailing upgrade announcements, you are better off using form feed post cards because they only cost $0.19 to mail.

Third-class mail requires at least 200 identical pieces be sent at one time. Addresses must be sorted by zip code. Thus, a good mailing-list manager is important. The cost of using third-class mail is $60 per year for the permit, plus postage for each piece sent. The highest postage rate is $.198 per piece for the first three ounces. Some bulk-mailing situations (many pieces going to the same city, for example) lower the cost per piece. For more information on third-class mail, get publication #49, *Third-Class Mail Preparation*, from your local post office.

By the way, when the post office says that you must mail identical pieces, it means that pieces must be the same size and weight. The contents may be different for each envelope, as long as each envelope is the same size and weight.

Fourth-class mail Fourth-class mail (parcel post) is used for packages and books. If you are mailing only your user's manual, book rate is the cheapest, and in many cases the fastest, way to send it. Material sent using book rate is delivered within five days, and would only cost you $1.48 for a two-pound package.

For international mail, send letters that weigh one ounce or less by letter air mail. Anything heavier (such as catalogs, disks, and registered versions of your software) should be sent via small-packet air mail. This includes packages to Canada and Mexico. The rates vary depending on the distance, but it is cheaper and just as fast as letter air mail. For more information on international postage rates, get a copy of publication #51, *International Postal Rates and Fees*, from your post office.

The United States Postal Service also publishes a free newsletter for mail-order businesses called *Memo To Mailers*. It contains information on changes in rules and regulations, plus tips on how to save on mailing costs. To get on the mailing list for this newsletter, write to:

U.S. Postal Service
P.O. Box 999
Springfield, VA 22150-0999

Depending on your circumstances, the post office might provide all of the services you need. The disadvantage of the post office is that they do not automatically insure packages. I have also found that, as the post office has become more automated, I get more mail returned to me as undeliverable. If you do not have the address exactly correct, the chances are increasing that it will be returned to you. In most cases, mail returned to me as having the "wrong address" was addressed exactly the way the address was given to me. People, following local customs, have gotten used to using addresses that are not technically correct. With hand sorting, the post office reliably delivered their mail. This is no longer true. Because of these insurance and delivery problems, many authors use UPS and over-night package-delivery services instead.

United Parcel Service

United Parcel Service (UPS) will pick up packages at your door daily. The big advantage UPS has over the post office is that every package is automatically insured and the packages are still processed by people. This means that if the address is not correct, the package will still, in many cases, be correctly delivered. I have had a package that both Air Borne Express and the post office were unable to deliver using an address I verified with the customer three times. UPS delivered it with no problems. Another advantage of UPS is that it will accept copies of your logbook as proof that the package was sent.

Although it might take more time to ship by UPS because you need to fill out a logbook, you do not have to stand in line as sometimes happens with the post office. UPS bills you on a weekly basis for all packages you have shipped and you can pay the bills monthly. With UPS, there is also a weekly fee of $5 that covers all pickups for that week.

UPS second-day air delivery is an essential service that many customers will require. The cost is only slightly more than ground delivery, and many customers are willing to pay extra to get their software in two days. UPS also offers overnight delivery that includes Saturdays. If you have a daily UPS pickup, using their next-day service becomes easy and relatively inexpensive.

Next day air services

I recommend that you sign up with an overnight air carrier such as Federal Express of Air Borne Express. It costs nothing to open an account and an account makes it easy should you need to ship something that requires overnight delivery. In addition, some customers will ask for (and pay extra for) this service, which can be essential for business software. I have also found overnight delivery useful for these reasons:

- When you want to let someone know they are important, such as a software reviewer, send their software by overnight express.
- When you have a big customer that needs a bug fixed yesterday.
- When a shareware disk dealer needs a new disk in time for a big computer show opening in two days.

You can find the phone numbers for all of the major overnight delivery services in the Yellow Pages of almost any phone book.

Using the telephone

How do you answer the phone? I am not talking about the words you say—although, if you want to sound professional, you should answer the phone using your company name. (I use, "Good morning, HomeCraft Software," before 12 noon.) I am talking about your attitude. What type of image do you project?

You want to convey the image of a cheerful, pleasant person who is eager to help. It is very easy to make your voice sound exactly the way it needs to sound to present this image—whether you are in a good or bad mood. Just smile. Smile when you answer the phone and you will sound like a person with whom people want to talk. The image you create with your body will also be reflected in your voice.

I learned this technique as a morning disk jockey. How do morning DJs sound cheerful and pleasant every morning, even when they are sick and are having a bad day? They smile when they are talking. It works in the opposite way also. If you are having trouble with a supplier and you want them to know that you are upset—but you do not want to say anything directly—clench your hands into a tight fist and your voice will take on an edge of anger and frustration.

Handling complaints

What happens when you pick up the phone and it is a user who has been struggling with a problem related to your software? The person is upset, maybe even angry with you. These can be some of the most difficult calls to handle. Most of us do not like complaints. They sound like personal attacks. We get caught up in the emotion of the personal attack on our competency or software. We might end up trying to prove the complainer wrong. We do everything except listen. If handled properly, complaints and problems can help your business grow. The most likely source of a registration is a person calling with a problem or complaint.

The best approach for handling an angry user is to stay silent and listen to the problem. Give the caller a chance to vent frustration, then go over the problem in a step-by-step manner. If you can, follow what the user is doing on your computer until you identify the problem. No matter how upset a user gets, remain calm and supportive.

The most difficult call I have had was from a user trying to install my hard-disk shell, YOUR MENU. Nothing was working the way he wanted and he would not stop complaining long enough to let me ask some questions. He would not try my suggestions, but insisted the software should work like WordStar. With a great deal of patience on my part, we worked through the problem and, at the end of the call, he gave me his credit-card number so that he could register as a user.

Most customers understand that software is occasionally faulty or has bugs. They will give you a chance, if you treat them fairly and with respect. Remember, the customer is always right. That does not mean they are technically right, it means that if you treat customers as if they are wrong, they will not be your customers.

Your company will be judged on your courtesy, the information you provide (give full explanations), and your responsiveness (avoid delays). Letters of complaint should be answered within 24 hours. If giving an answer takes longer, inform the user you are investigating and will be back in touch as soon as possible.

Phone services

Some phone services are beneficial while others are not. You should avoid call waiting. It is annoying to the person you are talking to, especially when that person is paying for a call to order your software. When you interrupt a call to answer your call waiting, you are telling the first person that they are not important to you. If you have so many calls that you must have call waiting, then it is time to have a second phone line installed. An answering machine on the second line can take messages while you are talking on the first line.

Call forwarding, however, is very useful. This allows you to have your phone calls automatically sent to another phone. You can visit relatives or go away for a weekend and still get all your calls without the callers knowing that you are spending three days at the beach, for example.

800 numbers

Do you need an 800 number? This is a difficult question. The answer is yes, all mail-order businesses should have an 800 number for customers to use to place orders. It will bring additional sales from impulse buyers. However, the other side of this question is that many shareware authors do not feel they can afford the extra expense.

If you are not sure about 800 numbers, the following criteria might help with your decision.

The value of an 800 number can depend on your software. If you have a unique program, you have less of a need for an 800 number. If you sell the same product as six other publishers, and all six of you advertise in the same magazines, then an 800 number is essential to help differentiate you from, or keep you equal with, the competition. A general rule of business is that you should make it as easy as possible for your customers to do business with you. An 800 number makes it easier for your customers to call you.

If you have a complex product that requires a lot of telephone support, you should have an 800 number. Build the cost of the 800 number into your registration fee.

An 800 number does help show that you are in business for real; it makes you appear less of a fly-by-night outfit. It gives you credibility. An 800 number is also very useful if you travel. Instead of using a credit card to check your messages, call your 800 number. The cost of using the 800 number will be significantly less, and this use alone can sometimes justify it.

An 800 number is good for building a mailing list. If the call is free, even people with a casual interest will call for information. Once you get them on your mailing list, you can put together a direct-mail campaign to sell them on your software.

An 800 number can increase your contact with customers. People who have questions (or complaints) are more likely to call when they do not have to pay for it. If you can resolve the problems over the phone quickly, these people are more likely to be repeat customers. (You want to keep people using your software so you can sell upgrades and enhancements.)

The most economical use of an 800 number is to restrict it to customers calling to place an order. A second, conventional number should be provided for users calling for information or help. However, if you want to expand your mailing list or improve customer service, allow everyone to use your 800 number.

Your existing phone can be set up to provide your customers with a toll-free number for reaching you. All the major long-distance companies have services that provide an 800 number that will ring on your existing phone. However, if you can afford a second line, it provides a way to tell whether the caller is using your 800 number or your regular number.

The biggest providers of 800 numbers are AT&T, MCI, and Sprint. Usually, several levels of service are available.

AT&T AT&T has four levels of service for 800 numbers. 800 Readyline delivers 800 service over regular lines and is compatible with local options such as call forwarding and call waiting. Intrastate and interstate calls are on the same line and require no new lines or hardware. The cost is $20 per month, plus $0.22 to $0.25 per minute—billed to the second. There is a $43.50 installation fee. A 5% discount is available if you spend more than $50 on long distance calls per month.

AT&T BASIC 800 service is similar, but uses dedicated lines.

AT&T Megacom 800 delivers service over digital lines.

AT&T 800 Masterline offers Canadian access in addition to intrastate and interstate access on a single dedicated line.

Call (800) 638-8326 or (201) 658-2664 to talk with AT&T.

US Sprint US Sprint offers FONLINE 800. You can receive intrastate and interstate calls on a single line. The cost is $10 per month with a $50 installation fee. US Sprint also offers ULTRA 800 for heavier users. It features overflow control that sends calls to designated local business lines should the 800 line be overloaded during peak calling periods. Contact US Sprint by calling (913) 541-6100.

MCI   MCI does not have bundled packages but instead offers an á la carte selection of services. Basic service is $20 per month and between $0.19 and $0.25 per minute. MCI is just beginning to offer a new service for residential phone lines that provides 800 service for $2 per month. You can reach MCI by calling (800) 888-0800 or (202) 872-1600.

Because competition is fierce in the phone business, things change rapidly; call each 800 – service provider for current information.

Questions you should ask

Questions you should ask long-distance companies when comparing services include:

- What is the monthly service fee?
- Is there a minimum monthly charge?
- What is the cost per minute, and how does this vary depending on distance and time of day?
- Are there any volume discounts? (For example, AT&T offers a 5% discount if you use more than $50 per month.)
- Are there any installation fees?
- What is the timing increment for billing? Some services bill by the minute, so if you use 62 seconds, you pay for a two-minute call. It is better to use a service that bills in smaller increments. For example, some bill by the second or for every six seconds.

Be aware that the cost varies depending on your location because of local phone company charges.

Taxes and the IRS

If you are running your own business, you will need to learn about local, county, state, federal, and possibly metropolitan tax laws. I can only discuss federal income tax here. You will need to find out about your state and local laws.

People starting their first business seem to run into two problems when filing federal income-tax forms: They file the wrong forms, and they do not correctly account for inventory.

Tax forms

Once you start a business, you can no longer file form 1040EZ. You must complete forms 1040 and 1040 Schedule C. Form 1040 is for people who itemize deductions. 1040 Schedule C is used to determine the profit or loss from your business.

Inventory

When calculating the profit or loss from a business, many people like to look at how much money they have received, subtract what they spend during the year, and the result is a profit or loss. You cannot do this. Any inventory you have must be accounted for.

Here is a simple example. If you are selling 386FX Widgets and spent $1000 to purchase 100 widgets last year, then your business expenses are $1000. If you had no sales, you might expect your business had a loss of $1000 for the year. That is not true. You still have $1000 of widgets in your possession. You have not lost anything, unless the widgets have lost value or become unsalable. The way you calculate your profit or loss is:

$$\text{Gross sales} - \text{Cost \& expenses} + \text{Inventory} = \text{Profit (or Loss)}$$

If, in the example above, you had sold ten 386FX Widgets for $50 each, your profit would be:

$$\$500 \text{ (sales)} - \$1000 \text{ (cost of goods)} + \$900$$
$$\text{(inventory at } \$10 \text{ each)} = \$400 \text{ profit}$$

Notice that although you made a profit, you have a negative cash flow. More cash has gone out ($1000) than you took in ($500). That is why, in an earlier chapter, I highlighted cash flow as being important. You can make a profit, but if you have a negative cash flow, such as in this example, you will soon be out of business.

Home-office deduction

You most likely will be running your software business from your home and will be eligible to deduct depreciation on your home. While this might seem to be a nice way to reduce your taxes, keep in mind that home-office deductions might not provide the advantages you expect. For example, when you sell your house, you might not be able to defer the capital gains tax on all of your profits. Under normal circumstances, you can defer paying taxes if you purchase another house within two years. If you have taken a deduction for using part of your home for your business, you will need to divide any gain on the sale of your house between personal use and business use. It does not matter how long you have had your business in your home. If you have deducted depreciation, you could save a few hundred dollars in taxes this year, but will have to pay several thousand dollars more in taxes if you sell your home next year.

Before taking a tax deduction for an office in your home, discuss your situation with your accountant. There are exceptions that you can take advantage of to save money. For example, if you took home-office deductions in the past, but do not take them in the year of sale, you might be able to defer paying capital gains tax on the entire gain.

Hobby or business

Whether you operate your software company as a hobby or a business can make a big difference in your tax bill. We all want to call our software publishing efforts a business. If your software company is defined by the IRS as a hobby, your tax deductions would be limited to the amount of income your software company earns. You cannot deduct losses from a hobby. But, if you are publishing software as a business, all of your business expenses are deductible. (If the IRS defines it as a sideline business, your business expenses might only be deductible after they exceed 2% of your adjusted gross income.)

What can you do to protect your status as a business and prevent the IRS from reclassifying you as a hobbyist? As far as the IRS is concerned, a business is any activity that results in a profit. However, you do not actually have to make a profit, you only need to show that you intend to make a profit.

The easiest way to meet this requirement is to make a profit. Based on IRS guidelines, if you make a profit in three of any five consecutive years, you are running a real business. It doesn't matter how big your profit is in those three years, as long as you make a profit.

If you have a business that is producing yearly losses, you will need to prove that your *intention* is to make a profit.

Here is a list of things you can use to prove you are running a legitimate business.

- Operate in a businesslike manner and keep accurate financial records. For example, you should have a separate bank account that is used only for your business. You should, at a minimum, be using a spreadsheet to track your sales and expenses.
- Act in a professional manner. For example, joining professional associations such as the ASP and your state's software association help establish you as a legitimate business.
- If you can show that you are making a serious effort to earn a profit, you have demonstrated you are trying to run a real business. For example, sending copies of your shareware to five or six distributors is not a serious effort. Sending disks to 200 distributors helps demonstrate a serious effort toward generating sales. Other activities such as advertising, obtaining VISA/MasterCard merchant status, registering a ''doing business as,'' and printing a catalog or brochure help demonstrate that you are making a serious effort to run a profitable business.
- Run your business as a business is expected to be run. Have business cards and stationery printed. Get a business phone that includes a listing in the Yellow Pages. Rent a postage meter and buy a photocopier. These are things nearly every business requires and they are the types of things you would not have unless you were seriously running a business.

You do not need to use everything listed, but, if you are losing money, you will need all the evidence you can put together to show that you intend to earn a profit and have the potential to do so in the future. The IRS's typical approach will be to try to show that you get personal pleasure from your business. If they can demonstrate this, it will count against you. A hobby is something you do for personal pleasure, even if it earns a profit. You need to prove that your motive is to earn a profit.

Employing your children

You can make your children's weekly allowance tax deductible by paying them to work in your business. A child with no other income can earn up to $3000 without paying taxes. To do this, you will need to keep good records showing the type of work they did, the hours they put in, and the hourly pay rate. The pay rate should be comparable with what you would pay someone hired from outside of your family to do the same type work.

Getting tax help

Many community colleges offer evening courses on taxes for people in small business. If you are not familiar with how businesses are taxed, I recommend that you take one of these courses. Although you might hire an accountant, you still need to provide correct information. For example, your accountant has no way of knowing the value of your inventory. If you mistakenly report a value of zero, that is the way it will appear on your tax forms.

I started this chapter by recommending that you learn more about running a small business and that is how I am ending the chapter. I have discussed some key topics that should help you get your business started. But, there is more to learn. In business, there is *always* more to learn. So read, take some courses, listen to audio tapes, and get involved in groups where you can discuss your business problems with others who have faced the same problems.

9
Legal considerations

There are no legal requirements for starting a business. No forms to fill out or papers to sign. Your business exists the moment you decide you have a business. However, what type of business you have and how you operate it might require some legal work.

I will start with some of the simpler topics and save the complex ones for later. I will assume that you are running your business out of your home.

Local licenses

Many different local laws affect businesses. I cannot even attempt to discuss local laws, permits, and regulations here. I will cover basic legal considerations in a broad fashion. You will need to check local requirements and laws yourself.

Zoning is usually not a problem for a home-based software business. If you do not have any external sign of a business, you usually can operate in an area zoned as residential.

Your city, town, or county might require a license for your business. Sometimes, this license is solely a source of revenue for local government. If you have employees, a local license might be required to ensure that you have safe working conditions. Enforcement of local licenses is often minimal or nonexistent. However, check with your city, town, or county clerk to find out what licenses are required, if any. Government penalties for not following the rules can be substantial, especially if your business turns out to be successful.

Sales tax

In the 48 states that have a sales tax, you are generally required to get a reseller's permit before you begin selling a product or service (specifics vary from state to state). In some states, computer software is not taxed. Contact your state's Department of Revenue for information. Also ask them for an application for a state tax-identification number.

Doing business as (DBA)

In many states or counties, you must file a doing business as (DBA) form, if you use a name other than your own name. You can do business using many different names. For example, you might use one company name for business software and another for educational software. However, you must file a DBA form for each name you use. This form allows the state to identify you should there be complaints or problems with your business. It prevents you from hiding behind a business name not linked to a person.

In many cases, you cannot open a business account at a bank without the proper DBA forms for the bank to put in their files. By the way, be sure to give the bank copies (not originals) of your DBA forms. I have run several businesses and, in every case, the banks have lost my DBA forms.

Where you file a DBA depends on your location. In some states, you file a DBA with the county clerk. In other states, a DBA is filed with that state's department of commerce. If you do not know where to file a DBA in your state, call one of the offices I mentioned. If you call the wrong one, they will tell you.

Export licenses

No licenses are required to export your software to most countries. Software falls under the general provisions of the export control regulations. You can mail it directly to the user via U.S. air mail. There are exceptions, though. For example, no exports are allowed to North Vietnam, Cuba, North Korea, or Iraq. These restrictions are not related to software, but are general export restrictions. If you receive an order from a user living in a country you suspect might be a problem, check with the U.S. Department of Commerce. Although the world situation is rapidly changing, question any order you receive from a communist country, a country not friendly with the U.S., or a country the U.S. has a serious dispute with, such as Iraq in 1990 and 1991.

One significant limit on exporting software is that you are not allowed to send software that includes DES encryption standards outside the U.S. For example, copies of the hard-disk backup program Fastback may not be shipped outside the U.S.

Copyrights

Copyright law is intended to protect your work from anyone copying, reproducing, or distributing it without your permission. It allows you to benefit from any financial rewards that are a result of your efforts. The 1980 amendments to the copyright law make it clear that software programs are protected under copyright law. An exact definition of the extent of this protection is still being hammered out in the courts and Congress.

A copyright begins at the moment you start to create your program or documentation. To make the public aware that you will protect your work, you just need to put a copyright notice on it. You do not need to file any forms with the copyright office. A copyright remains in effect for the life of the author, plus 50 years.

Copyright notice

A copyright notice consists of the name of the program followed by the word "Copyright". The word copyright must be written out—putting the letter "c" in parentheses is not acceptable. The only acceptable abbreviations are "COPR." and the letter "c'" enclosed in a full circle. List the year the program was first publicly distributed and all years in which a revision was publicly distributed. You should also include the name of the person or company holding the copyright (you or your business). Be sure the complete copyright notice is on one line. For example:

BOOK MINDER Copyright 1988, 1989, 1990 STEVEN C. HUDGIK

Include this notice as a part of a title screen that first appears when the software is booted and build it into your program code as a remark. According to the copyright office, the copyright notice does not need to be printed on your disk labels. However, you might wish to do this to help ensure it is noticed. Your manual can be copyrighted separately with its own copyright notice or as a part of the software package. If you include your manual as a disk file, be sure to include the copyright notice for the manual as a part of that file. In addition, you can copyright data files that you create for use with your software and text files for adventure games separately, if you wish. A separate copyright can be used in the case of a data file that is updated periodically, but the software remains unchanged. If you think you might wish to sell data files separately, it is a good idea to copyright them separately.

International considerations

Assume that copies of your shareware will find their way to other countries, even if you do not permit them to be distributed outside the U.S. The U.S. has officially subscribed to the Berne Convention, an international copyright agreement. Under this agreement, if you publish your work in the U.S., it automatically has copyright protection under the laws of other countries. The laws in other countries are different and provide different levels of protection. So do not assume you have the same protecton as you get under U.S. copyright law. To get the full protection available in some countries, you need to include an additional line that says, "All Rights Reserved." Be sure to include this statement just under your copyright notice.

Another suggestion for protecting your copyrights internationally came out of my discussions with the Department of Commerce. They recommend that the abbreviation GTDR be written on the outside of all packages containing copyrighted software shipped outside the U.S. This abbreviation stands for General Technical Data Restricted and helps protect your copyright in other countries.

Registering your copyright

Putting the copyright notice on your software and manuals provides only limited protection. You can stop someone else from copying your software, but you must do it at your expense and you cannot collect damages. If you register your copyright before the infringement, you can then sue for infringement in a federal court and collect damages and attorney's fees.

The filing fee is $20. You can file for a copyright yourself or have an attorney do it for you. It is a simple procedure and thus should not be expensive for a lawyer to do. To do it yourself, call the copyright office for information. Their number is (202) 479-0700 (8:30 A.M. till 5:00 P.M. Eastern Standard Time).

The copyright office also has a Forms Hotline for callers who know what forms they need. The forms Hotline number is (202) 707-9100. This number is answered by a machine 24 hours a day, 7 days a week. Ask for Information Package 113. It includes the necessary forms and booklets that describe how to file for a copyright.

Most questions concerning registering a copyright have to do with deposit requirements, the nature of authorship (form TX, line 2), and line 6 on form TX, derivative work, or compilation information.

Deposit requirements

The deposit requirement states that "one copy of identifying portions of the program" be submitted with your application. This requirement is defined as the first 25 and last 25 pages of program code. If your program code is less than 50 pages, then the entire listing must be submitted. The only exception is if this code includes trade secrets. There are three alternative deposit procedures for protecting trade secrets. If you need to protect a trade secret, call the copyright office for more information. The intent of the deposit requirement is to have a sufficient amount of code on file with the copyright office to prove infringement. In addition, the copyright office will also accept deposits of your entire program, on disk, as evidence that can be used in an infringement lawsuit.

If you have a question concerning the deposit requirements, call the copyright office. Very helpful people answer the phones.

Nature of the material created

Line 2 on form TX asks for the "nature of the material created" for which a copyright is claimed. I recommend using all-inclusive language such as "entire computer program and manual." If you get too specific, you might unintentionally exclude something. If you are too vague, you will be asked to clarify the information. Some things cannot be copyrighted. For example, do not include the words "program design" in your application or terms like "look and feel." This will cause it to be rejected.

Identifying pre-existing work

If your copyright notice contains more than one year, you will need to fill out section 6 of form TX. This section is used to identify any pre-existing work incorporated into your program. For example, if you use QuickBasic, the license granted you by Microsoft requires you to include their copyright notice. This should be included as a pre-existing work and is described in section 6 of form TX. This also applies if you have written and modified your software over several years and have included all these years in your copyright notice.

The importance of correctly and completely filling in this section was brought to public attention in the *Ashton-Tate vs. Fox* lawsuit. In this court case, the judge ruled that Ashton-Tate's copyrights on dBASE were not valid because Ashton-Tate's copyright application did not reveal that dBASE was partly based on pre-existing public-domain program code.

If you are not sure whether or not to include some items in section 6 of form TX, attach a letter that discloses everything imaginable. (Add the words "see attached letter" to section 6 of form TX.) The letter can be used to disclose the compiler used (which inserts some code), any toolboxes used, and any minor parts of the code written by someone else.

Why you should register your copyright

Registering a copyright is a legal formality that generally is not required for protection. If your work was first published before March 1, 1989, and the copyright notice was not included or the name or year date was omitted or had an error, you should see a copyright attorney. However, there are several advantages to registering your copyright. These include:

- If you register your copyright within five years of publication, registration establishes *prima facie* evidence in court of the validity of the copyright and the facts stated in the certificate. *Prima facie* means that, just by having the registration, it is assumed that your copyright is valid. It is up to any parties challenging your copyright to show that it is not valid.
- If registration is made within 3 months after publication of the work or prior to an infringement of the work, you will be able to collect the minimum statutory damages plus attorney's fees. Otherwise, you can only collect actual damages and loss of profits.
- Registration provides a public record of your copyrighted material. Putting your work in an envelope and mailing it to yourself so that it is postmarked does not establish a record of your ownership of published material. Registering it with the copyright office will accomplish this.
- If your work is of U.S. origin and is infringed in a foreign work originating in a country that is not a Berne Union country, registering is required for you to file suit.

Copyright summary

Laws that protect software are changing. For example, there have been some moves to allow certain aspects of software to be patented. Another example is that in the past you could not copyright screen displays. An interesting development is the June 28, 1990, decision by Judge Robert E. Keeton in the *Lotus vs. Paperback Software* copyright infringement lawsuit. This decision extends copyright protection beyond literal code to non-literal elements of a program, for example, the menu command structure of Lotus' 1-2-3 spreadsheet. The end result is that your rights to borrow user-interface elements from existing products have been legally reduced.

Although the court case has been decided, expect this to become a political issue. Congress will further clarify copyright law as it pertains to software, although it might take several years to resolve all the issues.

Copyrights and shareware

Shareware is copyrighted software with full protection under copyright law. In distributing your software as shareware, you grant a license that allows others limited rights. You should specifically describe those rights in a shareware license included in your documentation, introduction files, and possibly the opening copyright screen.

Some of the rights you might wish to grant others include:

- The right to distribute copies of your software, provided that no fees are charged for the disks.

- Allowing ASP vendors the right to distribute copies of your software without getting permission from you.
- Setting a certain time period for users to review your software. At the end of that time period, registration is required.

You might also wish to specifically identify actions you do not allow, such as distribution of your shareware outside the U.S.

By waiving some of your rights, you have not eliminated your copyrights. Except for the rights you specifically identify, all other rights are not waived. This type of selective waiver is enforceable. Shareware copyrights were upheld in the *Datastorm, Inc. vs. Software-To-go, Inc.* court decision several years ago.

Here is an example of a shareware license.

The author grants permission for this disk to be copied and distributed, if no fee is charged. Otherwise, you must get written permission from the author to distribute copies of this disk. If you use this software for more than 90 days, you are required to purchase a registered copy.

This license grants permission for the disk to be copied—as long as no fee is charged—to allow it to be shared among users. Disk dealers are required to get permission so that the author can send them the latest version and include them on a mailing list for future updates. If you require dealers to get written permission, be sure to respond to their requests.

Trademarks

A trademark protects your right to use a word, name, symbol, or device to identify and distinguish your product from those produced by others. If you start distributing your program without a trademark (TM) notice (a word, phrase, or symbol you use to identify it), you might lose the rights to your trademark. Under trademark law, you own the word, name, symbol, or device that identifies your software as soon as you use it in commerce. You do not need to register a trademark to own it. The purpose of using the (TM) notice is to make it clear to others this is your trademark. Without the (TM) notice, others might inadvertently start using your mark, and as a small publisher you would not have the financial ability to defend it in court. The (TM) notice is used prior to registration of a trademark to show that you intend to defend your mark against infringement. Once registered, the "R" in a circle is used to indicate the mark is a registered trademark.

What registering a trademark does for you is to provide notice nationally that this is your trademark. It also puts your trademark on the federal database so that when someone else does a trademark search, they will find it and know that the trademark is already in use. Once a trademark has been registered for five years, it becomes incontestable, with just a few exceptions, making it much easier to defend your mark.

For information about registering a trademark, write to the U.S. Department of Commerce, Patent and Trademark Office, Washington, D.C. 20231. Request the information package called *Basic Facts About Trademarks*. You can also call (703) 557-3158 to order this package.

Unlike a copyright, which can be registered regardless of whether or not the work is published, a trademark must be used in interstate commerce at the time the application is filed. Or, you must have a bona fide intention to use the mark.

An application consists of a written application form; a drawing showing the mark (the mark may be typed, if your trademark is a word); three examples showing actual use of the mark; and the required filing fee, which is currently $175.

Once you register a trademark, you will need to file a Section 8 Affidavit of Continued Use between the fifth and sixth year after registration. The fee for this is $100. A notice of this requirement is attached to the registration certificate that you will receive when your mark is registered.

Trademarks remain in effect for 20 years. You may renew your trademark for an unlimited number of 20-year periods. Currently, the renewal fee is $300.

Registering a trademark

As with a copyright, you can register a trademark yourself or have an attorney do it for you. I have registered several trademarks and have had problems filling out the forms and providing the necessary backup information. The application process is specific and you need to follow procedures exactly. When you file to register a trademark, your application is assigned an attorney in the trademark office. I have found these attorneys to be very helpful and understanding of people who do not have a legal background. They will guide you in putting together a proper application, *if* you have done most of the work correctly. They *will not* put together an application for you. An application with a lot of problems will be rejected and your application fee will be lost.

Some of the things that will cause a trademark application to be rejected include:

- If the mark consists of immoral, deceptive, or scandalous matter, or matter that might disparage or suggest a connection with persons, living or dead, institutions, beliefs, or national symbols.
- If the mark uses the flag or coat of arms or other insignia of the United States, or of any state or municipality, or of any foreign nation.

- If the mark uses the name, portrait, or signature identifying a particular living person without that person's written permission, or if it uses the name, signature, or portrait of a deceased President of the United States during the life of his widow, except by written consent of the widow.
- If the mark resembles a mark registered already, or a mark or tradename previously used by another and which is likely to cause confusion, mistakes, or be deceptive.
- If the mark is descriptive or generic. For example, I publish a program for cataloging stamp collections. I would not be able to register "Stamp Database" as a trademark.

You can also register your trademark in some states. The process is much faster and cheaper. However, because of their limited jurisdiction, state trademarks are weaker than federal ones. The major benefit of a state trademark is that it can be used to strengthen your case against trademark infringements. Applications are usually available from the state corporation counsel office or the office of the secretary of state.

For both copyrights and trademarks it is your responsibility to protect them. No one else will do it for you. Some trademarks, such as aspirin, have been lost over time when they became synonyms for products. A trademark is very specific and you must reproduce it correctly when you use it. Do not be sloppy or careless when you use your trademark as you can weaken your own rights to your trademark.

Choosing a legal form for your business

The three forms your business can take are a sole proprietorship, a partnership, or a corporation. How you run your business will affect your personal liability, your taxes, how you handle any profits, and how decisions are made. The best form for your business will depend on your situation. Talk to your attorney and accountant for help in making this decision.

Sole proprietorship

If you are the only person involved in your business, and you do not form a corporation, your business is a sole proprietorship as soon as you start operating as a business. The sole proprietorship is the most common way shareware businesses are organized. For legal and tax purposes, you and your business are one and the same. Your business operations and activities are treated as a part of your personal activities. For example, a sole proprietor is not a separate tax-paying entity. However, you do need to keep separate business records for business income, deductions, inventories, capital acquisitions, and dispositions. Your tax-reporting year must be the same for you and your business. For tax purposes, the profit or loss from your business is calculated separately using IRS Form 1040, Schedule C, and then combined with your personal income.

Note that in a sole proprietorship, if your business makes a profit and you have not already paid the maximum Social Security tax, you must pay a self-employment tax for Social Security. You might also have additional taxes to pay to your local or regional government.

Partnerships

If two or more people are involved as owners of the business, then the business is organized as a partnership. While you can form a partnership with a handshake, it is best to have a formal contract. Even if the partnership includes only family members, all of whom are on good terms with each other, put your agreement in writing and have an attorney write the contract. This is not a matter of whether you trust or do not trust the other people in the partnership. If you do not trust them, you should not be going into business with them. It is important because there is more to a partnership than agreeing to work together. For example, how will profits or losses be split? How is the work to be split? How are disputes to be resolved? What happens if one partner wishes to leave the business or passes away? An important consideration is that one partner can bind the partnership in a contract. This means that either partner can be sued for the acts of one partner. So, be careful. There are more issues than you might realize; having a specialist write the contract is the only way to be sure most possibilities are covered.

Forming a corporation

Whether you start as a sole proprietor or partnership, you might eventually wish to form a corporation. One of the major reasons to incorporate a small business is to protect you from personal liability. Generally, sole proprietors and partnerships incur personal liability. If your business is incorporated, it becomes an entity separate from you. Many other reasons can affect your decision about forming a corporation. These range from marketing-based reasons to tax advantages. To make your choice, you and your legal advisor should look at your specific situation.

In most cases, if you wish to incorporate, you should incorporate as a Subchapter S corporation. This allows you to operate in a corporate form, but not pay tax as a separate entity. This eliminates a lot of paperwork and avoids the double tax on corporate operations. To qualify as a Subchapter S corporation, your corporation must meet certain stock and income tests. For example, trusts, partnerships, and other corporations cannot own stock in your corporation. On the income side, there are limits on the percentage of income that can come from rents, royalties, dividends, interest, annuities, securities sales, and foreign sources.

There are booklets that tell you how to form a corporation for $50. I have read them and I recommend that you hire an attorney instead. The cost to hire an attorney to form a Subchapter S corporation might run from $400 to $1000 (depending on your location) and is well worth it. In addition to providing all the documents and filing the necessary forms, your attorney can advise you on how to conduct business as a corporation. For example, as a sole proprietor you do as you wish. Once you are incorporated, the powers of the corporation are described in its charter. If you wish to do something not allowed by the charter, it needs to be amended.

Warranties and liability

Nearly all software publishers offer no warranty on the software. You might wish to provide a warranty that states that the disks and manuals are free from defects of manufacturing, but do not warranty the software or content of the manuals. If you wish to reassure your customers that they are buying a quality product, offer a no-questions-asked, money-back guarantee.

It is important that you not warranty the software and manuals because you have no control over how they will be used. A warranty can provide the basis for a lawsuit. If you provide a warranty on your software, you could end up in lengthy and expensive court battles. In addition, damage awards can be high. Bugs in software have caused losses of many years of work, crucial data, and miscalculations resulting in significant monetary losses. As a small publisher, the first warranty lawsuit would probably put you out of business. Offer a money-back guarantee and you have limited your liability to refunding the purchase price of the software if a user is not satisfied.

Place a warranty statement in the front of your manual or on the disk envelope that states:

**"This software is provided as-is.
There are no warranties, expressed or implied."**

However, there is more to include in your warranty statement. Just because you have said that you do not provide a warranty does not mean you have avoided all warranty liability. The Uniform Commercial Code (UCC) creates implied warranties for all sales of goods and provides that you cannot disclaim these unless you *conspicuously* use specific words.

These specific words are called a warranty disclaimer. To be conspicuous, the warranty disclaimer should be printed in capital letters. Using all capital letters is not a legal requirement. The UCC does not define what is meant by conspicuous. Using all caps has become the accepted standard for meeting this requirement. In addition, you cannot use fine print. In most states, the warranty disclaimer must be a minimum of 6-point type.

You also want to be sure that your warranty disclaimer is in a location where most people can be expected to see it. The best spot is to put it in the first page or two of your documentation. If you would like to see an example of the type of wording that you should include, look at any of the software packages put out by the major publishers. Highly paid legal staffs protect these companies by being sure the wording in the warranty is the best possible. It is interesting to note that the wording used by the various publishers is relatively uniform.

Here is the warranty disclaimer that I use.

HCP SERVICES INC. DISCLAIMS ALL WARRANTIES RELATING TO THIS SOFT-WARE, WHETHER EXPRESS OR IMPLIED, INCLUDING BUT NOT LIMITED TO ANY IMPLIED WARRANTIES OF MERCHANTABILITY AND FITNESS FOR A PARTICULAR PURPOSE, AND ALL SUCH WARRANTIES ARE EXPRESSLY AND SPECIFICALLY DISCLAIMED. NEITHER HCP SERVICES, INC. NOR ANYONE ELSE WHO HAS BEEN INVOLVED IN THE CREATION, PRODUCTION, OR DELIVERY OF THIS SOFTWARE SHALL BE LIABLE FOR ANY INDIRECT, CON-SEQUENTIAL, OR INCIDENTAL DAMAGES ARISING OUT OF THE USE OR INABILITY TO USE SUCH SOFTWARE EVEN IF HCP SERVICES, INC. HAS BEEN ADVISED OF THE POSSIBILITY OF SUCH DAMAGES OR CLAIMS. IN NO EVENT SHALL HCP SERVICES, INC.'S LIABILITY FOR ANY DAMAGES EVER EXCEED THE PRICE PAID FOR THE LICENSE TO USE THE SOFTWARE, REGARDLESS OF THE FORM OF CLAIM. THE PERSON USING THE SOFT-WARE BEARS ALL RISK AS TO THE QUALITY AND PERFORMANCE OF THE SOFTWARE.

Some states do not allow the exclusion of the limit of liability for consequential or incidental damages, so the above limitation may not apply to you.

This agreement shall be governed by the laws of the State of Oregon and shall inure to the benefit of HCP Services, Inc. and any successors, administrators, heirs and assigns. Any action or proceeding brought by either party against the other arising out of or related to this agreement shall be brought only in a STATE or FED-ERAL COURT of competent jurisdiction located in Multnomah County, Oregon. The parties hereby consent to in personam jurisdiction of said courts.

The last paragraph is important because it requires that any legal action be made in a court that is local to you. Without this statement, you could be sued in a remote state. The cost of defending a lawsuit in a remote state is so high that you would be forced to settle without going to court.

The warranty statement protects you from not only warranty claims, but also claims for any other damages someone thinks might be caused by your software. However, keep in mind that you do not have ironclad protection from being sued. Anyone can sue anyone else for any reason. This wording just makes a suit against you much less likely to succeed and, thus, bringing suit against you is not worth the effort.

In addition to warranties and limiting your liability, you also need to protect your copyright. Your documentation should include the terms under which other people may use your software. The most important term is that your software may only be used on one computer (unless you have granted a site license). Check other software packages for typical wording. Here is what I use:

> This software and the disks on which it is contained is licensed to you, for your own use. This is copyrighted software. You are not obtaining title to the software or any copyright rights. You may not sublicense, rent, lease, convey, modify, translate, convert to another programming language, decompile, or disassemble the software for any purpose.
>
> You may make as many copies of this software as you need for back-up purposes. You may use this software on more than one computer, provided there is no chance it will be used simultaneously on more than one computer. If you need to use the software on more than one computer simultaneously, please contact us for information about site licenses.

Site-license agreements

A site license is a legal contract in which you and a registered user agree on the terms under which the user can install your software on more than one computer. These terms generally allow the user to install the software on a specified number of computers in return for payment of a specific site-license fee.

When you sell a registered copy of your software the registered copy is no different than retail software. It is copyrighted and the user may not give copies to other people or install it on more than one machine without your permission. As the copyright holder, you can set the specific conditions under which the registered version of your software may be copied. Most shareware authors treat their registered versions exactly like retail software; the software may be copied for backup purposes only. Some authors allow the registered copy to be shared with other users, but use of the software on multiple computers within one organization or on a network requires a site license.

Here are some typical questions and answers relating to copyrights and site licenses. For these examples I will be using a fictional program called FastWrite.

> *Question:* We have 100 computers in our company, but only 25 people are trained to use the FastWrite program. We want to install FastWrite on all of our computers so that the most convenient machine can be used at any time. How many copies of FastWrite do we need?
>
> *Answer:* This user must purchase 100 copies of FastWrite. According to copyright law, an application that is installed on a hard disk is a copy regardless of how often it is used. If you have copies of a program installed on 100 hard disks, you must own 100 copies.

Question: We have purchased a registered copy of FastWrite and installed it on one computer. Can we use the shareware version on the other computers in our office?

Answer: No. Purchasing one registered version of a program means the software may only be installed on one computer. It does not change the licensing conditions under which the shareware version is used. These conditions usually state that if a shareware program is used for more than a reasonable test period, it must be registered. Thus, every computer on which a shareware version is installed must have the shareware version replaced by a registered version or the shareware version must be removed.

Question: What happens when I receive an upgrade to FastWrite? Can I use the old version on another machine?

Answer: No. Upgrades and updates are improvements on the original software, not a new copy. Legally, they are the same program and you have not purchased the right to use it on additional computers.

Question: Can nonprofit groups and schools register one copy of a program and use it on multiple machines?

Answer: No. The copyright laws apply to nonprofit organizations and schools in the same way as they do to individuals and corporations. As the owner of the copyright, you can make a marketing decision to allow certain groups to use your software on more than one computer. Should you do this, you are essentially granting a site license to that group and not charging for it.

Question: We have installed FastWrite on our network, which has 50 terminals. Only one person is trained and authorized to use FastWrite. How many copies do we need to purchase?

Answer: There is no one answer to this question. Legally, the user only needs to purchase one copy of FastWrite because, in this case, it is installed on only one hard disk. However, as a part of the terms of your user license agreement, you can require the user to purchase additional copies if the software is used on a network. The number of additional copies they must purchase is a marketing decision you make.

In addressing the use of shareware on a network, some people reason that it would be possible to have a user at every terminal, all using the FastWrite software. Thus, the publishers should require network users to buy a site license that covers the total number of terminals. This approach simplifies the site license accounting because, if additional terminals are added, an additional site-license fee is required.

Another approach is to require a site license for the average number of people who might use FastWrite simultaneously on the network. With this method, you are dependent on the customer to provide an accurate estimate of this average.

A simple approach is to charge a one-time site-license fee for unlimited use of the software on a network. The unlimited-use license grants the user the right to put the software on as many computers within the organization as they wish.

Some publishers license their software for use on a network by a specified maximum number of people. A counter is built into the software that tracks the number of simultaneous users. If the maximum number covered by the site license is exceeded, the software is designed to prevent additional users from accessing the software. Other programs in these circumstances just flash a warning message on the screen.

How you approach network licenses might be different than these examples and depends on your marketing goals and the terms of your site license. In my survey of shareware authors, the most common response to the questions about site licenses stated that site licenses are negotiated on a case-by-case basis. There is no one right answer. Every site license can be different, with varying terms based on the needs of your customer and on what you feel is a fair price.

Sample site-license agreement

The following provides a sample site-license agreement. I recommend that you include a copy in each registered version of your software. This will make users aware that a site license is required to use the software on more than one computer and it provides an easy way for them to request and pay for a site license. Keep in mind that all contracts are negotiable. In some cases, the following example would serve only as a starting point which can be modified to fit the situation.

HCP Services, Inc.
HomeCraft Software
Site-License Agreement

If you wish to use this software on more than one computer, a site license is required. A site license is also required to use this software on a network. A site license allows you to copy and use this software within your organization on as many computers as contracted for. An unlimited site license allows unlimited copying of the software for internal use only. This is copyrighted software and any distribution or reselling of the software to third parties is prohibited.

HCP Services, Inc., grants _____ a site license for the use of the following software program(s):

This is a perpetual license for the use of the software within your organization, and is not transferable. This site license allows internal use and copying of the software for use by/on _____ users/computers.

This license is distinct from shareware use. It does not authorize the continued use of shareware. If, in addition to the software used under this license, shareware is in use, that shareware must be registered with HCP Services, Inc.

HCP Services, Inc., will provide technical support for one year from the date of this agreement to one person, designated as the key contact within your company or organization.

HCP Services, Inc., warrants that it is the sole owner of the software and has full power and authority to grant the site license without the consent of any other party.

HCP Services, Inc., disclaims all warranties relating to this software, whether express or implied, including but not limited to any implied warranties of merchantability and fitness for a particular purpose, and all such warranties are expressly and specifically disclaimed. Neither HCP Services, Inc., nor anyone else who has been involved in the creation, production, or delivery of this software shall be liable for any direct, indirect, consequential, or incidental damages arising out of the use or inability to use such software even if HCP Services, Inc., has been advised of the possibility of such damages or claims. In no event shall HCP Services, Inc.'s liability for any damages ever exceed the price paid for the license to use the software, regardless of the form of claim. The person using the software bears all risk as to the quality and performance of the software. (Some states do not allow the exclusion of the limit of liability for consequential or incidental damages, so this limitation might not apply to you.)

This agreement shall be governed by the laws of the State of Oregon and shall inure to the benefit of HCP Services, Inc., and any successors, administrators, heirs, and assigns. Any action or proceeding brought by either party against the other arising out of or related to this agreement shall be brought only in a STATE or FEDERAL COURT of competent jurisdiction located in Multnomah County, Oregon. The parties hereby consent to in personam jurisdiction of said courts.

Company _____

Address _____

City _____ State/Prov _____ Zip _____

Country _____ Phone _____

_____   _____
Authorized Signature   Authorized Signature

                                      Steven C. Hudgik
_____

Print or Type Name

                                      President, HCP Services, Inc.
_____

Title

_____   _____

Date   Date

On the back side of this agreement form I provide my proposed site-license fee schedule. In some cases, your customer might wish different contract terms that will affect your licenses fees. For example, the customer might ask you to provide printed manuals or support for each user. These can be included in the contract, but be sure to modify your fee schedule to include them.

Software rentals

Although not directly related to shareware, before finishing this chapter I would like to include an interesting legal note about renting software. After five years of intensive lobbying by the software industry, the 101st Congress approved the Software Rental Amendments Act. This legislation prohibits "the rental, leasing, or lending of commercial software without the express permission of the copyright holder." It is now against the law to rent, lease, or loan software without the publisher's permission. This means that the only legal method to try software before you buy it is shareware.

10
Business skills

This chapter will help you with some essential business skills: writing a business plan, selling, communication, and how to write a proposal. These are all things you can learn to do. They are also skills that continually need refreshing. Most of us do not use these skills everyday. As with anything else, if they are not used, they become rusty and are eventually lost. Keeping your skills shiny and ready to use requires regular maintenance. Take the time to read a book about one of these areas or listen to an audio cassette. You might even reread this chapter once in awhile.

Writing a business plan

I am going to take a different approach to business plans than what you will see in any other book or publication. Most books that discuss the writing of business plans are directed toward larger businesses—typically, with a million or so dollars in sales every year. I feel that for a small, one- or two-person company, this approach is overkill and leads to nothing being done about planning because a business plan looks so big and overwhelming. The approach I will describe is a two-step one. The first step provides a very simple business plan that is perfect for internal use by a one- or two-person company. The second step involves writing the more traditional detailed business plan that can be used externally. (*Internal documents* are those that are only seen by people within your company. They are never given to anyone who does not work for your company. An *external document* is one that can be given to people outside your company such as bankers or insurance agents.)

Before I start, there is a key element that needs to be addressed: why you need a business plan. There is a long list of reasons. Here are the six most important reasons to help you:

- Better know your business and yourself.
- Get to know your software better.
- To get to know your customers and understand your market.
- Learn the business skills you will need to run a business.
- Get the resources your company needs from outside sources such as banks.
- Provide a "blueprint" for what you want your company to do and where you want it to go in the future.

Notice that the first four items are things that help you directly. A business plan is usually thought of as a document that a "big" (meaning bigger than a one- or two-person home business) company uses to attract investors or other people interested in the company. The typical opinion has been, if I am not trying to attract investors, why do I need to bother with writing a business plan? In reality, for the small business, having a business plan is more important, because of what is learned in writing it, than how it is used. Writing a business plan is a good way to learn many of the skills you will need to run a professional and successful business. Think of it as a learning plan. As you work through each section, you will learn business skills, learn more about your business, and learn more about yourself.

This does not mean that a business plan has no value once it is complete. For example, a business plan can be a key ingredient in getting your VISA/MasterCard merchant status. It goes a long way toward showing a bank that you are a serious, professional business because it demonstrates to the bank that you have the skills needed to run a business.

The sixth item in the previous list, providing a "blueprint," is also a key point for a small business. What does this mean? Having a business plan will bring focus to your business. This helps in making decisions and in determining how you approach your product and customers. There was a discussion on CompuServe several months ago concerning the amount of time a user should be allowed to use a shareware program before registering. Most people were saying thirty to sixty days was a good time period. My opinion was that we should let users take as long as they want. I based this on the objectives I have in my business plan. They are:

- Get my shareware into the hands of as many users as possible.
- Make my shareware interesting and good enough that users will try it.
- Make my shareware good enough that they will continue to use it and not switch to another program.

I feel that these three objectives are the most important things I need to accomplish with my shareware. If I am unable to accomplish them, I will not have many sales. For me, how long users "test" my software before registering is not important—as long as they keep using it. If they switch to another program, then I have lost those users and there is no longer a possibility that they will register.

Your business plan is a blueprint for your business. It provides guidance and keeps you on track with what you want to do. It is easy to be distracted and go in the wrong direction. Your business plan serves as a reminder of where you want to go and helps to keep you heading in that direction. Studies done by Dun & Bradstreet have found that lack of direction is the major cause of business failure. The root cause of this is that most people do not understand the importance of planning.

If you are determined to succeed and make shareware more than a part-time "hobby," planning is important.

The mini business plan

Just as you will find a "quick-start" section in many software manuals, here is a quick-start section on writing business plans. You will end up with a mini-plan that will help you understand your business, your product, your market, and your customers better. It also serves as an excellent foundation for a full-blown business plan.

As a software consultant, I have helped people start software companies and launch new software products. I have almost always found that they have a product or idea that are excited about and are anxious to get started selling it. But, if they were to immediately start selling software, the chances are they will join the 80% of businesses that fail within their first five years. The problem is that they do not have the answers to some very basic questions. I have already talked about knowing your product and your market. But, there is more. When someone hires me as a consultant, I first ask that they fill out a questionnaire. I think of the answers to this questionnaire as providing a mini-business plan for small companies that do not need external financial help. It is also a good place to start for getting your thoughts together to write a full-blown business plan. The following ten items will help bring focus to your business. As you go through the items, do not just read them and think about the answers. Put your answers in writing. If you expect to benefit from these items, they must be answered in writing. Then, you should periodically review your answers to help maintain your focus and direction.

Background information   What is your company name and your name? What is your background? What are your qualifications for writing this software?

Purpose   Why did you write this software?

Short description   Describe your software in one sentence. It is surprising how many people cannot do this. This should be a short, concise statement describing your software. Imagine that you have a 10-second sound bite on the CBS evening news. What would you say?

Why do you need to be able to describe your software in one sentence? The average person cannot hold an image of more than one relationship in their head. A description that is longer than one sentence becomes too complex for most people to understand and remember. You need to be able to describe your software in a concise manner. If you cannot describe your software in one sentence, do not expect users to remember your software.

Long description   In one or two short paragraphs, describe your software, its purpose, its scope, the problem it solves and how it solves that problem, and the benefits users of your software will see.

Expand on the one-sentence description that you wrote for the third question. Include more details, but do not write a long-winded description. If the answer to question 3 was a 10-second sound bite, answer this question as if you were writing an ad for your software, but can only afford to buy two column inches of space. Keep it short and to the point.

Features   List ten features of your software that would be of special interest to users. Explain why users should be interested in these features. How do these features benefit users?

This can be a tough item. It is usually easy to come up with three or four features. However, if your software does not have at least ten features that users will find attractive, you are going to have a tough time selling it. Be honest with yourself. Only list features that you feel are truly of special interest to users. If you cannot come up with ten, then work to improve your software until it has at least ten features that are easily identifiable as being of special interest to users. To verify your answer to this question, send a survey to some of your users and ask them to list features they particularly like. Most users will only list four or five features. The reason you need ten on your list is that various features are of interest to different people.

Uniqueness   Describe at least one feature that is unique to your software. Why have you included this feature? How does this feature benefit the user?

To be successful, you must be able to differentiate your software from the competition. It must have at least one unique feature you can point to and say, ''Mr. User, you should buy my software because. . . .''

Your users   Describe the typical user of your software. What background knowledge, experience, and skill will the user need to use your software? Why will this person be interested in your software? Why would this user use your software instead of another program?

Marketing plan   What is your marketing plan for this software? Are you promoting it using shareware only, or do you also plan to advertise, send out press releases, have a trade show presence, or engage in other promotional activities? What are your yearly sales objectives? What is the registration price? What do users get when they register? How are you planning to package the registered version? What type of support will you provide?

The competition   Is there existing software (both shareware and commercial software) that is similar to your software? If so, list each program with a brief description. For each competing program, describe how your software is different or better.

Beating the competition   List any characteristic weaknesses and omissions in competing software. Does your software have the same weaknesses? If so, describe what has been done in your software to eliminate these weaknesses and omissions. Are these important to your customers? Why are they important?

Write out your answers in the form of a report. Put a nice cover on it and keep it handy. Just going through the process of answering them will help you know more about software, your market, and what you need to do to reach your targets. Keep a copy of this document handy and mark it up as you think of new things or as your situation changes. This mini-plan should be a living, changing document that grows as your company grows.

The mini-plan's purpose

The mini-plan forces you to think about what you are doing and why you are doing it. It forces you to think about your software, your prospective customers, and whether or not there is a match. Over 85,000 shareware programs have been released, but software libraries only carry two to three thousand at the most. Why? Because many authors have released software that no one is interested in. There is no match between potential customers and the software.

The mini-plan forces you to think about the competition. If you have written a DOS shell, you might get writer's cramp before you finish listing all of the competing software. This should help you realize that the DOS-shell market is not a good market to be in if you want to make some money.

Writing out a mini-plan forces you to think about a marketing plan and to commit to that plan in writing. No, it is not a contract requiring you to market your software in a certain way. But, by writing out your marketing plan, you better focus your thoughts about how you want to approach marketing your software.

Writing a full business plan

If you are going to use your business plan as part of a loan application or to attract investors, you will need to put together a full business plan using the standard format. You can get by with using the mini-plan to help organize your business and get your VISA/MasterCard merchant status, but, for almost anything else, you will need to put together a full business plan. In this section, I will show you how to do that.

Before we get started, I would like you to keep several things in mind. You cannot be casual about putting a business plan together. A business plan must use correct spelling, grammar, and punctuation. It must be well thought-out and organized. Your plan needs to be focused, clear, and specific. Do not say you will do something without describing how you plan to do it. Do not use superlatives. If you say that your product is the best in the market, explain why and back up your explanation with facts. As you complete each section, take the time to have your plan proofread by at least three other people.

If you are getting the impression that a business plan is an important document that cannot be thrown together over a weekend, you are right. Expect to take several months, at best, to complete your business plan. A business plan involves not only writing the plan, but also a lot of research, forethought, and careful consideration of what you want your company to do and where you want it to go.

First, I will discuss the major sections of a business plan, then I will talk about the mechanics of putting a business plan together.

The major sections of a business plan

I will start by showing you a brief outline of a business plan. This will show you the title of each section and provide a summary of what needs to be included in that section. Then I will get into the details of what to include in each section.

Section I. Mission statement   This is a short statement explaining why you are in business and what you want to accomplish.

Section II. Company description   In this section you should provide a brief history of your company and the products you make.

Section III. Product descriptions   Each product you make should be described here in detail. What does it do? What are the outstanding features? And, what makes your software different from the competition?

Section IV. Marketing plan   This section identifies who your potential customers are, what your objectives are, and how you plan to achieve these objectives.

Section V. Competitive analysis   This section is used to describe your competition and how they approach the market.

Section VI. Management   This is where you describe your background and experience as well as the backgrounds of any other key individuals in your company.

Section VII. Financial plan   This final section lays out the financial condition of your company, provides your financial plan, and includes your financial statements.

When complete, a typical business plan might run 30 to 60 pages. This might seem to be an overwhelming writing job. But you do not have to do it all at once. It is good to get started now, when you do not need to have a business plan other than for your own use. Then, as your company grows, you gain experience, and you learn about your market, you can add to your plan and build it a piece at a time. It is a less formidable task that way.

Now let us go ahead and take a detailed look at what goes on in each section. I will be discussing the writing of a business plan from the prospective of a one- or two-person home-based business.

I. Mission statement   In a handout called "Tips for Software (and other) Companies," Bob Wallace (founder of Quicksoft, Inc.) gives Quicksoft's mission statement as, "We help people create documents."

This is one of the shortest mission statements I have seen, but it includes all of the key ingredients. It states why Quicksoft is in business and what their overall goal is.

Although most mission statements are longer, you should try to keep it as short as possible and still express the basic concept of your business. Use the mission statement to explain the nature of your business in one sentence (two at the most).

Your mission statement is the foundation of your business and all else flows from this mission statement. Keep it short. I have seen some that run four or five pages and they become meaningless.

Here is the mission statement for my company, HomeCraft Software: "To build a business based on high quality customer service and honesty that supplies products and services to meet the cataloging needs of collectors."

When working on a mission statement, focus on writing something that you can refer to anytime you have to make a major decision. Are you looking at adding a new product? How does it fit with your stated mission? Are you looking for new ways to do business? Are they in tune with your mission statement?

Of course, over time circumstances will change and you will want to adapt your mission statement for a new situation. But, always give it a lot of thought before you change your mission statement. Do not change it quickly or on a whim.

II. Company description   Here is where you describe the past history of your company, why you started it, and what you are doing now. Start with an introductory section.

Who founded your company and when was it founded? Why was it founded? Have there been any name changes since your company was founded? If so, why did you change the name? How many people are there in your company now?

What markets has your company served in the past? Are you creating a new market or responding to an existing market? Who buys your products?

Next, provide a brief description of your products. What type of software do you publish? What benefits does your software provide users? Do you have any technological or innovative advantages? You do not need to go into a lot of detail here because there is a later section that deals specifically with describing your products.

Briefly describe shareware and how it works. (A more detailed description should be included in the marketing section, so be brief here.)

Describe any awards your software has received and include quotes from positive reviews.

Summarize your objectives for your company. What are the critical factors affecting your potential for success or failure? What risks and opportunities does your company face? What are your company's strengths and weaknesses? What barriers are there to your achieving your objectives? How are you going to overcome these risks, weaknesses, and barriers? What contingency plans do you have if you cannot fully overcome them?

By the way, do not try to do a snow job by only describing your strengths. If you ever have to present your business plan to a bank manager, for example, it will immediately be recognized as a fraud and you will lose the respect of the manager. Bank managers might look at 10 to 15 business plans a week, in some cases, and they know what to expect. All businesses have weaknesses and risks they have to face. If you do not include them in your business plan, it shows that either you are hiding something or you do not know what you are doing. Both circumstances are not good. There is no reason to emphasize the negative aspects of your business, but you should be honest.

What is the business environment your company faces? Briefly describe your market. Who is your competition?

Many of these questions will be answered in detail in later sections of your business plan. In this section, use only a sentence or two to answer most questions and only answer those that are relevant to your company's history or current status.

III. Product descriptions This section provides a detailed description of each of your existing products and describes any plans you have for future products or services. If you have multiple products or services, each should be described separately.

If you have already done the mini-plan I described earlier, use the sections from that document that describe your software as your starting point for this section. Include the description of your software that describes its purpose, scope, the problem it solves, and its approach to solving that problem. List the ten features in your software that are of special interest to users and explain why. Describe at least one feature that is unique to your software. Why have you included this feature? How does this feature benefit the user?

Describe any weaknesses your software might have and your plans to correct or overcome them. Do not try to hide weaknesses. All products have weaknesses. By showing that you are aware of your software's weaknesses and that you have a plan to address those weaknesses, you show you know how to run a business.

Describe the features of your software that others would call excellent features. Excellence is an important characteristic of any product. To be successful, all software has to offer some form of excellence in an area of interest to potential users. If your software does not have excellence in some form or manner, you have to ask yourself two questions. Should you get out of this product area? What can be done to develop the excellence that people will pay for and will allow this software to stay in the market?

Is your software ready to ship or is it in development? If it is in development, show a development plan and schedule. How long will it be until it is ready to ship to customers? How are you planning to handle beta testing and bug fixes? A development plan is a detailed schedule showing the various stages in the development of your software and when they are scheduled to be started and complete. Figure 10-1 shows a simple development schedule.

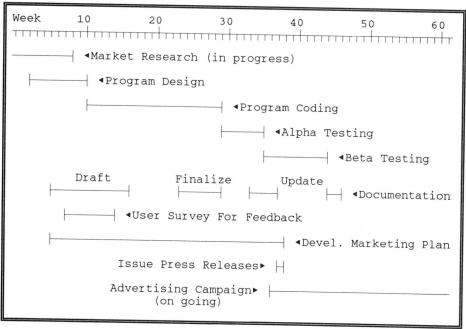

10-1 Simplified fictional development schedule. Horizontal bars are used to indicate the duration of each phase of developing a new software product.

Do you have any patents or licenses that affect this software?

How are your products different from the competition? A good way to present this information is to use a comparison table similar to those used by magazine reviewers. List your software and the competition's software across the top. Show the key features down the left side of the chart. Then, fill in the boxes. TABLE 10-1 provides an example using three competing products. Let us assume that we are comparing mailing-list managers and your product is called ZipBase™ (this is one of mine).

Table 10-1

This is a typical chart that can be used in a business plan to compare the features of several competing programs.

	ZipBase	FastBase	QuikMailer	MailMgr
Capacity	10,000,000	32,000	32,000	5000
Sort by zip code	yes	yes	yes	no
Drop-down menus	yes	no	no	no
# of fields	21	8	14	50
# searchable fields	21	8	4	2
Types of labels printed	3 built-in, plus user-definable	Standard Avery labels	User-defined	2 standard sizes
Printers supported	all	all	Epson	Epson & HP
Memory requirements	256K	512K	256K	640K

Do you anticipate any changes to your existing software? Are you planning any new software or other products? How often do you plan to issue updates or upgrades? What is your policy for discontinuing software? This is an important question. All products have life cycles. How will you know when it is time to discontinue or divest yourself of a product?

IV. Marketing plan   Most businesses skimp on this section and do a poor job. This happens because marketing information can sometimes be difficult to get or, in many cases, you might have to make an estimate. Put some extra effort into this section. Go looking for information about your market and your competition. Anytime you make a statement about your market or the competition, be prepared to back it up with facts.

Start this section by describing your target market. What are you selling? Who will buy it and why? What is your typical user like?

Target market. If you target a niche market, you must identify the niche. What are the characteristics of the niche? Why is this niche market right for your software? If you make a profit in this niche, will larger competitors enter it? What happens if larger competitors enter this market? Is this market ignored by the competition or not properly served by the competition?

What is the current economic environment affecting your target market and what are the economic trends for the future?

What is the market size? What has the size been in the past? What is the projected market size in 5 to 10 years? What are customers in this market buying (what benefits are they buying)? Why are they buying these benefits?

Provide a market-share analysis. What products are currently available? How many other suppliers provide this type of software? What percent of the market does each of these suppliers get? Based on the past, what are the market-share trends?

How do you get this type of information? All you have to do is ask. To find out about commercial software, request a copy of a publisher's annual report. Also, send for your competitors' brochures. Check with local software stores and ask about the comparative sales of competing software. Purchase a report on your competition from Dun & Bradstreet. Look for references to your competitors' software in magazines and newspapers.

To find out about shareware, talk with a few disk distributors and ask them about the sales of competitive software. They might not provide exact numbers, but you should be able to get a good idea of how one program does compared with others.

Objectives. Next, talk about your objectives, starting with your strategic objectives. Strategic objectives are the objectives you set in order to reach a specified target. Supporting strategic objectives are your tactical objectives, which are the things you need to do to accomplish the strategic objectives. A strategic objective states what you are going to do to reach a target you have defined. Your tactical objective describes the specific activities you will do to accomplish your strategic objective.

As an example, let us say you are targeting to have your software in the top five programs of its type within 24 months. To do this, you need to reach annual sales of $250,000. One of your strategic objectives would be to inform the market that your software is available and that you are ready to ship it. A tactical objective to support this strategic objective would be to send disks to disk distributors, start advertising, print brochures, and send out press releases.

Another strategic objective would be to arrange for the supplies needed to run your business. The tactical objective that supports this involves identifying suppliers and establishing a business relationship with suppliers.

Always list strategic and tactical objectives in the order of importance. Set your priorities so that the most important things are done first.

Critical success factors. What are the critical success factors in your business? In other words, what do you need to do to be successful? In this section, provide a break-even analysis that shows how much software you must sell on a monthly basis in order to cover your expenses for the first year. Also, show the same information on a yearly basis for the next three to five years.

Market analysis. This section should be a detailed analysis of your market. Your understanding of your market will be demonstrated in this section. Bankers and investors know that you will not be successful unless you have a complete and thorough understanding of your market.

One of the most frequent questions I am asked concerns how to find market information. Where do you look and what do you do to get facts about your market? The sources of information are everywhere.

You can talk with existing suppliers of similar software and get their brochures. Meet with competitors at trade shows or use information services such as GEnie or CompuServe. It might take some nerve to ask your competitors about their business, but you will be surprised at how much they will tell you. They are one of your best sources of information.

Read trade publications. For example, computer magazines are good sources of comparative reviews of mass market software and software that serves large markets. Industry-specific publications can provide details about niche markets. For example, if you make software that car dealers use to track inventories and customer preferences, you should be subscribing to *Automotive News*. How do you find publications? Go to your library and look in the *Standard Periodical Directory* published by Oxbridge Communications, Inc.

Talk with users of existing products. This includes the users of your products and your competition's. Attend user group meetings or post a survey on CompuServe or GEnie. Visit some of your potential customers. For example, if you make software that businesses use, stop in and visit the purchasing people in several corporations or use personal contacts to arrange appointments with people in the industry you serve.

You should also talk with potential users. This is a key area. You should have as many discussions as possible with users before and after you introduce your software. Their feedback should be incorporated into both your software and your plans. Find out what magazines they read. What are their tastes and preferences in software (i.e., do they prefer GUI's or command-line-driven software?). How much software do they buy? What type of computers do they have?

The marketing section of your business plan should also include an analysis of market opportunities. How is the market segmented (split)? Is it segmented by industry? Is there a difference between volume buyers and single-unit buyers? What are the growth prospects for each segment? Is this a mature market (no growth) or a new market with a high growth potential? What are the trends in each segment and why? Are there government regulations affecting your market?

Promotion and distribution. Promotion and distribution are an important part of marketing. How are you planning to promote and distribute your software? The answer might be obvious to you—you are using shareware to promote your software and you will handle all sales directly, via mail order. However, to someone outside your company, it will not be obvious, and in most cases, they will not know what shareware is. Describe how shareware works in detail and, if you are just starting, provide examples of successful companies that use shareware to market their software. Describe the role shareware disk distributors play and your plans for sending disks to distributors, BBSs, and user groups.

Also, describe any other methods you plan to use to promote and distribute your software such as advertising, the use of disk distributors to handle credit-card sales, or even sales through retail stores (if you can arrange it). If you are planning to advertise, list the publications you plan to advertise in and explain why. Are you planning to send out press releases? If so, to what type of media, how many, and on what schedule? Do you have any experience working with software distributors or dealers? Will you be selling your software internationally or limiting distribution to the domestic market? If you are limiting your market, explain why and the circumstances that would cause you to drop this limitation.

Are you planning to hire anyone to help with marketing or sales? If so, what are you planning to pay them? Be realistic in your estimates of what you plan to pay them. For example, do not make the hiring of an experienced marketing manager an objective and then state that you have budgeted $15,000 as the salary. It is not realistic and only shows that you are out of touch with the cost of doing business. Of course, if you can hire an experienced person at a low rate of pay, for example, a retired family member, provide a complete explanation.

How do you plan to ship your software? Will you charge extra for shipping and handling? What level of inventory do you plan to maintain? How often do you plan to turn over your inventory?

Sales objectives. Another part of the marketing section of your business plan is discussing your sales objectives. What are the sales targets you are shooting for? What levels of sales do you expect your company to have in one year, two years, and five years? How much income do you expect to be earning in one year, two years, and five years? At what point do you expect to be profitable? Do you want your shareware business to be your full-time job? If so, by what date? What are you going to do to reach these targets? What happens if you do not reach these targets?

Having a backup plan that comes into play when your first plan runs into problems is important and is sign a of a good manager. The future holds too many unknowns. There is no way you can establish a single business plan to achieve your objectives. Expect problems and have plans in place to deal with the unexpected.

What sales tactics do you plan to use? For example, one strategy would be to have a low registration fee in order to try to make a profit on selling upgrades. Another approach is to have a higher price and sell software based on the value it provides to the user. A third approach, focusing on customer service, might be appropriate if your market consists largely of novice users.

What type of product image does your software have? Low price? Out-standing customer support? Advanced features? Are you planning to change this image? What type of warranties and guarantees do you offer? How are you going to package your software?

Answer all of these questions and explain the reasons why you are taking the approach you describe. Back up your explanations with solid facts.

Pricing. Next, talk about your pricing. Relative to the market, is your software priced high, medium, or low? Explain. What is your billing policy? C.O.D.? Net 20, 30, 60, 90 days? Do you accept purchase orders? Under what conditions do you accept purchase orders? Do you accept credit cards? If not, is it important to you to accept credit cards? If so, what are you doing to get merchant status and how are you planning to handle credit-card orders until you can get merchant status?

Do you accept foreign checks and under what circumstances do you accept them?

Do you offer dealer discounts? What are they?

What is your exchange/return policy?

V. Competitive analysis You had better know your competition. Who are they? How do they approach the market? What are their strengths and weaknesses? What is their reputation in the market? What niches are they in?

What do you do better than the competition? People almost always buy because they feel a product is superior to its competitor's. Explain why your software is better and back up your explanation with facts and comparisons.

What type of history and experience does your competition have? Have they been in business a long time or are they new? You might think that it is best to show your competition as weak and in a poor position to compete against you. If you are creating a new market, this approach is good as long as you have the only viable product in this new market. However, if you are entering an existing market, showing that the competition is weak might mean that this is not a viable market. Showing that you have strong, successful competition can be important. It shows that you are in, or plan to enter, a good market.

VI. Management The first part of this section should identify the key people in your company. If you are a one-person company, this is where you get to talk about yourself. If someone else is involved in your company, you should discuss why they are involved and what their background is. For each of the key people in your business, answer the following questions.

Who are the people involved in your business?

What are their backgrounds, experiences, and qualifications?

What are their achievements and how successful have they been?

Will your company need to hire additional people in order to achieve the goals described in the previous section? Where are you going to get them? What are you going to pay them (remember, pay must match the skills required)? Will these employees need training? Will you purchase outside services (i.e., consultants, contract programmers, etc.)?

If you have three or more people in your company include an organizational chart.

In addition to people, your company needs material resources. In the next part of this section, describe how you produce the registered versions of your software. What equipment and facilities do you need to produce your software? Where are you going to get your supplies? Will you be hiring outside services or producing your software completely in-house? What type of quality control program will you have?

VII. Financial plan   This is one of the first sections most bankers will look at. It summarizes, in numbers, the current health of your company and your company's potential for the future.

Start by describing the financial history of your company. How was its start-up financed? Most shareware publishers are financed by the author. Did you write checks drawn on your personal account to pay the bills when you first started your company? How much money have you put into your company? What types of gross margins do you expect to have and what is the industry average? This is a tough question. Essentially, all shareware companies are owned by individuals and none publicly publish their financial statements. (I will be using future author surveys to try to get an answer to this question.) For most industries, a minimum of a 40% gross margin is typical.

What is your philosophy concerning debt? What debt does your company currently have? What is the source of that debt? What type of credit arrangements do you have with suppliers? What other business-related liabilities do you have?

Provide the following financial statements: projected revenue, projected cash flow, and a pro forma (projected) profit & loss statement.

What assumptions did you use as the basis of these financial projections? For example, did you anticipate deferring your own salary? What was the basis for depreciation? What was the assumed interest rate?

As a part of these statements, include the number of copies of your software you expect to sell and the estimated gross revenue for a given time period, for example, for the next year. Show what you expect your cash reserves will be, what the cost of goods sold (COGS) will be, what your operating expenses will be, and what your net income or loss will be (negative numbers—losses—are shown in parentheses).

Another financial statement that you will need to provide is a pro forma balance sheet. Describe how you plan to monitor and control funds. How will you handle accounting? How will sales be recorded? How will expenses be tracked? A shoebox accounting system will not impress your banker. At a minimum, you should be using a spreadsheet to track your daily (or at least weekly) sales and expenses.

How do you plan to finance your business? In almost all cases, a shareware business will be financed internally—meaning you provide cash as it is needed. What do you expect the financial requirements of your business to be and what personal resources do you have available for meeting these requirements? Are you going to need financing from external sources? If so, what do you plan to use for collateral and how do you plan to get that financing?

That is it. That is everything you need to put in your business plan. Now let us look at how to put it all together.

Producing your business plan

I have described the seven major sections of a business plan. Once you have those completed, there are a few other short sections you will need to add.

There should be a cover page that includes the title, the name of your company, and the date your plan was last updated. Even if your business plan is only for your own use, you should include a cover page to tell you which version (based on the date) you are looking at. If you will be distributing copies outside your company, the cover page should also include a control number. This number is used to track which copy was given to whom and whether it was returned or is being held in someone else's files. You could think of the control number as part version number and part ID number. This number should be recorded in a log book and include information about who this specific copy of your business plan was issued to. If you are concerned about the confidentiality of the information in your business plan, include a non-disclosure statement on the cover page. A typical non-disclosure statement should be:

> "The HomeCraft Software Business Plan is confidential and contains proprietary information. Neither this plan nor any of the information in the plan or appendices may be reproduced or disclosed to any other person under any circumstances without the express written permission of HomeCraft Software."

In the first section inside the front cover, before anything else, include an executive summary of the plan. This is the most important part of your business plan. If you are applying for a loan, for example, your banker will first glance at the executive summary and then turn to the financial section to study your pro formas. Only after they have looked at these two sections will they look through the rest of your business plan. If you have a poor executive summary, your business plan and your chances for a loan might be dismissed without anyone having read the details of your plan.

The executive summary should be as short as possible, and under no circumstances should it exceed three pages. It needs to be a concise and clear summary of what your company is about and it must give the reader some sound reasons that explain why they should read your plan. It should include the following information.

- Your company   A brief description of your company, your mission statement, when the company was formed, and how you market your software.
- Your products   What products do you sell and what are the distinguishing features? Is your software ready for the market or under development? Does your software have any unique features?
- Your market   What is the current size of your market and is it growing? What is your estimated market share? Do you sell your software domestically or internationally?
- Financial summary   What are your five-year projections for sales and revenues? Are you looking for financing and why? How long will you need financing? When will your company be profitable?
- The management team   Provide a brief description of your background and experience. If someone else is involved in your company, include a description of their background and experience.

Following the executive summary, include a table of contents. Then, include the body of your business plan based on the outline and questions I have presented. At the end of your business plan, include appendices that have information such as:

- Resumés of key people.
- Schedule of events.
- List of major customers/users.
- Supporting financial information, including detailed information about assumptions, receivable policies, payment policies, depreciation utilized, and any other information used to put together your financial statements.
- List of principle suppliers.
- Description of any insurance coverage you have for your company.
- Expense budgets.
- Any other documents or data that supports what you have written in your business plan.

When you are finished, put your business plan in a good binder or bind it using a GBC machine. Do not just staple the pages together.

Now that your business plan is complete, do not put it on a shelf and forget it. Read through it every couple of months. Reading your business plan helps keep you on track with what you want to do and it allows you to pencil in changes. As you gain experience and your company grows, your business plan will need to change. It will also need to be adapted to changes in your market and in economic conditions.

Selling skills

When I asked other shareware authors about the selling skills they needed, I was surprised at the number who said they did not need to know how to sell. They felt shareware did not require selling. Once they had sent out their disks to distributors, they could just sit at home and wait for the orders to come in. That is how they felt shareware worked. Many felt that you do not have to sell software in a face-to-face meeting with the customer. Just send shareware to disk distributors and wait for the orders. Who needs selling skills? Well, selling skills are important and I will tell you why in a moment.

Mention the word "selling" or "salesperson" and right away you have a problem. Selling and salespeople have a very bad image. When we think of a salesperson, we generally call up an image of a pushy guy trying to "sell" us something we do not want. The words "selling" and "salesperson" both are seen as negative words. Yet, these are two of the most important words for someone running their own business. And, the images they bring up are wrong!

Then there is the question concerning whether salespeople are born or if selling is a skill you can learn. We think of a salesperson as someone with a permanent smile—a back-slapping, glad-handing person with an aggressive attitude—telling jokes and being the center of conversation. These are things you are born with, right? That's right! These are skills you are born with, but they are not the skills that make someone a good salesperson.

Take me as an example. I am basically a quiet and shy person. I do not particularly like social functions, and I am terrible at making conversation. I prefer to read a good book and enjoy quiet times by myself. This is not the description of a typical salesperson. Yet, in 1989, I was the top salesperson for Combustion Engineering Power Services, Inc. I have made individual sales with values over 10 million dollars and, in 1989, I made a million-dollar-plus sale to a customer that no one else in the history of the company had been able to sell anything to. In the ten years I was responsible for the Pacific Northwest, I built a 75% market share for my company while facing four other major competitors. Overall, that is not a bad sales record for a quiet, shy type of person.

Sales skills are something anyone can learn and some of the best salespeople are the quiet, wallflower type of people. Although there might be more books written on how to be a good salesperson than any other type of business book, the basics you need to learn are very simple and easy to do. I can list everything you need to know in two paragraphs. But first, let me answer some of the other questions I have raised.

Why you need sales skills

When you are talking to your banker, trying to get a VISA/MasterCard merchant account, you are selling. You are selling yourself, your honesty, and your ability to run a business.

When someone using your shareware calls for help with a technical question, you are selling. You are selling the quality of your technical support and the ability of your software to do what the user requires.

When you are talking with a magazine editor, you are selling. You are selling your software as something the magazine's readers will be interested in.

When you are talking to a supplier about purchasing disks, you are selling. You are selling your image as a strong, stable company that can buy supplies on terms instead of C.O.D.

Selling is an integral part of any business and everyone, if they are good at what they do, needs selling skills. If you work for a big multinational corporation that has 100,000 employees, each of those employees has a customer they are serving and each needs some level of selling skills. For someone in an entry level position in the mailroom, that person's customers are the people they deliver mail to. What is the mailroom clerk selling? They are selling their ability to deliver the mail, and thus keep their job. They are selling their ability to do their job, and thus get a promotion. They are selling the mailroom's ability to deliver the mail, and thus keep the mailroom from being replaced by an outside contract service.

What are you selling?

In the software business, you are selling software. That was the easy answer, but what else are you selling? Not everything you sell has a price attached to it. Before you can sell your software, you must "sell" a lot of other things. The following is a list of things you should be selling.

- Your image
- Your belief that your software will be beneficial to your users
- Your reputation
- Your trustworthiness
- Your technical support capabilities
- Your programming skills
- Your ability to write good documentation
- Your background and knowledge in the field in which your software is marketed

I have deliberately picked eight items that are abstract—things that are not physical. Generally, before anyone buys a copy of your software, you have to "sell" them on all eight of these abstract items. Sometimes, it is easy—your shareware package sells itself. Sometimes, you are selling and might not be aware of it, such as when a user calls for technical support. Other times, when a user asks you to explain why your software is better than anyone else's, it is obvious you need to be wearing your sales hat.

What selling is

Selling is providing a service to a potential customer by matching that customer with a product or service that will benefit the customer. Notice that I did not say that selling is getting someone to buy something. Getting someone to buy something they do not need is not selling, it is fraud. I also did not say that selling is fast talking and a lot of hype. That is one of the images we have of salespeople and it is wrong.

The best salespeople are those who are themselves, who are honest and who have a sincere desire to help the customer. Do you have to be a joke teller and socialite? No. Be honest and be yourself, that is it. But, as with anything else, there are some skills you can learn that will help you do a better job. The following is a list of skills that should make you a better salesperson.

Be a good listener   Most salespeople talk too much. Good salespeople not only listen, but they pay attention to what the customer says and does. In many cases, while the other person is talking, we are thinking about what we are going to say next. We are only half paying attention to what the other person is saying. If we are going to provide this person with the best possible level of service, we need to fully listen to what they are saying, how they are saying it, and what they are doing.

Help the customer   A good salesperson's main motivation is a desire to help the customer. Good salespeople are service-oriented. Making money and the satisfaction that comes from closing a sale, do make us feel good. But, if these come before our desire to serve the customer, we will not be closing the sale, nor making money.

Be honest   The only thing a salesperson can directly offer a customer is trustworthiness. If a salesperson loses a customer's confidence in his or her trustworthiness, that customer never again will buy from that salesperson. Yes, you can make a sale by lying. It might even be the easiest sale you will ever make. It is easy to offer the best product, if you can make up features and benefits that do not exist. But, after that first sale, the customer will find out the truth and you will never sell anything else to that customer (we all would like to sell upgrades, right?). Even worse, your bad reputation will spread and soon you will have no customers.

Understand your customer's needs   Good salespeople are able to put themselves in the customer's shoes. Being able to understand the customer's problems and needs is important. It is the best way to truly understand how you can serve the customer and match them with the software you make that is best for them. In many cases, when a good saleperson's products are not appropriate for what the customer needs, that salesperson will refer the customer to a product made by another company.

Be positive   No one likes to talk with or do business with a grump or someone that always sees the negative side of things. That is why a positive attitude is important when you are working to sell your software. A good salesperson looks for the good in people and for the positive aspects of any situation. The worst thing that can happen to a salesperson is to lose a sale. But, when that happens, the good salesperson does not start blaming the loss on unfair tactics by the competition or stupidity on the part of the customer. A good salesperson takes a positive approach, getting feedback from the customer to find out what he did right and what areas should be improved.

When I was working in sales, I did something few, if any, other salespeople do. About once a year, I would visit with my customers and ask them to tell me what I was doing right and what I could improve. I would have my customers evaluate my performance and that is how I learned to do a better job for my customers.

That does not sound too bad, does it? In fact, being a salesperson, for most people, means being the person we are, not some fake image. Is there anything wrong with being someone who listens to other people? A person who cares about and wants to help other people? A person who is honest and can understand another person's point of view? A person with a positive attitude? Sounds like a really nice person to me. Somebody I would want to know.

These are only some of the skills you will need when you talk with customers, suppliers, editors, and many other people. Although sales training courses teach a variety of skills, such as how to ask open-ended questions, I feel there are two basic skills every salesperson needs. Things such as open-ended questions will develop from the characteristics I previously listed. For example, if you are honestly interested in a customer's welfare, you will automatically ask open-ended questions, because you are interested in learning more about that customer.

Two key things that I feel a salesperson must do are follow up on a sale and ask for the order.

You should always follow up—whether you win or lose a sale—to find out why. With shareware, many times you will not know you have lost a sale because users will simply delete your software. So how do you follow up when you are using shareware to market your software? The next paragraphs have five suggestions.

Call disk distributors and ask if they have gotten any feedback on your shareware. Find out whether your shareware sells a lot or just a few copies. Remember, however, that several hundred people might buy your software for each person that registers. All you are trying to find out from the disk distributor is whether or not your software catches people's interest.

Do a presentation about your software for a user group. During the presentation, pay attention to how the group is reacting to your software. Are they interested or are they drifting off to look at something else? Following the presentation, hand out a questionnaire.

Beta test your software and get feedback from your testers. Ask them whether or not they continue to use your software when they are done testing and find out why (or why not).

Send questionnaires to people on your mailing list who have asked about your software, but have never purchased it. Find out why they asked about your software and why they have not purchased it.

When an unregistered user calls with a question, but does not register during the phone call, ask if there is anything you could change in the software that would make it better fit his or her needs.

One of the most difficult things you should do is ask people to buy your software. It is called asking for the order. It is very hard to do and most salespeople do not do it. I once attended a seminar in which 15 other experienced salesmen were participating. Some had more than 20 years of experience in sales. We all were asked to sell a fictional product to the person running the seminar. Out of 15 salespeople, only one person—me—asked for the order. The others made their presentation, talked about the features and benefits of their product, gave the price, and that was it. They left the customer wondering about what to do next and, like most people, the customer put off making a decision.

When talking with unregistered users on the phone, I have several approaches for asking for the order. The one I use most frequently is, "If you'd like to order a registered copy now, we do accept credit cards and I can take your order on the phone."

Another way to ask for the order is to say, "We just started shipping the current version. I'd be happy to take your order now so we can ship it to you right away."

If you are not able to accept credit cards, you are at somewhat of a disadvantage, but there are still ways you can try to close a sale on the phone. For example, you could offer a free copy of another shareware program: "We have a special offer I'd like to let you know about. If we receive your registration check within the next week, we'll include a free copy of the *1991 Shareware Almanac* with your order." You could also offer a reduced price on your software and include additional utilities at no charge.

The two-paragraph summary

I said earlier that I could list everything you need to know about selling in two paragraphs. Well, here they are.

Be yourself and have a positive attitude. Be honest and concerned about the customer. Try to see things from the customer's viewpoint.

Whenever you can, get feedback on why the customer bought or did not buy your software. Do not forget to ask for the order.

That is it. Two rather short paragraphs at that.

Communication skills

Another important skill that will help your software become successful is the ability to talk up your software. We all envy those people who have the gift of gab. They can meet a complete stranger and be in a deep conversation a few seconds later. That is not the type of person I am talking about. I am talking about you and me, ordinary people who have learned a few communication skills.

> *Shareware authors need to be able to talk to people. I've met a lot of authors that when you get into a conversation it's like talking to a brick wall. They may talk up a storm on CompuServe, but you get them one-on-one and they don't say anything.*
> —Marshall Magee, president of Magee Enterprises (*AutoMenu*)

The ability to talk with people is a useful skill that can be learned. As a business person, it is important that you have the ability to talk with people and communicate your message. I mentioned talking and communication separately because they are two different things. You can be talking, but if the other person is not listening and paying attention, there is no communication. What is the best way to encourage communication? Talk louder? Talk faster? Kick the other person in the shin to get their attention? No, but here is a list of suggestions.

Ask questions and have people ask questions of you Does that make sense? If you want to communicate with someone, you should find a way to get people to ask you questions. The point is that you want to *tell* them something, not have them tell you things.

Asking questions makes sense. Before you can deliver your message, you first must get the other person's attention. Then, you must learn enough about them so that you can deliver your message in a way that interests them. How do you do that? You ask questions. Use your questions to learn about the other person's interests. It makes starting a conversation easy because everyone's favorite subject is themselves. Once you learn a little about what the other person likes and dislikes, you can deliver you message in a way that will interest them.

Make eye contact If you are talking with somebody, look at them. That does not mean to stare at them continuously, because that will make people uncomfortable. However, if you are looking around the room or looking at other people, that tells the person you are talking with that you are not interested in what they are saying.

Be aware of your body language   Some studies have shown that up to 85% of what is communicated is nonverbal. For example, if you are trying to have an open and friendly conversation with someone, but your arms are folded, your body is delivering a message that says you are upset about something. When you first meet someone, try to have a relaxed, easy posture. By the way, a simple way to learn about body language is to watch TV. Actors are aware of their body language and use it to help express the emotions of the character they are playing. In many cases, especially in sitcoms, they will use exaggerated body language. Key in on one character, identify the emotion they are expressing, and then notice what they are doing with their body.

Promoting software   As a software business person, you should talk up your software with anyone who will listen. It is an important aspect of promoting your software. "Oh, but I never know what to say!" That is how I feel. My natural inclination is to be a wallflower and avoid conversations. I am perfectly happy being a wallflower, just watching other people have a good time. But, if I am going to make my business successful, I have to step away from the wall and introduce myself.

That is all there is to it. That is how you start a conversation. Just introduce yourself. After that, ask the other person a few questions about themselves. What type of business are they in? What do they do? If you are at a meeting or convention, ask them if they are enjoying the meeting. If you are at a bus stop, ask them if they take that bus often. Mention the major news events of the day and ask for their opinion.

To be able to carry on a conversation, you will need to know what you are talking about. Knowing your subject builds your confidence and makes it easier to talk with individuals and in front of groups. If you want to talk about your software, you need to have an in-depth knowledge of your software and of the people who use it. Because you wrote it, you might think you know it all. That is not true, and I will talk about that in a moment. Knowing your subject also means having a wider breadth of experience than just knowing about your software. For example, you cannot talk about the day's news unless you read the newspaper. You cannot talk about the state of the computer industry unless you read a few computer publications. So do a little outside reading and be aware of what is going on in the world around you.

To be able to tell people about your software, you must know everything there is to know about it. Do not assume that, because you wrote your software, you know all about it. Knowing about it means knowing who uses it, why they use it, how they use it, and everything else you need to learn in order to write a business plan. As I said in the section on business plans, that is one of the main reasons for writing a business plan.

Sometimes it takes a lot of research, but knowing your subject gives you confidence. Knowing a one-sentence description of your software, and having thought about that one sentence in detail, allows you to intelligently answer when someone asks, "What type of software do you publish?"

Writing a proposal

Proposal writing is another area in which the initial responses I got from authors indicated they didn't feel they needed to know how to write a proposal. If you ever plan on your business being more than a part-time business, you need to know how to write a proposal. For example, would you like to sell a 5000-copy site license to United Airlines? If so, you will need to know how to write a proposal. Would you be interested in a purchase order from the New York City School District for 1000 copies of your educational game? If so, be prepared to write a proposal.

A proposal does not need to be a 50-page document, written in response to a formal request for proposals (RFP). Some proposals are single-page letters or, in some cases, nothing more than a photocopied price list. If you have a catalog, at times that might be considered your proposal. The form a proposal takes will depend on the situation. In this section, I will be describing a formal type of proposal that would be used in making a fairly large sale. However, except for the title page and executive summary, even a two-page letter proposal would still be based on the same format I describe here.

Why is it important that you know how to write a proposal? If you are planning to sell your software to business, you have to present a professional image to be taken seriously. Here is what Marshall Magee, president of Magee Enterprises, Inc. (*AutoMenu*), had to say about selling to corporations.

> *Corporations like to deal with a stable, established company. You need to assure them that you are going to continue to exist.*

What is the best way to help a corporate customer feel secure in doing business with you? Show them you know how to present a professional-looking proposal.

Types of proposals

There are two types of proposals. The first type is a proposal sent on an unsolicited basis, meaning the customer did not ask for your proposal. In most cases, this type of proposal is designed to persuade the reader that they need your product or service.

The second type of proposal is one that is sent to a potential customer who has an identifiable need and your proposal must convince them that your product or service will best fill that need. This is the type of proposal most shareware authors are likely to use. For example, this is the type of proposal you would send to a corporation interested in purchasing a site license for your software.

Solving the customer's problem

Before you start to write a proposal, you need to have your approach well organized. Most proposals are written to present a solution to a problem. For example, if you sell a DOS shell, the customer's problem might be that the average user in their organization is having problems accessing various programs on a hard disk.

You will use your proposal to describe your understanding of the customer's problem or need. Then, your proposal will present a solution and explain why your solution is a good approach. That's all there is to it, so let's get started.

As with so many other things, the first step is to define your objectives. Before you start to write a proposal, you must have a clear understanding of what your objectives are and what strategy you want to use in your proposal. To define your objectives, first ask yourself what are the main reasons this corporation should buy your software? Why is your software better than the competition's? What features of your software provide a unique benefit to the customer, that will help solve their problems? Is your software the most efficient, easiest to use, least costly, most capable? Do you offer the best support, outstanding training, or the most complete documentation? Out of these, or possibly other advantages your software offers, pick one or two overriding advantages and base your selling strategy on them. Your proposal needs to focus on the customer's needs. Don't try to be everything anyone could want. Your message will be diffused and the result will be a weak proposal.

Before you start to write your proposal, talk to customers and find out what they need. Look for the root cause of problems. In asking for your proposal, the customer might have only defined the symptoms. To be successful, you need to dig to find the causes of the problem. Ask them to describe the problem and then ask them to tell you what they think is causing the problem. Keep asking questions until you feel satisfied that you have found out why the problem exists.

With the problem defined and the key benefits of your software identified, you now have a focus for your proposal. Focus on the key benefits (assuming, of course, these benefits are what the customer needs to solve their problem). Carry this focus throughout the proposal. Emphasize it in your cover letter, in the executive summary, and even in the headings you use for each section of the proposal.

Proposal guidelines

Every proposal should have a title page as the front cover. This page includes the name of the organization to which you are submitting the proposal, the date of submission, the customer's RFP number or other reference number, your proposal number, and, if the proposal contains confidential material, you might also wish to add a confidentiality statement. Many times, a proposal will be re-written two or three times. Put a proposal number on each so you can easily identify which version you are working with. A typical proposal number might be 91-003-02. This means the proposal was written in 1991 and was the third proposal you did that year. The 02 indicates this is revision 2.

First, always keep in mind that your proposal, whether it is a price list, a catalog, or a 50-page site-license proposal, should always look neat and professional. Appearance counts. The appearance of your proposal provides a strong first impression about the quality of your company and how you do business. Do not submit proposals printed on a dot-matrix printer. Do not send copies of your copier smudged or streaked.

If the proposal is longer than 8 to 10 pages, you should include a table of contents. Use the table of contents to provide a detailed outline of the key information in your proposal. This will help the reader find information and serve to jog the reader's memory about the contents of your proposal.

If your proposal includes exhibits, client lists, or screen shots, include a page listing these. Also list any extra material, such as brochures, so the reader can tell if something is missing.

The first section of a proposal is generally an executive summary. Use this section to summarize the key details. Describe the important benefits your software provides and describe the facts that support your claims. If the schedule is important, highlight your schedule and your ability to meet that schedule. Assume that the only section the decision maker will read is this section. You will need to mention all the essentials, but do not clutter this section with details. Just highlight the one or two key reasons why the prospect should do business with you.

Description of requirements   Use this section to summarize your understanding of the customer's problem. Include an analysis of the problem based on the conversations you have had with the customer. If you feel there are several problems, describe them and tell the customer why you feel this way. By doing this, you are laying the groundwork for the alternative solutions you will be describing in the next section.

If you have made any assumptions, list them here. Also list any customer requirements such as the number of users, type of material to be delivered (for example, printed manuals), and the schedule.

Proposal   This is the section in which you describe the software and services you are offering. Discuss your proposed solution to the customer's problem in full detail, focusing on the customer's goals and the results they can expect. List the advantages of your solution and tell the customer how to measure or evaluate the results of using your software.

Cover all the details. Do not let the reader make assumptions because they might be the wrong assumptions. Discuss every benefit, even if it appears to be an obvious benefit. It might not be obvious to the reader. Help the reader focus on the key benefits you want to emphasize. For example, if the key benefit is that your software is easy to use, use a chart to show how quickly users can learn your software compared with other programs. If cost is a key issue, show a per-unit cost breakdown. Evaluators might not always think to break things down or might be distracted by someone else's proposal whose focus is in a different area.

Make sure the proposal answers the key questions. Put yourself in the customer's place and visualize the questions you would have. But be careful, some proposals try to have all the answers—before they have the questions. Be sure that you understand your customer's concerns, problems, and needs before you start writing your proposal. If you show that you understand the customer, the customer will feel more confident that your solution is the correct one.

Should you be concerned about giving too much information? No. Be open, honest, and give the customer the full details. Your proposal must be specific enough to show that you clearly know what you are talking about. Do not be vague. Vagueness is usually used to hide a lack of knowledge.

Do not include extravagant claims that you cannot back up with facts. Avoid words and phrases such as "best" or "undisputed leader" unless you can provide proof. Unless your competition agrees that you are the leader, you cannot be the "undisputed leader." A good way to support your claim is to include copies of reviews and quotes from letters from users. You should always get permission from the magazine that did the review before you copy it. I have found that, in most cases, magazines do not charge for this as long as you give them proper credit for the review and have their permission in writing.

Also, be careful not to use hedging language or vague qualifiers. For example, never say, "our software should perform to the specification requirements." Either it will perform as required or it will not. Anytime you use the word "should," you are telling the reader you are not sure your software is right for them.

Never knock the competition. Knocking the competition just shows a negative attitude on your part. Let the qualities and benefits of your software speak for themselves. Yes, you can compare products, if you have facts. But never bad-mouth the competition.

Options You might find that the customer is asking for something that will not solve the problem. In all cases, always propose what the customer asked for. If you then have a better solution you would like to offer, offer it as an alternative. In the option section of your proposal, describe each option in the same detail as you did for your base proposal.

Other options you might want to include in a proposal for a site license include:

- If the base proposal does not include printed manuals, you can offer an option to supply printed manuals. Or, if they are included in the base proposal, offer an option that reduces the price if the customer duplicates the manuals.
- Offer an option to provide user support based on an hourly rate.
- Offer an option to provide on-site training.
- Offer an option for other software you publish which the customer might find useful. Many times you can put together a package price that is more attractive should the customer buy two site licenses.
- Offer an option for customized screens, customized programming, or customized user manuals.

References and experience list   If you have sold similar site licenses to other companies, include a list of references. The best references include the specific names and phone numbers of people who can be contacted. If this is not possible, only include a list of previous customers if it is a substantial list. This means the list must have some recognizable names on it and it must be at least 10 to 15 names long. It is best, however, to have enough names to fill a page—even if you have to use large print.

If you, or other employees in your company, have any specialized experience that applies to the situation, describe that experience in this section.

Pricing   Include a separate section that lists the prices for your base offering and for any options that you have proposed.

Terms and conditions   This section should contain a copy of the site-license contract you are proposing. (See chapter 9 for a sample site-license agreement.)

Miscellaneous exhibits   The final section of your proposal contains any brochures, copies of reviews, magazine articles about your company or software, your resumé or anything else that supports your proposal and demonstrates your track record.

The cover letter   Whenever you send out a proposal, always include a cover letter. If it does nothing else, the cover letter says, "Here it is." It documents that you sent your proposal and to whom it was sent.

But a cover letter can also do more! Include a few brief sentences that summarize what you are proposing. Emphasize the key benefits of doing business with you. Also use the cover letter to answer any anticipated questions about the proposal in general. If you are unable to propose exactly what the customer asked for, explain why. Also explain any omissions or changes in your proposal. Put yourself in the reader's place. After you have examined the proposal, what questions would you have? At the end of your cover letter, thank the customer for asking you to submit a proposal.

11
Writing and testing software

Software users, in general, want ease of use, good documentation, and technical support. In some respects, these three are the same. They mean that users want software that has a short learning curve and that can be quickly put to use for its intended purpose. By the way, that is the number one item on the list—software must provide a solution to a problem. It must be useful and nontrivial. Otherwise, there is no reason for the user to purchase the software.

What users want

The following comments are from users, and they basically say the same things about what users want.

I like well-written documentation.

I want to see four things in the software I purchase. 1) Good documentation. 2) Ease of use. 3) Good support. 4) Cost, but only if the above three are equal or the price difference is substantial.

I definitely go with the program that is easier to use.

I think wide use of the program is important. If it is not widely used, your ability to get support is limited to the technical support department of the company.

Once users decide they need to purchase new software, they want true ease of use. This means that most users in your target market can intuitively use existing software, that the documentation is easy to read and complete, and that quality support is readily available. The problem with the phrase "easy to use" is that people have various definitions of what it means. When I asked other shareware authors how they defined "easy to use," these are some of the answers they gave:

> *I like to think "easy to use" is when I start the program up and can do something useful with it without having to resort to using the manual. I don't mind using the manual for advanced features, but I want the startup and basic use to be obvious.*
>
> —Tom Simondi, author of TUTOR.COM

> *Easy to use is when the computer novice does not have to wade through 300 pages of text and make 10 calls for assistance. An author needs to listen to the calls and letters he gets and ask, "What can I do to prevent the user from having this problem?" In designing a program and its documentation, you have to apply KISS—that means Keep It Simple Stupid. Even complicated programs such as a payroll system can be easy to use. I am thrilled when users of my ZPAY 3 program call and tell me how easy to use the program is.*
>
> —Paul Mayer, author of GRAB Plus and ZPAY3

> *I don't think it is easily defined. Perhaps something along the lines of intuitive enough such that the average user can figure out how it works based on what appears on the screen.*
>
> —Bob Falk, author of *EasyFormat* and *ProPak 2.0*

Finding out whether or not your software is easy to use

There are no specific step-by-step instructions you can follow to make your software easy to use. The definition of "easy to use" is different depending on the experience and background of the end user. A program that is easy to use for a business user might not be easy for a home user. What is intuitive for one person is unintelligible to another. The only way you can know whether or not your software is easy to use is to test it. Find someone with no computer experience. This might be your spouse, a friend, or even students in a computer or business class at your local high school. (My thanks to Paul Mayer for this suggestion.) Get their comments. Pay attention to what makes them frustrated. What questions do they ask? Note the areas they have problems with. Then change your software so that the next user does not have the same questions or problems.

Another approach to finding out how easy to use your software would be to release it to a few distributors and get feedback as people start to use it. Then once you have confirmed that your program is easy to use, or after you have improved it, release it to a larger number of distributors. Keep in mind that you might be imposing on these early users. Be prepared to put extra effort into providing them super service. If they make suggestions, make changes in your software and send out free updates ASAP. By the way, do not use this type of testing to debug your software. Releasing buggy software just frustrates users and results in a bad reputation for you. The purpose of this type of testing is to find out if your software is easy to install, easy to use, and whether or not it has all the functions users need. To encourage feedback, include a special offer such as a reduced or free registration fee, and be sure to properly identify the software as a pre-release version.

> *If they have a problem or can't understand something, see what you can do to make it easier. If you can modify the user interface and change program actions to minimize technical support calls, then you have a winner.*
>
> —Paul Mayer

Making a program intuitive and easy to use is especially important with shareware. People will put your disk in their computer, give it a quick try, and if they can get it started without reading the documentation, they are more likely to use it. The way most people learn a new program is by first trying to use it. They read the manual later to learn about the more advanced functions.

Get feedback

Remember, what is easy for you might not be easy for most users. Test, test, test and listen to the feedback. Try different approaches in designing your software and test them. When talking to users or testers, remember what I said in the section on handling complaints. Do not get upset. Users will find lots of problems and they will have some complaints and suggestions that are not justified. Always stay calm and keep in mind that different people see things differently.

It is often easy for users and testers to identify problems; but, you need to find solutions. This is not easy. Sometimes, the solution to one problem creates difficulties in another area. Once you have released the final fully tested version, keep listening to users and continue looking for ways to improve your software and make it easier to use. The feedback and improvement cycle never stops.

This chapter provides some guidelines to help you make your software easy to use. I am not going to try to show you how to write program code or discuss the specifics about programming languages. After all, this is a marketing book, not a programming book. However, the principles covered here can be applied using any programming language.

Benefits of good software design

The benefits of writing good software are that you can more easily get people to pay the registration fee and that you can avoid spending all your time on the phone providing support. I have talked with people who have written a program and do not want to release it because they do not want to answer questions on the phone all the time. Or, they release the program and specify that all questions must be mailed to the author; no phone number is given in the documentation. This is fine if you run your business as a hobby. However, if you are serious about publishing software and making money doing it, you will need to include your phone number. If you have any intention of selling your software to businesses, you must include your phone number.

The solution to the telephone support problem is to listen to the questions users ask and then change either your documentation or your program to eliminate the questions. It takes some time, but you will have a better program. And, when the phone rings, it will be a call from a user wanting to register, not someone with a question.

Getting started

The first rule of writing good software is do not rush. Take the time to write a good program. Find other people to test it or, if you are on your own, put it aside for a few weeks before you test it. Anytime you get an uncomfortable feeling in the back of your head telling you that some part of the program does not work right, change the software. Do not ignore feelings that make you uneasy about parts of your software. Take the time to listen to your inner voice.

Keep in mind that since you designed and wrote the program, it will all seem intuitive to you. An outside opinion, possibly that of your spouse, is useful in determining whether or not the software really is intuitive. Try to have someone that is not familiar with the program use it without looking at the manual. What problems and questions do they have?

Software installation

The first thing a user does with a new program is install it. They are anxious to get started, so reading the documentation generally takes a back seat to getting the program installed and running. There are four key points concerning installation that you need to pay attention to:

1. Make installation as easy as possible.
2. Make the installation instructions easy to find.
3. Assume the user has no knowledge of DOS or DOS commands.
4. Make as much of the installation process as possible automatic. For example, your software should automatically detect a computer's video card type.

Making installation easy

The simplest programs to install are contained on a single floppy disk that can be immediately run directly from that floppy disk. All you need to do is tell the user to make a backup copy and then give them the command that starts the software. I've found that over 80% of the software I've looked at falls into this category.

Although most people have hard disks, don't assume that users will want to install your software on their hard disk. Many users like to try the software first, before installing it on their hard disk, especially if they are trying shareware. If your software is a TSR (Terminate and Stay Resident) program that should be installed as a part of the user's PATH statement, give them a way to try the program before they install it.

If your program can be copied directly to a hard disk using the DOS COPY command, let the user know this. Many experienced users prefer to copy a program directly instead of going through the installation process. However, no matter how simple your program is, always include a way for the software to be automatically installed. Use a filename that is intuitive for starting the installation. For example, it has become common to use the first letter of the program's name and the word "INSTALL". For my Play 'n' Learn software, the installation file is PINSTALL. I have also used HDINSTAL to indicate a hard-disk installation file and FPINSTAL for a floppy-disk installation file. However, I recommend having only one installation file and, if there is a difference between the hard-disk and floppy-disk installation procedures, having the first question be, "Are you installing this software on a hard disk or a floppy disk (H/F)?"

The installation process should provide a series of questions that prompt users to enter the information needed to install your software. With each question, a default setting should be provided and explained on the screen. For defaults, use the most common response. For example, when you ask users to enter the letter designating their hard disk, the default should be **C**.

When a user has responded to all of the installation questions, put a summary of the user's responses on the screen. Give the user the opportunity to change any of the responses or accept them all as correct.

During the installation of your software, especially if it is a time-consuming process, put something on the screen to tell the user what is happening. Watching a blank screen while your disk drive churns away can be disconcerting. Include short status statements such as, "Copying files . . ." or "Checking for CONFIG.SYS file . . .". These let the user know that the installation is proceeding and, most likely, functioning properly.

Make the installation instructions easy to find

Your installation instructions should be the first section in the front of your manual. If you feel the user needs to have an understanding of DOS before they install your software, put a DOS tutorial in an appendix at the back of your manual. The installation instructions can then refer inexperienced users to the appendix. If you want to explain shareware and talk about the ASP, and if it is more than a one-page summary, put that information in an appendix.

For shareware disks, I also recommend including a brief description of how to install and start your software in a READ.ME file. Give the user the word they need to enter to start the installation process. If there is something the user should know before installing your software, refer them to a specific page in your manual. Also, tell the user how to start your software and use it directly from a floppy disk, if that is possible.

DOS and DOS commands

Using the DOS DIR command might appear to be simple to you and me, but many people do not know what it is. With the release of DOS version 4 and Windows version 3, many people buying their first computer never see the DOS prompt. They do not know what a DOS prompt is and might not know how to get a DOS prompt on their screen.

Even users who have earlier versions of DOS might not be familiar with DOS commands. In the past, they might have installed other software by following the instructions in a cookbook-like way. If you ask the user to type a DOS command, be extremely detailed in providing step-by-step instructions. Describe each keystroke and provide an illustration of what the screen should look like.

Be careful when asking users to do something with CONFIG.SYS or AUTOEXEC.BAT files. For example, my database software requires the CONFIG.SYS file to have a FILES = 20 statement. I explain this in my documentation and tell the user how to create or modify their CONFIG.SYS files. My software will also automatically create the necessary CONFIG.SYS file during the installation process, if the user asks it to do this. What could go wrong?

I get calls from users who get error messages telling them to add a FILES = 20 statement to their CONFIG.SYS file. They tell me, yes, they do have a CONFIG.SYS file. When I have them use the DOS TYPE command to list the contents, it shows a FILES = 20 in the CONFIG.SYS file. After I have asked a few more questions, I find that they are running my software on a floppy disk and they have put the CONFIG.SYS file on that floppy disk instead of on their DOS disk.

You have to write your installation instructions just as if you were writing a cookbook. Do not leave out anything. Have a complete novice test your instructions to ensure that you have not left out something that is obvious to you, but not to a beginner.

Make installation as automatic as possible

If your software needs to know specifics about the hardware being used, have the installation software automatically detect as much of the hardware configuration as possible. For example, your installation software should be able to determine the type of video card installed.

If your software uses a COM port, give the user the option of entering the COM port number or having the software find the right COM port. For example, if you publish telecommunications software, have your software automatically check each COM port for a dial tone.

If your software can use EMS memory, it should automatically check for EMS memory. Do not assume that the user knows what EMS memory is or what a COM port is. Use your installation software to automatically detect as much of the configuration information as you can.

There will be some external peripherals that your software cannot identify, such as a printer or a modem. For these types of peripherals, provide a list of brands and model numbers and allow users to select the one they have. Printers are a good example.

Printers

If your software needs to use special features provided by some printers, display a list of printers that your software supports. Printers that use the same drivers should be listed separately. For example, most Panasonic printers are Epson compatible. However, you should list each Epson and Panasonic printer model separately. Many users will look for their specific brand and model number. If they do not find it, they will assume their printer is not supported by your software. I once helped a friend who could not get WordPerfect to print. He had an Epson RX-80 and that printer was not listed among the printers that WordPerfect supported. WordPerfect did list the Epson MX-80, but he did not know that an RX-80 and an MX-80 were the same. By the way, this person was trying to print a draft of his doctoral thesis, so he was not unintelligent.

I have seen a lot of shareware that requires the user to enter printer control codes during the installation process. This is a poor choice and I recommend that it be avoided. You might allow printer control codes to be entered to accommodate people with oddball printers, but you should provide drivers for all of the common printers such as Epson and Hewlett-Packard.

Be sure to test your print drivers before releasing your software. I have had people purchase my software because they could not get someone else's software to work with their printer, although it was supposed to. Most printer manufacturers have developer-support programs that will loan printers to software publishers for the purpose of testing print drivers.

You can contact Hewlett-Packard by writing to:

HP ISV/IHV Program
16399 W. Bernardo Dr.
San Diego, CA 92127

You can contact Epson by writing to:

Epson America, Inc.
Developer Relations
2780 Lomita Blvd.
Torrance, CA 90505

In most cases, printer manufacturers that do not have a developer support program will be willing to send you a copy of their user manuals. This will allow you to write drivers and then, hopefully, find a friend or a beta tester with a printer on which you can test your drivers. Another way to test print drivers is to visit a computer store when they are not busy. If you have a program that will automatically test your driver in a few minutes—in other words, you do not have to sit there and manually test the printer driver—many times, they will let you run a test.

An approach I use for handling printers is to only send standard ASCII characters to the printer. No fonts, no bold, just print ASCII characters and form feeds. This works fine for applications that only require information to be listed. If you do this, keep in mind that dot-matrix printers use 66 lines per page while laser printers only use 60 lines per page. You might want to let the user indicate whether or not they have a laser printer, otherwise, all printed reports should be limited to no more than 60 lines per page.

AUTOEXEC.BAT and CONFIG.SYS files

Never modify a user's AUTOEXEC.BAT or CONFIG.SYS file without first getting permission from the user. If the user tells the installation software that it is okay to modify these files, always make backup copies of the original files. Tell the user the filenames used for the backup copies so they can recover them if necessary.

Never change users' PATH statements without telling them. For example, I have tried software that was divided among several directories on the original floppy disk. During the installation, the PATH was reset to accommodate the directories on the floppy disk. After installing the software, I found my computer no longer worked as it should, and I eventually discovered this was caused by a change in the PATH setting. Rebooting the computer restored my old PATH, but finding the problem was very frustrating and should not have been necessary.

Verify the configuration

Once the configuration of the user's computer has been determined, display the configuration settings on the screen. Give the user the opportunity to change any of the settings before they are installed.

Program design

The best summary that I have seen of practical suggestions for writing an easy-to-use program was written by Rosemary West. Rosemary is the author of 17 shareware programs, including one called Book of Changes. When I was looking at shareware to see what other authors included on their disks, her programs impressed me as being very easy to install and use. Here is what she has to say.

I'm not sure what "easy-to-use" really means since I get a lot of different opinions from users. Most seem to like menus with simple descriptive words. The kind of menu that puts a short explanatory message at the bottom of the screen as you scroll through the choices is popular.

People don't like to go more than a couple of layers deep into menus.

Very few people use F1 for help.

Most users seem to feel a program with a pretty screen is better even though it performs exactly the same as one with an unpretty screen.

Cluttered screens seem to confuse people. Screens that use color or highlighting to draw attention to important items are a big help.

Documentation that includes extremely simple explanations about how to copy disks, how to get the software onto the hard disk, how to start the program, etc., are very much in demand.

Make your software intuitive

Today, people won't put up with lack of menus, with command-line-operated programs, and with simplistic stick-men graphics.
—Roger Jones, president of Shareware To-Go

For shareware, designing intuitive software is particularly important. People get to try your software before they pay for it. If they cannot quickly get it running, they are likely to move on to the next program.

Two types of people will look at your program: those who read every word of the documentation before starting, and those who try to use the program without reading any of the documentation. I have found that there are a surprising number of the first type of person, people who read manuals. But, the majority of people are of the second type. Most people want to put your shareware disk in their computer and give it a quick try to see if they like it, before they commit to spending a lot of time with it. That is the advantage shareware offers users, the no-risk trial. But it makes your job harder.

Your program must be easy to use. If you want users to try your shareware, they must be able to get started without reading the manual. They must be able to use enough of the basic features of your software to get a good feel for how it works. They must be able to use the software well enough that they become interested in spending more time learning how to use it. Most importantly, they must not become frustrated and stop using your software.

Keep in mind that users want to spend as little time as possible learning new programs. People will stay with their existing software, even though it has fewer functions and is less powerful, to avoid the hassle of learning a new program. If you have a program that is unique and has no competition, you might be able to get away with it being difficult to learn—but do not count on it.

Making intuitive software

What does it take to design intuitive software? For most programs, the user must be able to figure out how to use the basic functions with only a minimal amount of reading the manual. The best way to accomplish this is to provide a series of menus or prompts on the screen that identify the functions available. Pull-down menus are becoming very popular as a user interface, but be careful. Be sure to let the user know how to pull down a menu.

Do help screens make your software easier to use? I agree with Rosemary West when she says that very few people actually use help screens. They seem to be important in helping your software get a good review in a magazine, but they do not seem to be used. The problem with help screens is that they only can display a limited amount of information and it usually does not directly apply to what you are trying to do. Most users find it easier to use the reference section of the manual to find the information they need. I dropped the help screens from my software almost four years ago and have not had one user ask for the help screens to be put back in, although users have asked for a lot of other changes in my software during the past four years.

Instead of relying on help screens, you are much better off to make the user interface easy to understand and intuitive. The one place where help information is useful, however, is in your error messages. I will talk about error messages shortly.

To make software intuitive, be sure to follow established standards for user interfaces. For some software, that is easy. For example, if your software is designed for use with Microsoft's Windows or to run on a Macintosh, Microsoft and Apple have published standards describing how the user interface must look and operate. Unfortunately, few standards exist for IBM DOS programs. Some authors follow the "WordStar standard," although this standard seems to be in decline. Others follow the "WordPerfect standard," but WordPerfect does not follow some of the traditional function-key assignments, such as using F1 for help. No one follows a "Lotus standard," because Lotus Corporation likes to sue people over user-interface standards.

To determine what standard your software should follow, review other software in the same category as yours and see how they handle the user interface. Also, look at the interfaces used by the best-selling retail programs. These will be the programs that large numbers of people have. Thus, more people will be familiar with the standards used by these programs.

One standard that you should never violate is that the ESC key is only used to escape (or exit) the current function. Never use the ESC key for selecting a program function. Never use the ESC key to start a program function. Never use the ESC key as a toggle key. ESC should only be used to exit from or stop the current function or to exit from the program.

Whatever you do, be consistent. Function keys should activate the same function throughout the program. For example, do not use F5 to select a filename in one case and then F2 to select a filename in another part of the program. Maintain the same style and arrangement of information on all your screens. Do not change things around so that the user has to hunt for information with each new screen.

To help users know what they are supposed to do, always list the possible alternatives on the screen and provide a default based on the most likely choice. For example, if the user wants to select a new filename, list all the filenames in the selected directory and show the current filename as the default.

Intuitive software should appear to be simple. Do not clutter the screen with prompts for numerous functions. Include prompts only for the basic functions and allow the user to access menus or screens for more complex functions by using ALT key combinations or pull-down menus. In designing your software, work to keep it simple. Some magazine reviewers like to compare software based on the number of functions each program offers. This has led developers to focus on adding features instead of designing software that solves problems. First design your software to solve the user's problems in as easy a manner as possible. Once you have done that, then you can add features for reviewers to count.

Another important part of designing intuitive software is to make the program run in a way that matches how people think. For example, when we make a typographical error, we want to fix it right away. We do not want to wait until we get to the end of a document and then go back to fix it. Always allow users to correct errors at any time. Always allow users to back up and correct mistakes on previous screens. Always provide a way for users to change their mind. For example, it is very frustrating to start a large database sort and then realize there was something else you wanted to do, but you cannot stop the sorting process. Users should always be able to exit from whatever the computer is doing by pushing ESC. The best programs allow users to exit or shell to DOS, use another application, then return and continue the original function, picking up where it left off.

Also keep in mind that everyone thinks differently and that each of us is comfortable with different ways of doing things. Build some flexibility into your program. Allow users to select the screen colors they prefer. If your software includes sound effects, allow the user to turn them off.

Handling errors

Error trapping and handling is one area many shareware authors have a problem with. There are just so many things a user can do to screw up your software. Plus, I have found that different versions of DOS report the same error in different ways, making it more difficult to identify a specific cause.

Error trapping is an important part of software design. When users try your software and run into an error, they need to know what caused the error and how to avoid it in the future. If they get an error message and cannot get out of it, the most likely thing they will try is rebooting their computer. If that does not fix the error, they will probably delete your shareware program and move on to the next program.

The first step is to design the software to avoid errors. The fewer error messages the user sees, the better. You do this by designing your software so that it does not accept incorrect keystrokes or keystrokes that take it beyond a boundary condition. For example, in my database software, when someone tries to type beyond the end of a field, the software beeps and no longer accepts keystrokes.

Another way to avoid errors is to design software that includes features users expect in your type of software. For example, if you have written a word-processing program that does not provide word wrapping, users will continue to type beyond the right edge of the screen, possibly creating an error condition.

Even when you have done everything you can to prevent errors from happening, users will still find ways to get into error conditions. For example, they might try to access a function that is not appropriate for what they are doing at the time. Or, they might not have installed the software correctly. That is why you have to trap errors.

Trapping errors is easy; the hard part is explaining to the user why the error occurred and how to avoid it in the future. Every error should display an error message that provides the user with some help. In some cases, the explanation will be easy, the user was trying to print something and the printer was off. Other times, you might have to refer the user to the manual for a discussion of possible causes. Whatever you do, do not just display an error code and expect the user to figure it out.

Compile

With compilers available at under a hundred dollars, it is surprising that anyone writes software that is not compiled. However, a lot of GW-BASIC code is still released as shareware.

Here is what the president of one of the largest shareware disk distribution companies had to say about compiling programs

People won't put up with GW-BASIC. We had an author, who is well known now, who submitted a program to us about a year ago. It was a wonderful program. It was in the area of financial planning. A GREAT program, but it was in BASIC.

I called him and said, "You're telling the user they should plan on an income of $100,000 a year and you don't even have your program compiled! You can't expect a person, who is fairly well heeled and in the upper middle class, and who you want to use this disk, to first load BASIC. They're not going to fool with it."

That author compiled his program and now has seven successful shareware programs. His income from shareware now exceeds what he makes as a financial planner.

—Roger Jones, president of Shareware To-Go

Always compile your programs so that they run as stand-alone .EXE files. Compiled programs also offer you many advantages because you can use some of the many programmer's libraries that are available. Libraries such as Crescent Software's *QuickPak* can add pull-down menus, error trapping, math functions, and access to DOS functions with little programming effort on your part. They will make your program look professional and help your software run faster.

Cleaning up

Sometimes, I concentrate so hard on getting something done that I forget about some of the final details. For example, you might design the greatest software that has ever existed for printing financial reports. It uses special fonts for titles and automatically carries totals from one report to the next. But, if you do not send a form feed to the printer at the end of the last page, you will have frustrated users. Yes, it is the little things that can bring down the best software.

You have to clean up after your software. Always return the computer's settings and the settings of any peripheral equipment to their default condition. For example, never leave a printer set to print in a special font or graphics mode. After all, that is what the master reset printer control code is for, to reset the printer back to its default settings. Use it!

When the user exits your software, close all files and return the video display to its default mode. Erase any temporary files your software might have created and clean up the computer's memory. If your software has done anything that affects the PATH statement or other internal settings of the computer, return them to their original condition. When your software is done running, the user should find no evidence that your software was used (other than the data or document files it might have created).

Finally, remember to keep things simple and thoroughly test your software!

Testing software

If you are a software author, you know that it typically takes 20–30% of your time to write the program code and 70–80% to test and debug it. Testing and debugging software is, by far, the most time-consuming and frustrating part of writing software. However, if approached logically and in an organized manner, the time spent on testing software can be minimized.

The best approach to testing software is to get someone else to help. Generally, you are too close to your software to do a good job of testing it. However, if you are like me, you will probably do some of the initial testing yourself as you work with the program. The following are some guidelines to follow when testing software.

Be organized

Always write down what you do and what happens when you conduct a test run. Do not plan on remembering what happens. I find that using a spiral-bound notebook is very helpful. It keeps all of my notes about bugs, new features I want to add, user comments, etc., together in one place. If I run into a bug that I remember fixing previously, I can quickly look through my notebook to find the notes describing what I did the first time I "fixed" that bug.

Try each function, feature, and capability individually. This might seem obvious, but I have seen many authors plunge ahead, testing a variety of features all at one time. It might seem faster to try to do more than one thing at a time, but in the end it will take more time. Trying each function one at a time—in a methodical, orderly manner—helps you isolate and identify the cause of problems quicker.

Test boundary conditions

A boundary condition is a point at which any movement, beyond that point, takes your software outside of normal operating conditions, while movement in the other direction easily falls within the operating conditions that your program can handle. For example, let's assume that you've written an accounting program and this program is designed to handle only positive numbers. A boundary condition occurs at the numbers – 1, 0, and + 1. Although your manual tells users to never enter a negative number, what happens if they do? What happens when zero is entered? What happens if a user enters the numbers 243,837,878,8287,888? This is a number that is far larger than your software can handle and it goes beyond the upper boundary.

Another boundary condition might distinguish among numbers, letters, and other keyboard characters. How does your software handle receiving a letter as the input when a number is expected? What happens when you enter punctuation? What happens when Ctrl or Alt key combinations are pushed?

Look for boundary conditions throughout your software. What happens when the user attempts to move the cursor off the top or bottom of the screen? Can the cursor be moved beyond the left and right boundaries? Be sure to check all of the keys that are used to position the cursor. While the cursor movement might be fine when using the arrow keys, the Tab, PgUp, or PgDn keys might move it beyond a boundary or produce an unexpected response.

The first use of a program or function is a boundary condition. A function might work fine the first time, but produce odd characters, wrong calculations, out-of-memory messages, or invalid filename errors the second time it is used.

Exiting a program is another boundary condition. Does your software allow users to exit without saving the file or document they were working on?

The largest and smallest amount of memory the software can cope with is also a boundary condition. I test the memory limits of my software by first installing a small RAM disk. I increase the size of the RAM disk until my software runs out of memory and no longer runs. This tells me exactly how much memory my software requires. Keep in mind that as you use a program, it might open more files or require additional memory. Do not just boot your program and check for the opening menu. Use it awhile to ensure that all of its functions work with the available memory.

Look for boundaries of time. How does the software handle the thirtieth and thirty-first at the end of a month? Can it handle the 28 days of February, and what happens in a leap year? What happens at noontime and midnight? How does your software handle the end of a year? Plus, keep in mind that we are only a few years away from the new century. Will your software be able to handle the twenty-first century?

Look for boundaries within data and document files. Can your software read the first record in a database correctly? The last record? How does the program mark the end of a record or the beginning of the next? What happens when the software tries to read data or a document that is not in the correct format?

Test output

Try all of the printed reports offered by your software to be sure that they all print correctly. Are all the page breaks correctly skipped? What happens if the printer is turned off or disconnected? What happens when the printer runs out of paper? Keep in mind that when a computer sends something to a printer, it opens a file. If the CONFIG.SYS file does not have a high-enough number in the "FILES=" statement, you will get an error when trying to print a report. How is this error handled?

If your software uses a serial port, test to see what happens when the wrong serial port is specified. Does the software confirm that the specified port exists and that the information being sent actually was sent and received?

When storing information on a disk, can your software handle nine-character filenames or four-character filename extensions? If the user types an invalid filename, you want to be sure that the information does not end up in a file with an unrecognizable filename. What happens when the user tries to save a new file using an existing filename? Does the software provide a warning that the old file is about to be erased?

Never make assumptions when testing software. Never think that because you wrote the code, and that it was a simple piece of code, that it will function fine. Test everything. Make no assumptions. If you make a code change, test the function you modified *and all related functions*. Often, a change in one section of code can result in problems that show up in another area.

Types of software errors

It is impossible to list every error a user might make. In fact, that list might be infinite. Every time I have seen someone announce that all possibilities were covered, a user manages to come up with something that was not anticipated. Being aware of the general types and categories of errors will help you do a better job when testing your software.

User interface errors As you test your program, be aware of how it feels. To do this, you might need to put it aside for a while, otherwise, its operation will always feel natural. If there are areas in the program in which something feels awkward or confusing, then you need to make some changes. If you have someone else who can test your software, ask them to watch out for areas they do not feel comfortable with or in which they feel like something is missing.

When testing software, pay attention to how the software keeps the user informed about what is going on. Are the error messages clear or are they insulting? I have seen software that intentionally insults the user in an effort to "help" the user remember how to avoid making certain errors. Do not do this—it makes the user feel negative about you and your software.

How does the user learn to use the program? The best way to test this is to give your program to a novice and watch as they try to install and use it. Is the documentation complete? Does each screen provide a simple explanation of the functions available from that screen? Is it easy to get lost in the program? Are some commands easy to confuse with others. Are there places you can reduce the number of keystrokes required? Under what circumstances does the user make mistakes?

Error-handling errors   It sounds strange to say, but there can be errors in your error-handling routines. Try to intentionally cause errors and see how your software responds. Do you get the right error message? Are you able to correct the error or do you end up in an endless loop of error messages?

Be sure to test all of the error-recovery routines. Do they properly recover from the error? Does recovering from an error result in the user possibly losing several hours of work?

Calculation errors   On my old CP/M computer, I used to have a terrible time dealing with the computer's rounding errors. I had spent $3000 for a computer that could not even do arithmetic correctly. You should be aware that computers can lose precision as they perform calculations. This happens as a result of rounding off and truncation errors—even if the program code is correct. Look for these errors and change your code to avoid them.

Errors in handling data   If you load a document into your word processor and then just let it sit for a few days, you might come back to find some things changed. No, the cat did not walk across the keyboard and no one touched your computer. It is possible for parts of the computer's memory to change randomly for no visible reason. Possibly, there was a spike in the line voltage. Maybe some radio interference caused a change. I have even seen computers that have been left on stop functioning for no apparent reason and then work fine when rebooted.

As your program handles data, watch for errors. When reading data from a file, be sure it is valid data. If, for example, the file has been erased, your program could read the remnants of old files and interpret this as valid data.

Version control

Version control is something many shareware authors ignore. But, it is important. Here is where the good documentation of past problems and how you fixed them can be invaluable. For example, a bug you thought you had fixed can reappear if an old version of one subroutine is linked with the latest version of the rest of your program.

Also, check your opening screens to be sure the program has the right copyright message and version numbers. Make sure these match those in the documentation. Use version numbers to help you track changes, bug fixes, and updates. Some authors include a file on their shareware disk that lists all of the versions and the changes made in each version. Even if you do not put this file on your disk, it is a valuable record that you should have.

Making a shareware distribution disk

It is obvious that your shareware distribution disk will contain your program and documentation. But, other information should be on your disk and you need to pay careful attention to what you name the files on your disk.

> *In shareware, the naming of some of the programs is absolutely terrible. I can't tell you how many times a great disk has been submitted to us with the most archaic, technical, totally oblique name. A name that wouldn't begin to make it on Madison Avenue. Let's face it. Shareware, like anything else, has to be merchandised. You can't merchandise it with a name that turns people off or leaves them totally blank as to what the program does.*
> —Roger Jones, president of Shareware To-Go

> *There is value in maintaining consistent file-naming conventions for your software. I've also seen a lot of software succeed because people have used a unique and descriptive name.*
> —Bob Mahoney, president of Exec-PC BBS

Naming files

When naming your files, you should use a name that helps describe what your software does. Then use that name as a part of naming all of the related files on your disk. I will use my Play 'n' Learn software to provide some examples. The files on my Play 'n' Learn disk include:

    PLAY.EXE
    PLAYPGM.EXE
    PLAY.DOC
    PLAYREAD.ME

Notice that they all start with the word PLAY. By making the filenames similar, I ensure that they will stay together in a directory listing and it makes it easier for a user to identify them as belonging together. Why is this important? Because your files might be combined with other programs on a compilation disk or the user might dump a bunch of programs together in a directory on a hard disk.

The word PLAY also helps to identify these files as something fun to use. Instead of using PLAY, I could have used the initials of the program name, PNL. This would have resulted in the following filenames:

    PNL.EXE
    PNLPGM.EXE
    PNL.DOC
    PNLREAD.ME

Which set of filenames more clearly conveys a fun and interesting image. For me, at least, PNL does not create any type of image. The word PLAY does a much better job of describing the software and attracting attention.

Notice that I called the documentation file PLAY.DOC instead of MANUAL.DOC. I do this because it keeps the manual close to the program files in a directory listing. Another reason is that a lot of authors have already used MANUAL.DOC and your manual file could easily be erased and replaced by someone else's file when programs are combined in the same directory of a hard disk.

If you feel you must include an AUTOEXEC.BAT file or CONFIG.SYS file on your disk, be very careful. In testing the software that I have reviewed in chapter 14, one of the tests I ran was to have a computer novice install and use the software. A couple of days ago, I got a call from one of my testers. His computer had stopped functioning. It booted okay, but the DOS prompt looked different and all of his software had disappeared. After having just paid $300 for WordPerfect, he was rather upset that it was no longer on his hard disk. He was also very angry with me for giving him a program that wiped out his hard disk.

I took a look at his computer and it was immediately obvious what had caused the problem. The program he was testing told him to copy the files from the floppy disk to his hard disk, which he did. He copied them directly to the root directory on his hard disk. This shareware disk also contained an AUTOEXEC.BAT and CONFIG.SYS file. They replaced the files in his root directory, his PATH setting was gone, and his computer could no longer find the files he normally ran, even though they were still there.

If you want to supply an AUTOEXEC.BAT or CONFIG.SYS file, give them other names and provide an installation file that will rename them. For example, for my Play 'n' Learn software I would use PLAYAUTO.BAT and PLAYCON.FIG. This helps keep them grouped with the other Play 'n' Learn files and identifies their function.

Documentation

Chapter 12 discusses how to write good documentation, however, providing on-disk documentation brings up some special concerns. For example, be sure that your documentation is in straight ASCII, with no formatting commands or control characters included. You should be able to use the DOS TYPE command to list it on the screen with no unusual characters, colors, or sounds appearing. To ensure that your documentation contains no control codes other than the control code for a formfeed, send the manual to your printer by typing

COPY FILENAME.DOC LPT1:

You should replace FILENAME.DOC with the name of your documentation file. I recommend that a formfeed be used at the bottom of each page.

Because of the different number of lines printed by dot-matrix and laser printers, this is the only way to ensure that the printing is correctly positioned on each page.

Do not count on users knowing how to copy your manual to the printer using the method I have just described. Include a batch file or program on your disk that will automatically print the documentation. A batch file with a single line containing "COPY FILENAME.DOC LPT1:" is adequate.

The manual you provide on your shareware disk should be the same as is supplied with the registered version of your software. The first page should be a title/cover page that also includes your copyright notice. Even the shortest manuals should have a table of contents and that comes just after the title page. The next page or two should identify the software as shareware, provide a brief description of shareware and how it works, include your terms for distributing your shareware, and have a warranty and disclaimer as was discussed in chapter 9. Include any further details about shareware, the ASP, site licenses, and other programs that you publish in appendices at the end of your manual.

Each page of your manual should be numbered. Place page numbers in either the upper right or lower right corners of the page or centered at the bottom of the page. This is where most people expect to find page numbers.

If your manual is more than 12 to 15 pages long, include an index.

Other files

Several other files should be included on your disks. These are files that are not related to the operation of your software, but which provide more information about your software and the conditions under which it may be distributed. Two files that should be included on every disk are:

    PACKING.LST
    VENDOR.DOC

In addition, you might wish to include files such as:

    SYSOP.DOC
    INTRO.DOC
    OTHER.DOC
    GO.BAT or START.BAT

The PACKING.LST file contains a listing of the files you put on your disk and a short description on each file. You can also include the dates and size of each file. The PACKING.LST file accomplishes two things. It allows users to determine whether or not they have a complete copy of your software and identify any additional files added to the disk by someone else.

VENDOR.DOC provides the terms and conditions under which vendors may distribute copies of your software. It also contains information that will help the vendor such as a short and long description of your program, the system requirements, the registration price, and your address.

Try to keep this file short, preferably no more than 80 or 90 lines. VENDOR.DOC files that are too long become ineffective because disk distributors will not be able to find the information they need. Put the important marketing information at the top of the page. This includes the program name, the recommended BBS filename, the short and long descriptions, and how to contact you. The terms and conditions covering distribution of your software should be on the lower half of the page. Keep the terms for distributing your software short and to the point. You want to provide legal protection for your software, but also keep in mind that when vendors are faced with a choice of two programs to carry, they will usually carry the one with the least restrictions.

The following is an example of a VENDOR.DOC file.

PROGRAM NAME: Play 'n' Learn

VERSION: 2.15

PUBLISHER: HomeCraft Software, P.O. Box 974, Tualatin, OR 97062
            (503) 692-3732   CIS 71450,254   FAX (503) 692-0382

PREFERRED BBS FILENAME: PLAYNL.ZIP (or ARC)

SYSTEM REQUIREMENTS: IBM PC, XT, AT, PS/2 or compatible with 256K of memory, CGA video (or better) and DOS 2.10 or later.

SHORT DESCRIPTION: A set of eight educational games for children 18 months to 3 years old.

DESCRIPTION: A program designed to introduce very young children, 18 months to 3 years old, to the computer and to help them learn about the alphabet, numbers, colors, and shapes. Games include simple keyboard response activities, color matching, shape matching, an "etch-a-sketch" type painting game, a lottery game based on the alphabet, plus an arcade-type game called Underground Alphabet. Reviewers have called Play 'n' Learn "one of the best available programs for very young children."

KEYWORDS: Educational, Children, Alphabet, Preschool, Kids

CONDITIONS UNDER WHICH THIS SOFTWARE MAY BE COPIED AND DISTRIBUTED:

Individual users may freely copy this disk and share it with friends and family.

Nonprofit groups (including user groups and BBSs) may distribute copies of this disk. A fee of no more than $5 may be charged to cover disk copying costs. If the files on this disk have dates more than a year old, we request that you contact us for a free upgrade to the current version.

Disk distributors and dealers must have written permission before selling copies of this disk. When you contact us, you will receive a free copy of the latest version and you will be placed on our mailing list to receive updates as they are released. Disk distributors may charge no more than $10 per disk for copies of this software. If, as a distributor, you supply copies to other resellers, the end price to the user may not exceed $10.

Anyone distributing copies of this software, whether for profit or as a nonprofit organization, must conform to the following:

The files on each disk may not be modified or adapted in any way. All of the files provided on the disk must be distributed together. Individual files or groups of files may not be sold separately. Additional files may be added and this software may be combined on a disk with other programs.

This software may not be represented as anything other than shareware and the shareware concept must be explained in any ad or catalog that includes this software and on any packaging used to display the disk.

You must immediately stop selling/distributing copies of this disk upon notice from the author or HCP Services, Inc.

REGISTRATION: $15.00 (includes shipping)

REGISTERED USERS GET:

[X] Current Version   [ ] Printed Manual
[X] Bi-annual newsletter [X] Free phone support
[X] 1 yr free updates   [ ] Discounts on other software
[ ] Free hard disk shell   [ ] Tech support via fax

< end VENDOR.DOC file>

The SYSOP.DOC file provides distribution information for BBSs. In many cases, this file is nearly a duplicate of the VENDOR.DOC file with the references to distributors taken out. If that is the case, a SYSOP.DOC file only adds to building clutter on your disk and should not be included.

For software that is primarily distributed by BBSs, such as communications software or file compression software, the SYSOP.DOC file becomes very important to include. For example, some authors feel it is very important that BBSs have only the latest version of their program. They will personally call several hundred BBSs and upload the current version to each. In cases such as this, the author might not wish to have BBSs distributing software without permission and a SYSOP.DOC file becomes the method for notifying sysops of the distribution conditions.

The OTHER.DOC/INFO.DOC file and many of the VENDOR.DOC files that I have seen include advertising for an author's software. In some cases, this advertising takes several pages. The purpose of the VENDOR .DOC file is to quickly provide vendors with the information they need to distribute your software. Long files defeat the purpose of the VENDOR .DOC file in that vendors do not want to spend a lot of time reading through a file trying to locate the important information. If you are going to include promotional material about your software or other software you publish, include this information in another file.

As with anything else, there are no hard-and-fast rules, only general guidelines. We all approach our businesses differently, have different objectives, different products, and different markets. The key is to know your objectives and your market and adjust your distribution strategy to support your objectives.

Distributor identification

I like to put the distributor's name on every disk I supply to a distributor, BBS, or user group. My registration form is designed to read this name from the disk, thus allowing me to identify which distributor, BBS, or user group provided the disk that resulted in a registration. I can tell which distributors, BBSs, and user groups generate a lot of registrations and which generate few or none. Because I have already put the name on the disk, I also try to do the distributor a favor by displaying their name on the copyright screen each time the software is booted. Figure 11-1 shows the copyright screen for my software *For Record Collectors*.

```
    F O R    R E C O R D    C O L L E C T O R S
         PC / MS-DOS   Version 4.00

    Copyright 1988, 1989, 1990 - Steven C. Hudgik

    Copyright 1982, 84, 85, 86 & 1987 by Microsoft Corp.

    Published by HOMECRAFT COMPUTER PRODUCTS - Tualatin, OR




    SHAREWARE DISTRIBUTED BY: The SOFTWARE LABS
                              3767 Overland Ave.
                              Los Angeles, CA 90034
```

11-1 The opening screen for all of my software gives the name and address of the distributor. When the user prints the registration order form the distributor's name is automatically printed on it allowing me to track which distributors sell disks that result in users registering.

It is sometimes interesting to notice where disks come from. For example, I just received a disk a user obtained from a distributor on the East Coast. The distributor was registered with me and I had provided them with update disks on a regular basis. But, this disk contained a three-year-old version of my software and the name of a distributor in Texas. A quick call to the distributor helped get the correct version back into their library.

Having the distributor's name on my disks has also helped me identify distributors that might have a bad master disk. There have been several occasions when users sent me bad disks for replacement and I have been able to identify them as all coming from one distributor.

Why do users send me their bad shareware disks? Because I guarantee that they will have a good copy of my program or I will replace their disk at no charge. It does not matter where they got the disk or who they got it from. If they are having a problem, I will replace the disk. I do this because, if users cannot try my program, they generally will not register. Plus, it is a good way to identify people who are interested in my software and get their names on my mailing list.

For additional information about what to put on your distribution disk, see chapter 13, which discusses the Association of Shareware Professionals. The ASP has minimum standards concerning information that must be on a distribution disk.

12

Software documentation and support

How do you make your software easy to use? I discussed this in the last chapter, where I said that you need properly designed software and *good documentation*. So, how do you write good documentation?

The user's manual must provide easy-to-follow instructions *and* build the user's confidence in your software. When you put together a good user's manual, both you and the user benefit. The user will find your software easier and more enjoyable to use. You will get more registrations and spend less time providing support.

When you are writing the documentation for your software, you have a big disadvantage working against you. You know your software better than anyone else. As a result, many things that require explanations for other people to understand will appear intuitive to you. Your manual is the way you "teach" your users how to use your software. Yet, you might not be the best teacher.

In the late 1970s, I spent several years working as a supervisor in the training department of a large corporation. I noticed that, in general, the best person to teach a subject was someone who had difficulty learning that subject. People who can quickly learn things generally do not make good teachers because they expect too much to be obvious to their students. They do not understand the frustrations and difficulties most students face in learning a new subject.

It works the same way with software documentation. The reason user manuals have such a bad reputation is that they are written by people who are very close to the software. In those circumstances, it becomes almost impossible to write a good manual. The writer does not understand the user's frustration and bewilderment about how the software works and what it really does. What seems obvious and perfectly clear to the writer might baffle some users.

The basics of writing good documentation

You say that you are a one-person company and there is no one else to write the manual? The answer is to test, test, test, and test some more. Use the same approach I described for writing easy-to-use software; test, listen to feedback, and change your manual to include the improvements suggested by users and testers.

Also, never have your first manual printed in quantity. Have a quick-print shop run off a few copies and put them in three-ring binders. This type of binder is more expensive than other methods of binding, but it is professional-looking and it allows you to make corrections and changes by replacing individual pages. (I will discuss methods for binding manuals shortly.)

The best approach for a one-person company is to write the best manual you can. Then test it. Here are some guidelines for writing a good user's manual.

Basic questions

To start, go back to the same type of questions that I have been asking throughout this book.

- Who are your users? What level of experience do they have?
- What are your users' needs? Why do they want to use your software?
- How will the documentation be used?
- Put yourself in your users' places. What suggestions do you think users would have for your manual? What problems will they run into?

Who are your users?

A user is anyone who has to do something with your software. These are the people who will need to read and use your manual. People such as those who will install your software, possibly a consultant or a computer-store employee. People who use the program. And possibly, there might be support people, for example, in a corporate information-systems group or a neighbor just trying to help a friend get started. All of these people might possibly need to use and understand your manual, depending on the type of software you publish.

By now, I have asked you to get to know your users enough times that you should be feeling this is important. In writing a user's manual, you need to know who will be reading it. Picture one person who is your typical user and write the manual for that user. The language and style of your manual will depend on who that person is and what type of background they have. The following describes seven basic types of users. Depending on what type of software you have written, there might be other categories that would apply.

Expert users These people have used similar software and are familiar with DOS and DOS commands. There is very little you need to tell them other than the specifics of how to run your software.

Experienced users Users who have used similar software. They might or might not be familiar with DOS and DOS commands. You can have people who are highly experienced with some types of software, but who know nothing about DOS system commands. For example, many business users work on computers set up by a consultant or a specialized group within the company. To run a program, the user selects it from a menu. They never see the DOS prompt. As a result, they do not know how to format a disk or copy a file.

Novice/beginning users These are people who have limited or no experience with other software or with computers. Your instructions will have to be very detailed and written in a cookbook style. In most cases, you should assume that your user is a novice.

Business users You can run into a variety of situations in businesses. In some cases, there will be an "expert" who knows it all. Some business users have an internal support group that provides help. In some cases, the support group even provides documentation specifically written to support your software. In other cases, the support group installs the software on a hard disk so that it is "ready to go" and the user is left on their own to learn how to use it. Other businesses rely on consultants or the store where they purchased their computer to get the computer setup and running. Once it is running, users might be on their own or they might contract with the consultant or store to provide additional ongoing support.

A situation in which you might be writing a manual for a business user would be if you have sold a site license for a customized version of your software. Because of the customization, you need to provide a customized manual.

Home users Home users generally do not have anyone else around to help them. They must learn to use the software by themselves and will sometimes spend hours trying to solve a trivial problem caused by an error in the manual. Anytime you write a manual for home users, write it in the same cookbook style as you would for a novice.

Occupation Users can be categorized by the type of work they do. For example, a construction company might want to use accounting software to run their field payroll. This is a totally different type of user than, for example, an accountant who wants software to maintain the books of a dozen small businesses.

Programmers Do not assume that because someone writes program code they have a complete understanding of computers. Even when writing documentation for programmers, you cannot take shortcuts. Your documentation still must be thorough and complete. Never assume that someone else knows everything you know.

What are your users' needs?

Why will users buy your software? What problems do they need to solve? How will they use the software? Where will they use the software? Yes, you need to know who your users are and what their needs are. When writing your manual, use language and examples that your users will understand.

Examples are important to include in a user's manual. They help clarify the topic you are explaining. An example allows the user to try the software by following the example. Many times, I have found that I could not understand what the manual was saying, but by following an example I could quickly learn how to use the software. The best examples are those that show how to use the software such that it does what the user needs it to do.

For example, if you are publishing a new spreadsheet that you expect will primarily be used by businesses, do not show an example of balancing a home checkbook. Pick an example that is a real-life situation for your user.

In the situation I mentioned earlier—of an accounting program designed for use on a construction site and another designed for accountants—the examples used in each case would be completely different. A construction superintendent will not understand examples designed for an accountant. You have to use examples that relate to the requirements and situations a user has to deal with.

How will the manual be used?

Once you have a feel for who will be using your software, next try to imagine how they will use the manual. Will it be used for training or can they run your software and use the manual as a reference guide? Do you have different types of people using your software who have different needs? If a variety of people will be using your manual, what is a typical situation? You will need to write a manual with various sections, each designed to meet the needs of different users.

User's manuals can meet three type of needs: They can provide training, they can serve as a reference guide, or they can be sectioned—divided to accommodate users with different requirements. Most manuals are written to meet a combination of two or all three of these needs. The most common combination is a manual that starts as a training manual to get users started. Then, in the second half of the manual, it is designed as a reference guide.

Before I go any further, let me define the different types of manuals.

Training manuals   Training manuals start with the basics and teach people how to use the software. With shareware, you have no way of knowing what level of computer experience a person will have. To get a maximum number of registrations, you should assume that a user has little computer experience and no experience with your software. To help these novice users get started, always include a training section in your manual. The training section should describe how to use your software in a step-by-step fashion and use lots of examples.

Reference manuals   Reference manuals allow users to quickly look up the information they need without reading the whole manual. An example of a reference manual is the section of your DOS manual in which DOS commands are listed and described alphabetically. Just as your manual should have a section written as a training guide, it should also have a reference section to allow experienced users to quickly find the information they need.

Sectioned manuals   Sectioned manuals allow different types of users to go to specific sections that cover just the information they need to know. An example of this would be the manual for the PostScript language interpreter that I am now testing (*GoScript*). This manual is divided into sections based on the type of word processing software a user has. Each user only needs to read the section that discusses his word processing software.

Put yourself in a user's place

Most users want to get their software running as quickly as possible. They will read the first few pages of the manual, then put the disk in and start running it. Users are smart. This is the best way to learn. You cannot learn and remember how to use a new program by just reading the manual—you have to combine written instructions with actions. That is why the first part of any manual should be done in a training-manual style, providing quick-start instructions. As users become more experienced, they will look up the information they need in order to use more advanced features—using your manual as a reference.

I am in the process of trying to learn a new communications program. The author of the manual started out by saying he knew I was anxious to get started and he would thus provide quick-start instructions. He then went on to take 75 pages to discuss background information that had nothing to do with running the software. I never found the quick-start instructions. You have to do more than just promise quick-start instructions, you have to deliver them in clear, easy-to-understand language at the front of the manual.

Organization

There are five ways to organize a user's manual:

1. *Organize information in the order of importance*. Discuss the most important functions and ideas first. Unless you have a very

limited and specific user base, this is a difficult approach because what is important to one user might not be important to another.

2. *Arrange topics in order of difficulty.* Start with the easy-to-use functions in your software and move on to the more complex. This is a good approach for a training manual whose sole purpose is to teach beginners.

3. *Arrange topics in order of frequency of use.* First, discuss functions users will need, and use, most often. Then, move on to the less frequently used functions. If you can count on your users having past experience with similar software, this approach will work for some types of software.

4. *Use chronological order.* Begin with the first function or action the user needs to perform and work through all of the functions in your software in the order they would normally be used. This is a good approach for most manuals and users. It allows the user to lay the manual open next to the computer and follow the step-by-step instructions that show how to use your software.

5. *Divide your manual by subject.* This type of organization is appropriate for reference manuals. It allows users to look up information as they need it. This type of manual is usually not intended to be read from cover to cover.

What is the best organization? It depends on your software and who your users are. In general, it is best to start with sections organized by frequency of use. These sections describe the major functions most often used. The rest of the manual might be organized by subject or difficulty of use. Within a section, the information may be organized differently. For example, within sections that are organized by frequency of use, there could be step-by-step instructions organized chronologically.

In the previous chapter, I said that one of the rules of writing software is "do not rush." This applies to the documentation also. It is important to keep that rule in mind. The documentation usually comes last. The program is nearly finished and will be ready to ship as soon as the manual is complete. The temptation is to quickly write a manual and get the software out the door. Like good software, a good manual takes time. Be prepared to rewrite a manual five, six, or more times to get it right. If you do not have a good understanding of grammar, hire an editor or proofreader to help you polish your manual. I recommend reading *How To Write Computer Documentation For Users*, Second Edition, by Susan J. Grimm, (New York, NY: Van Nostrand Reinhold Company, 1987). Even if you are an accomplished writer, have someone else proofread your manual. A fresh viewpoint helps to spot mistakes that you might miss and to point out illogical breaks in organization.

Writing the manual

All user's manuals have a similar organization. The first page inside the front cover should be the title page containing the name of the software, the copyright notice, and the company's name and address. The next page normally contains the user license. Following that is the table of contents.

Table of contents

The best way to start writing a user's manual is to put together a table of contents. It will serve as an outline and will help you get the manual organized before you start writing. Do not feel that, once it is written down, the table of contents becomes fixed. It is a flexible summary of the manual that changes as you write the manual.

The introduction

Next write a short, one- or two-paragraph description of the purpose of your software. This will become your introduction. It will describe what your software is intended to do. It should tell users about any assumptions you have made about their knowledge or any background information they will need. And, it should highlight any special features provided by your software. The purpose of these opening paragraphs is to let users know they have the right program for what they want to do.

In the next few paragraphs, provide a description of how to get around in your manual. Tell the user how your manual is organized. Where do experienced users go to quickly learn how to use the software? Where do novices look to find background information? Direct users of older versions to an appendix that contains information on the differences between the old and current versions.

Also, describe any conventions and abbreviations you use in the manual. If certain types of commands are always in bold type, this is the place to tell the reader. If optional commands are in brackets, let the reader know now.

The installation section

The first section of your manual should describe, in detail, how to install your software. Provide complete, step-by-step "cookbook" instructions. Describe each keystroke the user must make. Include keystroke-by-keystroke instructions on how to use any required DOS commands, even for things as simple as formatting a disk or changing the DOS prompt to another drive.

Assume the user knows nothing about computers, DOS, or software. Be complete and detailed. I once issued an update for one of my programs that requires a hard disk. The installation instructions for the update said to replace the MUSICPGM.EXE and UTILITY.EXE files that were on the hard disk. I described how to use the DOS COPY command to copy the new files from the floppy disk to a hard disk. But, I forgot to tell users to set their hard disk to the directory containing the program to be updated. I assumed that everyone knew that my directions were for copying files to the current directory. As a result, I received several calls from users who could not get the update to work. They had copied the new files into the root directory.

If your software can be installed onto floppy disks, provide a separate section for floppy-disk users. Combining the descriptions of a hard disk installation and a floppy disk installation in one section is confusing to some users.

The quick-start section

Quick-start instructions are very important. Users are anxious to get started with their new software. They want to make something happen, without having to read the complete manual. So that users can quickly find it, this section should be at the front of the manual, immediately after the installation instructions.

The quick-start section provides a short overview, describing how to start your program and utilize the most often-used functions. Do not go into a lot of detail about any one function or feature. Just provide enough information to allow the user to get started and do something useful. For example, for a word processing program, you might describe how to write a one-page letter and print it. The operation of the Del and Ins keys might be discussed, but marking and moving blocks should not be discussed until later, in the main part of the manual.

Do not tell the user that you are going to provide quick-start instructions and then spend a lot of time discussing DOS commands, how a computer works, how shareware works, the background of your software, and the history of your company. While this might be important information, it is not information the user needs to run the software. Put information such as this in appendices in the back of your manual.

Main body of the manual

After the quick-start section, your manual can be organized to best suit your users and the type of software that you have written. If your software is basic and intuitive, the balance of the manual might be a reference guide. If you need to provide more detailed explanations, background information, and instructions for advanced features, you should continue with a training-manual style.

General guidelines

The best way to write a manual is to imagine that you are talking to a single reader. Do not try to be a writer. Hold a conversation with the reader as if he was sitting next to you. Imagine talking to someone sitting next to you and describing how to use your software. Also, imagine the questions he might ask—and answer them. Test your manual by reading it aloud to see how it sounds. You might even try taping yourself as you read the manual. Then, play back the tape and try to follow the instructions. As you listen to the tape you might get a new perspective on your manual.

Ask questions. Questions are a natural part of any conversation and help to hold the attention of the reader. They also stimulate the reader to try to answer the questions before looking for the answers. This helps your readers remember what you are telling them.

Avoid slang, clichés, computer jargon, and acronyms. In most cases, your users are more interested in doing something useful with your software. They are not interested in seeing how big your vocabulary is. They are not interested in the technical workings of your software. Use words and language you would expect your readers to use in everyday conversations. If you must use a computer word, provide a definition. If you are going to use an abbreviation, the first time you use it provide the full wording with the abbreviation in parenthesis. Here is an example:

> Young children enjoy using HomeCraft's Play 'n' Learn (PnL) software. However, many grandparents are also enjoying PnL's Underground Alphabet game.

I talked about having consistency in the design of your software. Your documentation must also be consistent. It must match what the user will see on the computer screen. The use of capitalization and language should be consistent throughout your manual. Some shareware users will interpret what you write literally, so do not try to be creative in your use of synonyms. I have heard of many cases in which a shareware author has written in his manual, for example, "type the word PRINT", and a user then types "THE WORD PRINT". I know this sounds absurd, but if you would like to hear more horror stories about documentation, just drop in on the shareware forum on CompuServe. What you need to do in your documentation is be consistent and provide clear and simple explanations.

In reviewing shareware, I have seen many manuals that provide all the technical details about the inner workings of the software. However, unless you are publishing utilities or libraries for programmers, users will not care about *how* the software works, they just want to use it. Providing simple and clear explanations that describe how to *use* the software is particularly important with shareware. If your manual is too technical, most users will lose interest and move on to the next program. You need to keep users interested in your software and that means helping them to get started as quickly as possible. If you want to describe the inner workings of your software, do it in an appendix.

Keep it short and concise. Good writing uses as few words as will clearly deliver the message. A long manual is not necessarily a good manual. In many cases, a long manual is a sign of wordy documentation that is repetitious and difficult to read.

> *Some authors must have fantastic teams of writers putting together the documentation. It's so incredibly impressive in its size. But in some of it, the documentation is preceded by so many pages or screens filled with warnings, copyright notices, what is shareware, what our company policies are, and how to order, that I give up. I just want to figure out what the software is doing. I just want to see what it is before I go any further. But, it's so hard to find out in the documentation what the program does that sometimes I give up.*
>
> —Roger Jones, president of Shareware To-Go.

The beginning and end of your manual

Once you have completed the main body of the manual, you can add the pages that go in the front and rear sections. When the final page comes out of your laser printer, and the page numbering is set, update the table of contents and put together the index. The warranty disclaimer discussed in the legal section should be added to the front of the manual. Also, include a description of any warranties or guarantees you offer, such as a 90-day no-questions-asked, money-back guarantee. Add a title page that includes the name of the software, your name, and your company's name and address. Follow this with a page that has the copyright notice, version number and date, and information about how users can contact you for support or to register.

In the disk version of your documentation, include a short explanation of shareware, information about the registration cost, and tell users how to register. If you offer additional services, such as site licenses or custom programming, mention them at the front of the manual, but put the details in the appendices.

You might also include an appendix with a listing of the files that should be on the disk, even if this is already included in a PACKING.LST file. Also describe any files that will be created by your software.

Testing your manual

Test, test, test. That is the only way you will know whether or not you have a good manual. Have your spouse try to install and run your software. If your spouse is tired of being the guinea pig for your software, try asking someone else in your family, or your neighbor, or pay one of your neighbor's kids to spend a few hours using your software. Find someone who knows nothing about your software (and, if possible, nothing about computers) and have them install it and use the key functions.

In most cases, testing your manual will be integrated with the testing of your software. When someone has a problem using your software, you will need to determine whether it is a problem with the software or with the manual. Whenever I get a user calling for help with my software, I evaluate my manual and software for changes that would have eliminated the need for that user's call. Over the years, I have improved both my software and manual to the point where I now get very few support calls. Most of my support calls come from shareware users who have an older version of one of my programs.

Publishing your manual

Never use a dot-matrix printer to print your manual. Use a laser printer or, at a minimum, a daisywheel printer. A laser printer is best because it allows you to change point size for chapter and section headings. (Point size is a measurement of how big a printed character is. There are 72 points to an inch.) Incorporating larger, bold-print section headings helps make your manual easier to read.

Be sure to include page numbers. In laying out your manual, if it is printed on both sides of the paper, make sure all chapters begin on the right-hand page. The chapter title should be in bold and placed about halfway down the page.

Although it is cheap, try to avoid a photocopied manual with the pages stapled together. This should be done only for software with a very low registration fee. The quality of photocopying can nearly match that of printing, so I have no problem with photocopying, but instead of stapling a manual, put it in a binder or bind it in some other manner.

Binders

If your manual will be updated more than once a year, use a three-ring binder. If you make several hundred copies of your manual, you can get binders with the cover preprinted to your specifications. Another option is to use view binders. These allow you to slip a cover page behind a clear plastic sheet on the front. You end up with a professional, glossy-looking cover. Figure 12-1 shows an example of a cover from one of my early CP/M programs. It is a two-color cover printed on cover-stock paper. It is simple and inexpensive, and although it is not good enough to sit on a retail shelf, a cover similar to this one gives a better impression than a photocopied cover.

This cover in FIG. 12-1 was used in 1985 and 1986. The total cost of the artwork was under $75. The picture is from a clip-art book. My printer did the typesetting for $40. The paste-up and camera work cost another $35.

12-1 This is an example of the instructions given to a printer for a two-color user's manual cover.

By the way, three-ring binders are usually heavily discounted. You should be able to get binders for 60–70% off of a manufacturer's list price. If you are going to use a three-ring binder for your manual, have the printer use a three-hole-drill paper. It will save you from having to punch holes in all the pages. (The printer buys paper with three holes already in it.)

If your manual is under 50 pages, another option is to use a paper report cover with metal prongs that fit a standard three-hole punch. Although it is not as professional-looking as a three-ring binder, it is much better than stapling your manual together.

Before you buy binders, first find out how many pages you have. Then get a binder that is the right size for your manual. To make your manual easy to use, put dividers between each chapter.

Once you feel that your manual requires no additional changes, wait two or three months before printing it in large quantities. It seems that, just when you think there can be no more changes, a user will call with a new problem that requires another change in your manual.

Other binding methods

If your manual is less than 200 pages, there are less expensive ways to bind it. The following is a list of the different ways a manual can be bound.

Perfect binding   Perfect binding means that the pages are glued together and the cover (front, spine, and back) is all one piece. A paperback book is an example of perfect binding. The disadvantage is that your manual will not stay open by itself. This makes it harder to read while working at a computer.

Saddle stitching   Saddle stitching uses staples in the spine. Many catalogs are bound using saddle stitching. Use this method of binding if your manual is less than 100 pages. For shorter manuals, saddle stitching is a good, inexpensive binding method.

Spiral binding   Spiral binding is similar to what you see in spiral tablets. It works well for manuals under 200 pages. The advantage that spiral binding has over perfect bound or saddle stitched manuals is that the spine does not crack and the manual will stay open to any page. To provide some durability, the cover can be printed on heavy paper and it should be 1/8-inch larger than the paper used for the contents.

A system similar to spiral binding is *GBC* binding. A GBC-bound manual uses a "plastic comb" to hold the manual together. A single machine punches the holes in paper and holds a plastic comb open while you insert the pages. This machine costs about $280. GBC binding has several advantages. If your software changes, you can easily open the plastic comb and replace pages in the manual whenever your software is updated. For users, a GBC binding allows the book to lay flat and, unlike a perfect bound or saddle stitched book, it will stay open.

The cover

First impressions are important and your manual's cover is where users will get their first impression of the registered version of your software. It helps to use color in the cover. Anyone can run off black-and-white copies. By using color in your cover, you show that you have taken the time to be professional. You present an image of a serious company that cares about quality. To save money, you can have the cover printed in one color, such as blue, red, or green. Many times, you can find a printer that runs different standard colors on different days. If you use a standard color and your order can be combined with others, you can save quite a bit on press setup charges.

Having a two-color cover printed is not difficult. You can design it yourself and print the masters that you need on a laser printer. When printing a two-color cover, there are several approaches you can take.

One approach is to keep both colors completely separate. If the printing for each color never comes into contact with any other color, you can use a single master. Circle the lettering or areas you want printed in color. For example, if I were to print this page in two colors, with only one paragraph in blue and the rest in black, I could give it to the printer as you see it now. All I would have to do is indicate which paragraph is to be printed in blue and that the rest of the page is to be printed in black. This is the easiest and cheapest way to produce a two-color page.

Another approach involves using black ink and almost any other color. This method allows you to produce a cover on which the two colors overlap. In this case, you will need to produce two separate masters with your laser printer. One master contains the words and graphics that are to be printed in black. The other master has the words and graphics that are to be printed in the second color. When you lay one page on top of the other and hold them up to the light, everything should line up and be correctly positioned.

If you do not have a laser printer, have your covers typeset. A printer can usually do this. Provide a sketch of what you want and indicate which colors go where. Figure 12-1 shows an example of the two-color cover of a program I published in 1985. I used black and green, with the large HMM in green and the name of the software printed in black on top of the green. What you see in FIG. 12-1 is the instructions I gave to my printer.

When printing one color on top of another, always use black as one of your colors. Black completely blocks out any color printed underneath it. If you do not use black, you will get a third, usually very ugly, color.

You can also design a cover with multiple colors and a very tight registration. Having a tight registration means that the different colors come into contact with each other, but do not overlap. Designing this type of cover without professional equipment is almost impossible. I recommend that you hire a professional if you are going to produce a three- or four-color cover.

Another possibility is to include photographs on your cover. Including photographs will be more expensive than line art because they will have to be screened. Screening means that the photograph is converted into a pattern of dots. If you do not need high quality, you can scan a photograph into your computer, but in most cases, the 300 dpi capabilities of a laser printer are not good enough to produce a quality image for a cover.

Reproducing color photographs requires a color separation. This is a process in which the colors in the photograph are separated into their component primary colors. Using a color photograph on your cover is the most expensive way to design a cover.

Providing support

Should you answer the questions of, and provide support to, users that have not paid a registration fee? It is to your advantage to help unregistered users. Many times, they just need a question or two answered and they will register at the end of the phone call (if you accept credit cards). Keep in mind that you cannot expect users to register unless they can get your software to first work to their satisfaction.

In supporting unregistered users, some authors have a policy of just providing information about installation plus enough to get the user far enough along so that they can evaluate the software. If the unregistered user wants more information, the author asks for a credit-card number to charge the registration fee to. If you get a lot of calls from unregistered users and feel that you must do this, here are three possible approaches.

1. Improve your documentation and software so that you reduce the number of support calls you get.
2. If a user complains and asks for more help, blame it on company policy. Say that it is company policy that only registered users can get support beyond what you have already supplied. You cannot break this policy due to your commitments to other users.
3. Change your support policy and provide more help for unregistered users.

Of these three options, I prefer and recommend a combination of numbers 1 and 3.

Returning phone calls

What if unregistered users call and leave messages on your answering machine? How do you handle these calls from unregistered users? Should you call collect? Should you ignore the call and hope they call again? Maybe your answering machine message can tell them they must try again later. I suggest that you call them back at your expense, even when they offer to accept a collect call from you. You never know what the sales potential is. In particular, anyone willing to pay for you to call them collect is very interested in your software. Call them right away!

As you can tell, I recommend answering all questions from unregistered users. In helping unregistered users, I have found that a high percentage soon send in the registration payment. Plus, it is a great way to get feedback. You can learn more about how to improve your software by listening to a user's questions than the user can learn from you. As a consultant, I give away my time for free just so I can hear the questions someone wants to ask me. That is how you learn about your customers, what their needs are, and how you can better serve them. It is how you learn how to make your software and documentation better and it is how you find out about bugs. Besides, calls from unregistered users might be more important than you expect.

> *A couple of years ago, I got an EPLEX on CompuServe from a non-registered user. He asked some questions and I answered. He wrote again the next day, and again I answered. Then the next day, and the next day, and. . . . Well, I finally said, "Hey, you're not registered and everything I've answered is in the manual. What gives?" After that, he told me he was a reviewer for PC Magazine and he was evaluating the way I answered my support questions.*
> —Paul Mayer, author of *GRAB Plus*

Treat all callers as if they were magazine reviewers and you will be doing the right thing. By the way, when unregistered users call, always get an address if you can. For example, offer to send more information about your software. Once you have their address, you can include them as a part of your direct-mail campaign. A direct-marketing approach that I have found to work well is to send some unregistered users copies of my newsletter. When they read about the current update/upgrade, they often will be interested enough to register so that they can get the new features in the update/upgrade.

At a minimum, provide support through the mail. A quick response is a key to building user loyalty and satisfaction—so try to answer all mail within 48 hours.

Telephone support

I highly recommend that you provide telephone support. Many people want instant gratification. If they are trying your shareware and cannot call when they have a problem, they might move on to the next program and you will lose a sale. If you are running a part-time business, have an answering machine take your calls when you are not available. Working a full-time day job while trying to provide support on your lunch hour and during the evening is difficult. But, if you want to build your business, you will need to put this extra effort into it. Make it a rule that all messages left on your machine are answered within 24 hours.

Should you restrict the hours that you provide telephone support? You can, but be flexible when people call outside those hours. Remember that international callers have drastically different hours than you. You might try using an answering machine to screen calls during your "off" hours.

If you do not wish to provide telephone support, you might have to get an unlisted number. If your name and address are in your documentation, users will get your phone number from directory assistance. However, keep in mind that any user that took the trouble to get your number from directory assistance is probably very interested in your software.

I have tried issuing shareware disks that included only my address and others that included both an address and phone number. The number of registrations I received increased noticeably when I provided a phone number.

Another way to provide support is via CompuServe, GEnie, or DELPHI. These services can be convenient to you and the user because you both can retrieve and answer messages. Plus, they are a lot cheaper for the user than a long-distance phone call (unless you provide an 800 number).

Types of calls

The following are some of the types of support calls you can expect from users.

Some users state that they will not read the instruction manual and that they want you to take them through the installation. All you can do is talk them through the installation, step by step. You might lose money supporting these users, but you need to help them in order to maintain your reputation. Fortunately, there are very few people like this.

Some users will read the entire manual and still not understand how to use your software. No matter how well you write the manual, there will be some people who do not understand parts of it. We all occasionally have mental blocks that prevent us from seeing something that is right in front of our noses. There is also the problem that people see things differently. What might be a simple set of instructions to one person, will be meaningless to another. Although the answers are in the manual and seem obvious, help these people by taking them step by step through the problem area.

You will also have users calling who quickly browse the manual and get stuck with a problem. They don't want to spend any more time reading the manual, so they call you. If you answer their questions and point out the pages in the manual where their questions are answered, you can get them back to running the software on their own.

There are also users who will completely read your manual a dozen times and still not find what they need—because you did not cover it. All you can do is answer their questions and write an addendum to your manual.

Regardless of the type of person calling, answer all questions in a cheerful, pleasant manner. Most unregistered callers are not trying to cheat you, they are just trying to learn how to use your software. With those users who appear not to have read the manual, do not get upset or angry. Remember, people can read a manual cover to cover and still miss things. Answer their questions and then refer them to a specific page in the manual for additional information.

A typical support phone call

User: How do I start an alphabetical listing of my database? It's not explained in the manual anywhere.

Support Person: Start by going to the Printed Reports/Search screen by selecting #3 on the main menu. Do you have your computer in front of you?

User: Yes.

Support Person: What's on the screen now?

User: The Printed Reports/Search screen.

Support Person: Can you see the prompts across the bottom of the screen for the function keys?

User: Yes.

Support Person: Do you see the prompt that says "F3/F4—Lists"?

User: Yes. It's in the middle at the bottom.

Support Person: The F4 key will start an alphabetical listing. Go ahead and push F4.

User: I pushed it.

Support Person: Did a menu appear in the lower right corner of the screen?

User: Yes. It says F1, alphabetically by zip code. F2, alphabetically by name. F3, alphabetically by business name.

Support Person: How would you like the list to be alphabetized? By name?

User: Yes, I'll push F2.

Support Person: What is happening on the screen now?

User: Robert Appleton's name and address are on the screen.

Support Person: Look in the lower left corner of the screen. Do you see the prompt that says "F1—Search Again"?

User: Yes.

Support Person: Push F1, and you'll see the next name in alphabetical order.

User: Yes. It works.

Support Person: Good. The alphabetical listing is working fine. By the way, if you need to know more about this, there is more information on page 45 of the manual. It tells you how to use the other types of listings and how to print the report.

Notice that the support person first answered the question then referred the user to the manual. Your first objective is to solve the user's problem. A secondary objective can be to help the user learn how to use the manual.

Do they have their computers in front of them?

When going over problems with users, always ask them to be in front of their computer with your software running. This might not always be possible, but it will make it a lot easier for you to help them. If they are not in front of their computer, ask them if you can call back when they are. However, in a few instances, the user will not have a phone near his computer and you will have to do the best you can.

I recommend that you ask users to be in front of their computers when you are helping them. Many times, users will insist that they have done everything correctly, exactly as described in your manual. Yet, when you walk them through the problem area, the software works fine. Without realizing it, they had missed something, usually something very simple, that prevented them from getting the software to do what they wanted.

Having users actually work through their problems with you on the phone is also very helpful to you. For example, sometimes users get error messages mixed up. They will tell you the message on the screen said one thing, but when you have them run the software, you find out it was actually a different error message.

By the way, if you hear a lot of static and buzzing on the phone line, the user is probably talking on a cordless phone. Ask the user to step back from the computer a little bit. The person should stay within reach of the keyboard, but move as far away from the CPU and monitor as possible. Also, ask if there is a second person near the computer and, if there is, ask that person to move away. A person's body can act as a reflector, trapping the radio frequency emissions from the computer and bouncing them into the cordless phone.

Problem solving

If you do not immediately know the answer to a user's question, have the user repeat the steps that caused the problem while you are on the phone. You might want to have the user try several things so that you can eliminate the possible causes of the problem. As you give directions, tell the user specifically which keys to push, including all spaces, punctuation marks, and the Enter key. If what is described as happening on the screen is not what you expect, have the user repeat back to you the names of the keys that were pushed. Many times, the user is pushing the wrong key and does not know it. For example, I have asked users to type an asterisk but found they were typing a number 8 (shift plus the number 8 key is the asterisk). Constantly check what is on the user's screen by asking the user to describe it.

If people are having problems with DOS commands, you should help them get going, at least well enough to use your software. You then might direct them to books that help explain DOS. For example, I have recommended that users pick up a copy of the *PC Crash Course and Survival Guide* (available in many software stores). It provides good, simple explanations of the important DOS functions.

Keep a log

Always write down each question a user asks. This will provide a record of the problems that users have. You can then use your log when improving your software or manual. I also use my log to help me put together a question-and-answer book that someone else can use to help people calling with questions. This book becomes a quick-reference guide for technical support.

I also keep a log because I do not necessarily change my software or documentation every time someone calls with a problem. Unless it is an obvious problem, such as a bug, I generally wait until several users have asked for the same change.

Support check list

The following is a check list of what to do when handling a support call.

- Provide users with a step-by-step description of what to do to solve a problem. Do not try to make them feel bad because they did not read the manual. The first objective should always be to help users solve problems. Everything else is secondary to this.
- Ask users to have their computers in front of them with your software running. This makes solving a problem much easier for both you and the user.
- Involve users by asking questions. This helps to get them thinking and sometimes they will come up with the answer themselves. Asking questions also confirms that what you think they are doing is what they really are doing. If you are stuck, it also gives you time to think and it might turn up new information that will open up other possible solutions. The most common question you can ask the user is: "Can you tell me what is on your screen now?"
- Never act like something is obvious. Avoid phrases such as "of course" or "everyone knows." These phrases make other people feel stupid and, generally, the problem is just that they have no past experience with what they are trying to do. The best situation is to solve the user's problem and leave the user feeling good about himself or herself.

- As you work through a problem, explain what you are having a user do and why. Do not just give a string of keystrokes. Help the user understand and he will not have to call back with the same question.
- Do not assume that a user knows how to use DOS commands. Many users do not know how to change directories or copy files. When you tell a user to type CD <space> DOS to change to the DOS directory, explain what the letters "CD" mean. And always specifically explain each character and **space** that needs to be typed.
- If unregistered users call, help them. If they have older versions of your shareware that has bugs, offer to send new disks with the latest shareware version, at no charge. It not only solves the problem, but you get their addresses to use in a direct-mail campaign in the future.

Tough problems

What do you do if someone has a problem that seems impossible to solve?

You could ask them to describe the steps they took to get into the problem (determine the cause). Then have them repeat these steps, and describe what happens, with you on the phone.

You could have users go back to the first screen that your software displays and have them repeat and describe each step. Follow it on your computer. In some cases, where the selections made during the installation process were important, you might want to walk users through the installation procedure to re-install your software.

If a problem consistently is repeated, it is most likely a software problem. If the problem varies and seems random, it most likely is a hardware problem. The most common hardware problem that I have run into is a fragmented hard disk or a disk with bad sectors. These problems will cause all sorts of odd errors ranging from locking up the software to data disappearing. Start by asking the user to run CHKDSK. This is somewhat like checking to be sure the TV is plugged in when someone complains it does not work. However, be aware that CHKDSK only checks for a limited number of problems. It does not, for example, detect fragmented disks.

If CHKDSK reports no problems, ask users if they have PC Tools or Norton Utilities. If so, they should use the utilities provided by these programs to defragment their hard disk and check it for problems. If they do not have either of these, I usually recommend that they buy one of them or a similar program. As with any other machine, a computer needs periodic maintenance and this is the type of software you use to perform that maintenance.

Other potential problem areas to check are the CONFIG.SYS and AUTOEXEC.BAT files. Some users have memory-resident software running and do not know it. Have them take things out of these files one at a time, reboot their computers, and try your software again. It can be time-consuming, but many times this has solved a mysterious problem.

Take logical steps to isolate problems. What causes a problem? What functions can be used and not cause a problem? Sometimes, it is like solving a Sherlock Holmes mystery. You have to put a lot of small clues together to come up with the final answer.

Make sure that users are typing commands correctly. Remember that there are two types of slashes. Watch out for spelling errors (users will swear they spelled it right). Have users retype commands and spell commands as they type them.

For printer problems, first make sure a printer is on-line. I have had users tell me their printers were connected, turned on, and ready to go, but they still could not get a printed report. The problem turned out to be that their printers were not on-line. Check for the simple things. These can sometimes be the causes of big problems.

You should be aware that sometimes your suggestions will solve a user's problem, and if it was a simple solution, that user will not want to appear "stupid." If the user seems to want to end the conversation, let the caller go. It usually means that the problem was solved, or that the user noticed something else that was causing the problem (like the printer not being plugged in).

Provide super service for anyone who calls or writes. Consistent super service will increase your sales. It can bring you additional sales from add-on products or utilities. It builds your reputation for outstanding service. Plus, never forget that the single most important goal of customer service is selling! Sell your image; sell your product; sell add-on utilities; sell your reputation. To effectively do this, you must be professional, friendly, helpful, and courteous. We have all read about WordPerfect Corporation and the reason why they are the leading word processing software. It is because of their support! With every support call they handle, they are selling their image of super service and that image sells software.

Improving your software and manual

Pay attention to the questions users ask when they call for help. This is the feedback you need to improve your software and documentation. If you change your documentation to cover the problems callers have, you will get fewer calls. For example, include a section in the back of your manual for the most often asked questions. Or, publish a newsletter that includes answers to frequently asked questions. You will not only help current users, but you can then include back issues of the newsletter with the registered version of your software. These will help answer users' questions until you can modify and reprint your manual.

Remember to smile when you answer the phone. No matter what mood you are in or how you are feeling, if you smile when you answer the phone, you will sound pleasant.

Sometimes when people call for help, they will want to talk—a lot. A five-minute question can turn into an hour-long phone call. Although the user might be paying the phone charges, you might not have time to spend on a long, nonproductive call. I was once told about a way to hang up on people without making them feel bad. Hang up when you are talking—no one hangs up on himself, so the caller will assume it was a bad connection. (It does work, but I am just joking.) A better approach is tell the caller that you have to go to a meeting or that you have an appointment to make another call. Give them a good business reason for terminating the call.

International support

Treat users in other countries just as you do users in this country. Answer all mail within 48 hours and return phone calls. When I look over my phone bill to spot the expensive calls, the international calls do not stand out. I run up higher bills with people that just want to talk a lot.

To support international users, you might find that using a FAX machine is the best approach. It allows users to send you questions during their normal business hours and you can reply during your normal business hours. Be sure to tell people to leave their FAX machines on all the time because of the time differences.

Making use of the Email services provided by CompuServe, for example, is the cheapest and most convenient way to support international users. With the appropriate software, you can get your mail from CompuServe using less than a minute of connect time, read and answer it off-line, then spend another 40 to 50 seconds of connect time sending your response.

Getting paid for support

Among some of the larger software companies, including some shareware publishers, the concept of having users pay for support is growing. The bottom line is that support costs a lot and you cannot put just anyone on the phone to answer users' questions. The support staff must be trained to not only know the answers to technical questions, but also to know what questions to ask in order to determine what the real problem is. In many cases, you must answer the support calls because you are the only one that knows the answers—and this takes valuable time away from other important activities, such as marketing and product development.

The most popular way to charge users for support has been through the use of 900 numbers. For business users, some software publishers offer support contracts with price tags in the $5000 to $10,000 range. Buying a support contract gets the user priority phone and FAX support, low-cost major upgrades, and sometimes, access to electronic bulletin boards.

The pay-for-support concept is in its infancy and just starting to grow. I personally believe this concept will expand and become more accepted. As for how this will affect you as a one-person software publisher—plan on continuing to provide personal service until your company reaches $1 million in annual sales. The ability to provide free customer support, where the user can talk directly to the author, is one of the advantages of shareware that you can use to compete with, and beat, the big companies.

Updating/upgrading your software

Typically, people use the words update and upgrade interchangeably. In this section, I am going to define each as having a specific meaning.

An *update* brings software up to the current version. It provides minor changes and improvements in the software that do not involve printing a new manual. An update does not change the primary part of a version number, but does change the secondary part of the version number. For example, if the current software version is 2.3, then an update might change this to 2.4.

An *upgrade* is a major revision to software that adds additional features and results in either a new manual or a significant addendum to the manual. An upgrade results in a change in the primary part of the version number. For example, if the current software version is 2.3, an upgrade would change this to 3.0.

Then there are bug fixes. Bug fixes might or might not result in a version-number change. If the version number changes, the hundredths part of the number is increased, for example changing from version 2.3 to version 2.31.

My survey of shareware authors showed that most authors only send out bug fixes after a user complains. On the user side, users are getting tired of paying for bug fixes under the guise of receiving an update/upgrade. It is a difficult problem. Mailing a bug fix is expensive (just over a $1 per 5 1/4" floppy disk, if bulk mail is used), yet users feel they should get bug-free software that performs correctly.

How should you handle bug fixes? First, try to avoid them by thoroughly testing your software and not rushing the testing process. That is the cheapest way to handle bugs—fix bugs before they get to users. If a bug gets through your testing process, here are some suggestions.

Ideally, I would like to see all publishers fix bugs as soon as possible and update all the users who might be affected. However, I also realize that most authors might not have the budget to allow them to do this. I have noticed that even the big companies rarely send out bug fixes—they require you to buy an update that also includes the bug fix. For example, there are bugs in Windows 3.0. Microsoft will supply the update, version 3.00a, to any user that calls and complains about the bugs in version 3.0.

That is also exactly what my survey of shareware authors found that most shareware authors do.

I try to do a little better than the big companies. If I find a bug that might result in damaged files or loss of data, I immediately send a fix to all users who might have software with the bug. I will not subject my users to the potential of losing days, or weeks, worth of data.

If there is a bug that significantly affects the operation of a major function in my software, I send a fix to all affected users, but I wait for a convenient time. For example, I have included disks with bug fixes with my newsletter. It does not increase the bulk-rate postage costs, making the mailing of updates much more affordable. If people call for help because of a problem caused by a bug, I send them a new disk right away.

If the problem is a small bug in a part of the program that is rarely used, I fix the bug, but I do not send out disks. If users call with problems caused by the bug, I send them a new disk.

How often should you have an update or upgrade? Updating software is a continuous process. As you think of ways to improve your software and get feedback from users, incorporate these new ideas. You might start shipping the updated versions to new users as soon as the changes are ready. In some cases, authors update their software almost weekly. I update my software continuously and a policy that I have found to work well is to offer users updates for a minimal cost, usually $5 per disk, anytime they wish to buy an update. I describe the improvements in a newsletter that I send to all users every six months.

You should not issue more than one major upgrade during a year. The cost for an upgrade can vary depending on what you are giving users. If it is just a new disk, you might stay with the same $5 price you charge for updates. If the upgrade includes major new features and a new 300-page manual, you might charge $50 or more. Generally, your users should be able to purchase the upgrade at 50% off the list price or less.

One approach to issuing an upgrade is to start shipping it to new users first. It is very disappointing for a new user to buy a program and then receive an upgrade announcement a few days or weeks later. You should also offer users who purchased your software recently a reduced price or a free upgrade to the new version. You might end up with a schedule that looks like this:

June 1—start shipping new version to new users

June 1—mail newsletter containing the upgrade announcement to existing users

July 15—start shipping the upgrade to existing users. Users who purchased your software between January 1 and March 1 can purchase the upgrade for half price.

How you handle the schedule for upgrades will depend on your situation.

You might have users that need the new features an upgrade provides ASAP. In this case, get the upgrade announcement out as soon as you can and offer it free to anyone that purchased your software in the last couple of months.

In all cases, be sure that you are treating your customers fairly. Although upgrades can provide a significant source of revenue, do not feel like you can "milk" your users by charging high prices or by issuing frequent upgrades. You will find your users slowly dropping away and switching to other software and, as your reputation spreads, new user registrations will be dropping off. Always be fair and follow good business practices.

13
Professional associations

In chapter 7, I talked about how important it is to make contacts, to get to know people, and to get people to know you. That is one of the main reasons for attending conventions and trade shows such as COMDEX. The best way to get to know people within the software industry is to join a professional association.

The Association of Shareware Professionals

If you want to learn more about how to be a successful shareware author, if you want to find the answers to questions about marketing your software as shareware, and if you want to help promote the shareware concept and help improve shareware's image of quality and professionalism—then join the Association of Shareware Professionals (ASP).

Every industry has its trade associations in which members can meet, make contacts with, and get help from, other people with similar interests. For shareware authors, this group is the Association of Shareware Professionals.

The Association of Shareware Professionals was formed by a group of shareware authors in 1987. It is now a group of about 300 authors (and growing) who believe in the shareware concept and that have agreed to abide by a professional code of ethics.

ASP objectives

The ASP has four purposes:

- To set standards for shareware authors and vendors
- To pool information and serve as a resource for shareware authors

- To educate users and, in particular, deal with misleading advertising put out by some disk vendors and misleading information published in the press
- To protect the shareware concept so that it remains a viable and growing method of marketing software

The most important thing the ASP represents is that its members are professionals who act in a professional manner. Members must meet a minimum "code of ethics" and standards to maintain their membership. Applicants for membership are reviewed to ensure that they meet the requirements and standards.

The ASP works to educate users by publishing information in various files posted on BBSs, through discussions on CompuServe, through exhibits at trade shows, and through a vendor program that has gotten many vendors to stop listing shareware in the same category as freeware, demos, and public-domain software.

Through continuing discussions on CompuServe and via the ASP newsletter (ASPects), members help each other, answer questions, support each other, and help solve problems. Even if you are not a member, you can ask questions and "listen" to conversations by going to the shareware forum (GO SHARE) on CompuServe. You will find plenty of good advice and interesting discussions.

The ASP has taken significant steps to protect shareware. For example, as a result of ASP's efforts, the wording of a bill recently passed by Congress was changed. Without the change in wording, shareware would have lost copyright protection and would have been lumped in with public-domain software. This could have had a significant negative impact on shareware and, essentially, eliminated shareware as an effective means of distributing software.

Why you should join the ASP

Throughout this book, I have mentioned the ASP and recommended that all authors be members of the ASP. I have mentioned benefits such as professional contacts. The following is a summary of why you should be an ASP member.

Learn how to be successful As I have already mentioned, the ASP is the place to learn how to be a successful shareware author. This is the benefit mentioned by every ASP member I interviewed and, in most cases, the only reason they gave. In my interviews there were many success stories about how registrations doubled or tripled after an author joined the ASP and started to apply new methods.

Exposure The ASP sponsors events that give you the opportunity to gain exposure from the press and the public. They have had a booth at both

COMDEX and PC-EXPO. Authors can use the booth to help promote shareware and to promote their own products. The ASP also sponsors a party at COMDEX that gives authors the opportunity to meet the press and other authors.

Protect the shareware concept of marketing software   One of the more important benefits is that the ASP has been fighting to keep the word "shareware" in the public domain. ASP has filed protests on three different continents to prevent people from using it as a trademarked word.

If a magazine publishes an article that misrepresents shareware, the ASP will respond with a letter that, in many cases, gets published in the magazine's letter section. It helps the author of the article to better understand shareware and, through publication in the letters section, hopefully, clears up the misinformation.

You will be identified as meeting professional standards   Another benefit is that by agreeing to the ASP standards, you tell potential customers that you are meeting standards of professionalism and quality. Your users know they will not get crippled software. They know they can get support. They know you operate in an ethical manner. Although today the ASP label on software has limited effect, as users become better educated and more aware of what the ASP stands for, the value of being able to identify yourself as an ASP author will grow.

Why join if you are already successful   In talking to some highly successful authors who are not members of the ASP, they told me that they did not need to be a member of the ASP because they had "already made it." There was nothing further they could learn or gain from ASP membership. Unfortunately, this is not true. The ASP continuously provides you with benefits, even if you have achieved great success. The ASP's efforts in Congress, in protecting shareware, and in working to get shareware recognized as a professional way of marketing software benefit all shareware authors and publishers. So, even if you have made it and know all there is to know, your membership in the ASP helps support shareware and ultimately helps you.

Disk distributors and BBSs

The ASP also offers membership to disk distributors and BBSs. One of the reasons vendors and BBSs join the ASP is because many ASP members automatically send their disks to all ASP-member vendors and BBSs. Authors do this because they know an ASP vendor or BBS will not misrepresent their software. The need for the vendor or BBS to contact the author for permission to distribute the software is eliminated. It is a great way to reduce paper and I am all for anything that reduces paperwork!

How to join the ASP

To join the ASP, write to the following address for an application. You can also download a copy of the application form from CompuServe.

Executive Director
Association of Shareware Professionals
545 Grover Rd.
Muskegon, MI 49442-9427
CompuServe PPN: 72050,1433
(616) 788-2765 (fax)

If you write for membership information, you will receive a disk that contains files with the following information:

Introductory letter The following is a letter that is included in the ASP application package. It provides an excellent summary of the ASP and on being a shareware author. This letter serves as an introduction to the disk that the ASP sends out to prospective members. The files described in this letter are available by writing to the ASP and requesting an application. You can also download them from the shareware forum on CompuServe.

Dear Author,

Thank you for your interest in becoming a member of the Association of Shareware Professionals (ASP). We are a group of shareware authors that are working to improve the image of shareware as an alternative way of purchasing high-quality software.

Many of us operate by ourselves and have a "regular daytime" job and operate our software businesses during the evenings and weekends. Others of us, through hard work and "the right product" are running our shareware business full time, and a few even have a dozen or so employees. The term "right product" means that the author has developed a product that is highly needed, has wide appeal, is highly acclaimed, and that the author worked hard at marketing and became highly successful. Not all of us (myself included) are in that category.

Many of us target our software to a niche in the software market. We realize that our expertise is in that niche and are willing to write to that limited market. We can't all write good word processing, database, communications, or spreadsheet software. We have discovered that we can be compensated for our efforts through registrations, without the HIGH cost of advertising and distribution associated with the "traditional" methods of software distribution. Most of us really enjoy the direct contact with our customers. This allows our shareware to live and grow in ways that are just not possible with the "traditional" methods of distribution.

I have placed several files on this disk to help you prepare your software and documentation for ASP membership.

APPLIC.FRM READ THIS FILE!!! This is the full file that describes in detail what is expected of the ASP author's software and documentation. One of the MOST important sections contains ASP's No Crippling policy. This is the sticking point on many applications. All of us FIRMLY believe that the potential registrant MUST be able to make an accurate "buy" decision based on a freely distributed shareware disk.

Some shareware has created a bad name for our industry by being highly crippled as a registration incentive. If your shareware does not meet the No Crippling policy, you should either meet the requirements or withdraw your application.

Speaking for myself, when I revised my software to fully document and include ALL features on the shareware disk, my registration rate went up significantly!

APPLIC.TXT This is the last few pages of APPLIC.FRM and is the application form itself. Fill this out and CompuServe mail or U.S. mail (on disk) this file to our Executive Director after you have filled it out. In accordance with the instructions in APPLIC.FRM, sign a paper copy of APPLIC.TXT and mail with the disk containing the filled-out APPLIC.TXT file. BE SURE to either mail the disk or Email the filled-out APPLIC.TXT file or your application will be delayed until you do send the file. Myself and the reviewers are all volunteers and having this ASCII file will save us a lot of time {many thanks!}.

Please COMPLETELY describe your shareware in the section titled Major Features. Take as much room at this point in the file as you wish. If you just say "see attached" and include a paper write-up, I will return the disk to you to complete. I have a tough time stuffing brochures into my A:drive {grin}.

Please COMPLETELY describe ANY differences between your freely distributed shareware disk and what is sent to registrants. If you leave this blank, the application will come right back to you.

SHAREW.PRN Your documentation should contain a description of the shareware concept. You may wish to include a warranty and you must include something that lets the registrant know what he/she will get for registering. Paul Mayer developed the text in this file as an example of this type of text wording. Feel free to include portions or all of this file in your documentation.

GUIDE.EXE This self-extracting file contains a WEALTH of information put together by Nelson Ford. Just type GUIDE (enter) and this file will self-uncompress into a set of text files. It will give you a lot of ideas for preparing and marketing your shareware.

REASONS.TXT A collection of messages from the ASP's open forum on CompuServe that give many good reasons to join the ASP.

The address of our Executive Director is:

Executive Director
Association of Shareware Professionals
545 Grover Rd.
Muskegon, MI 49442
CompuServe PPN: 72050,1433

Thank you,

George Abbott
ASP Author Membership Coordinator

ASP membership application

Statement of purpose of the ASP The ASP is an association for shareware authors with the general goals of educating shareware authors and distributors and the public, setting standards, sharing resources and information among members.

Definition of shareware For the ASP's purposes, "shareware" is software that meets the following general criteria:

- It is a "complete" program, i.e., it performs all of the major functions normally expected of a program of its type, unlike a "commercial demo" which normally has a major function disabled. (The distinction is sometimes a judgment call, and the ASP has a procedure for arriving at such a judgment if necessary.)
- It is copyrighted (as opposed to uncopyrighted software which is "public domain").
- It may be copied for others to try out, subject to copying restrictions which the author may or may not choose to require.
- Registration fees may be required from the user as a condition of continued use of the program beyond a trial-usage period. Not requiring such a fee or requiring fees only from specific types of users, such as businesses and government, but not individuals, does not disqualify a program from being considered "shareware."
- Compliance with specified standards may be required from anyone copying the program for a fee or in conjunction with any business enterprise.

Membership criteria Membership is open to programmers who are authors of at least one "nontrivial" program (in the judgment of a Membership Committee) which is currently marketed and supported as shareware, who agree to abide by standards adopted by the association, and whose membership, in the judgment of the Membership Committee, will not be detrimental to the goals or reputation of the ASP.

Access to CompuServe is not required, but it is anticipated that this is where much of the decision-making process will take place because of relative ease of access. We encourage those who do not wish to use Compu-Serve or cannot get access to it to join the ASP anyway. Communication will also be accomplished via newsletters and possibly by other means.

ASP membership requirements These requirements are followed by all members of the ASP. When accepted as a member you will be required to abide by them.

These requirements apply to ALL programs you produce which are distributed as shareware (even if the ASP name or the word shareware are not used). By applying, you are confirming that all your shareware programs meet these requirements. The one program you submit is evaluated for the non-triviality test (which only applies to that program) and standards of professionalism (which apply to all programs).

The following are the general standards that ALL ASP authors (full members) have agreed to follow. Each was passed by at least a 2/3 vote of those members voting and is binding on all authors. They consist of a support policy, a policy on payments, a policy on no-crippled software, an ombudsman policy, and some miscellaneous items.

ASP software support policy

1. All ASP members' shareware products must provide support (included in the purchase price) for a minimum of three months from the date of registration. If the support is by telephone, there may be a limitation on BOTH the total connect time and the period after purchase during which it is available without additional cost, so long as the connect time is at least 30 minutes during the required three months. Support may be provided for a fee after this initial period has elapsed. The support policy must be clearly stated in the shareware documentation.

2. Support during the initial period may be one or more of the following:

   ~ mail support
   ~ telephone support (if this is the only support provided, at a minimum, an answering machine must be available 4 hours per day; this support may be limited to thirty minutes of connect time at the option of the author)
   ~ for communications products, or ones associated with a communications product by a BBS or major communications service
   ~ by any alternate method approved by the Board of Directors by a two-thirds vote (of those directors voting)

3. The minimum level of support required by this policy involves answering questions and fixing serious bugs during the minimum three-month period. For problems involving a specific hardware or software environment or feature, the author may choose not to

modify the program. In that case, if the report is within three months after purchase, then the author shall offer to refund the user's purchase price.

4. Any money sent to an author to register an unsupported product shall be promptly returned with an explanation that the product in question is no longer supported.

5. Known incompatibility with other software or hardware and major or unusual program limitations are noted in the documentation that comes with the shareware (evaluation) program.

ASP registration payment policy

1. The documentation must clearly describe how to register the product and what goods and/or services the user will receive for registering.
2. Fees must be expressed in fixed monetary amounts. Voluntary payments or contributions may not be solicited, although phrasing such as "if you use and like this product, please register" is allowed.
3. Multiple levels of registration may be set, as long as each level individually satisfies the above two requirements.

ASP policy on no crippling The principle behind shareware is "try before you buy." ASP believes that users have a right to try a fully functioning shareware program in their computing environment. Accordingly, ASP authors agree that:

1. The executable files (and/or items linked in with executables) in their shareware and registered versions will be the same (with the exceptions noted below).
2. All the program's features will be fully documented.
3. Registration encouragement procedures which, in the judgment of the Board, are either unreasonable or unprofessional are not allowed.

Exceptions to a strict interpretation of this policy are as follows:

- To save disk space, tutorial and additional explanatory material may be left out of the shareware documentation.
- The shareware version may have registration encouragement procedures absent from the registered version (or which can be disabled with a code only provided to registered users). The term "registration encouragement procedure" means a method for alerting users of their duty to register the program. Permitting registration encouragement procedures is not to be construed as a means of avoiding the anti-crippling requirements.

Specific ASP guidelines for registration reminder screens Registration reminder screens should:

- Be displayed no more than twice each time the program runs (or twice per day for long-running programs such as TSR's).
- Not require more than two keystrokes to bypass.
- Not have a forced minimum display time of more than three seconds. In other words, the RRS itself should not take control of the computer away from the user for more than three seconds.

Practices such as creating undocumented hidden files or printing a registration form without the user's knowledge or consent are prohibited. It is NOT necessary to have any of the above—a simple "Strike Any Key To Continue" is the least objectional to the user.

The registered version may include sample files not included in the shareware version.

If source code is offered with the registered version, it may be withheld from the shareware version.

The author may provide two shareware versions: one a small version which the author designates as the distributed version in normal circumstances (e.g., language tools in C only available in one model) so long as the full shareware version is available from some public source (possibly for a small distribution fee) and may be copied for trial purposes. The small version's documentation must clearly describe how users may obtain the full shareware version.

The author may provide an enhanced retail version of the program so long as it is not (in the opinion of 60% of the Board of Directors) merely an attempt to circumvent the no-crippling policy.

Registered users may be provided with bonus utilities unrelated to (and which do not change) the basic functionality of the program.

Registered users may be given utilities that provide a convenience but which are not essential.

Exceptions are approved by the ASP Board of Directors by a 60% vote (of those voting).

ASP ombudsman policy

1. The board shall set up the office of Ombudsman and appoint someone to that position. The Ombudsman's sole role shall be to mediate disputes between ASP members and their customers. The Ombudsman shall report to the board situations where he feels board action or knowledge is appropriate.
2. All ASP members and vendor associate members are required to cooperate with the Ombudsman when approached by him/her.
3. The shareware version of any shareware program produced by ASP author members must contain the following text as part of some

file on the disk. (The shareware version means the one intended for trial use.)

This program is produced by a member of the Association of Shareware Professionals (ASP). ASP wants to make sure that the shareware principle works for you. If you are unable to resolve a shareware-related problem with an ASP member by contacting the member directly, ASP may be able to help. The ASP Ombudsman can help you resolve a dispute or problem with an ASP member, but does not provide technical support for members' products. Please write to the ASP Ombudsman at 545 Grover Road, Muskegon, MI 49442 or send a CompuServe message via CompuServe Mail to ASP Ombudsman 70007,3536.

4. Inclusion of Ombudsman statement.
   a. Versions of ASP shareware sent to users when they register with the author or his direct agent shall also have the Ombudsman statement quoted in point #3, but these statements may be in a written form included in the registration package.
   b. Packages of the registered version (essentially identical to those sent to registered shareware users) intended for sale in retail establishments or primarily retail mail-order firms need not have an Ombudsman statement included. However, if the version contains any reference to shareware, it must also contain the Ombudsman statement.
   c. Members are free to include the Ombudsman statement in printed documentation, ads, and other mailings if they wish.
5. The first sentence may be replaced by "<Member's name> is a member of the Association of Shareware Professionals (ASP)." If a member's company qualifies under the company name policy, the company name may be used instead of <member's name>.
6. ASP-approved vendors must include the following statement with their catalogs and newsletters and are encouraged to include it with all disks sold:

Company X is an approved vendor and associate member of the Association of Shareware Professionals (ASP). ASP wants to make sure that the shareware principle works for you. If you are unable to resolve a shareware-related problem with an ASP member by contacting the member directly, ASP may be able to help. The ASP Ombudsman can help you resolve a dispute or problem with an ASP member, but does not provide technical support for members' products. Please write to the ASP Ombudsman at 545 Grover Road, Muskegon, MI 49442 or send a CompuServe message via CompuServe Mail to ASP Ombudsman 70007,3536.

7. The Ombudsman statement may not be hidden in a file or other manner which 60% of the Board of Directors regards as obscure.

ASP miscellaneous standards A program should be thoroughly tested by the author and should not be harmful to other files or hardware if used properly. Any discussion of the shareware concept and of registration requirements is done in a professional and positive manner.

The program's author will respond to people who send registration payments, as promised in the program's documentation. At a minimum, the author will acknowledge receipt of all payments.

The author will keep the ASP apprised of changes in his mailing address and of any changes in the status of his programs.

Membership dues The ASP has annual membership dues. First year dues are currently $50 per year, prorated from the quarter the applicant is accepted for membership. Subsequent yearly dues are currently $75. The $50 dues check must be sent in with your application.

Mailing-list option The ASP intends to provide mailing lists to outsiders. The mailing list, provided as labels and not in electronic form, shall be provided by whomever is keeping the official ASP membership list (currently the Secretary). The list shall consist solely of names and addresses and not phone numbers. Members shall have the option of being included in the mailing list or not as follows:

Your name will be included on this list UNLESS you indicate that you do not want it included by checking the box on the application.

At any time, any member may change their "include/exclude status" by notifying the keeper of the list in writing or via Easyplex.

How to apply for membership Three easy steps to apply for membership in the ASP are as follows:

1. Read and understand the above guidelines. If you are in compliance with the guidelines, then you may apply for membership. ALL of your shareware programs must comply with the ASP requirements, not just the submitted program.
2. Fill out the application below and mail it together with a copy of the program you elect to use as your submission for review. You must preprint any on-disk .DOC files to assist in a speedy review process and include this with the submission. It is also required that you complete the form below, answering ALL QUESTIONS. To save you time, the file APPLIC.TXT has been placed on this disk and is the actual application form shown at the end of this file. Place just the filled-out APPLIC.TXT on a separate disk to send in with your signed paper copy of the application. You may send the application form on CompuServe to the ASP Executive Director and eliminate the additional disk if desired. However, if you elect to

submit the application via CompuServe, the program submission package must be mailed or shipped within five days of the electronic filing of the application form. Place just the filled-out APPLIC.TXT on a separate disk to send in with your signed paper copy of the application.

In brief, your application will consist of:

a. One copy of the application form printed, dated, and signed.
b. A $50 check in USA dollars drawn on a USA bank.
c. Your on disk .DOC files preprinted.
d. Your program on disk for review.
e. If you noted on the application that the shareware version and registered version are different, you must also include a copy of the registered package.
f. The completed application form on disk with the disk labeled "APPLICATION FORM". (May be sent on CompuServe via Email if desired.)

3. Last but not least, if you have a CompuServe account listed, check your Email regularly for messages from the ASP Membership Coordinator.

The ASP membership application The following is a reprint of the ASP membership application (the APPLIC.TXT file mentioned earlier). It is provided here to give you a feel for what the application is like. If you are interested in joining the ASP, please send for the current application.

To apply for membership in the ASP, fill out the following form following the above instructions and send it to:

Executive Director
Association of Shareware Professionals
545 Grover Rd.
Muskegon, MI 49442 – 9427

or Email on CompuServe just the following completed form to:

ASP Executive Director [72050,1433]

The initial $50 payment is for the first year's dues. The year starts with the date your application is received at the ASP and ends on December 31st of the same year. If you are approved, any unused full-quarter amounts ($12.50 per quarter) will be credited to the next year's dues. If your application is not accepted, all but a $15 processing fee will be returned to you.

Email of the initial application will be accepted. The signed form must be included in the review package and received within one week of the Email application. When Emailing, please transmit only the part of the form following this line of dashes.

ASP Membership Application

(Please do not modify the format of the following block of info.)

Your Name .... _____ (30 characters)

Company Name .... _____ (30)

Street Address .... _____ (30)

P.O. Box .... _____ (20)

City .... _____ (20)

State, Ctry, Zip .... _____, _____ _____ (2, 15, 10)

Phone, day .... _____ (14)

Phone, evenings .... _____ (14)

CIS PPN .... _____ (10)

MCI & Other .... _____ (20)

If you list a CIS PPN, the Membership Coordinator and Committee may contact you via EPLEX—Please check your EPLEX regularly between the time you apply and your application process is complete.

If membership is approved, members normally have their name and program listed for CompuServe. This is limited to 24 characters and normally would appear as such: John Doe (Your Program)

How do you wish your listing to appear?

CIS Name/Program. _____

ASP provides mailing lists to outsiders such as disk vendors. Your name will be included on this list unless you indicate that you do not want it included by checking this box:

I do not wish to be included on the external mailing list [   ]

If you have more than one shareware program, please provide the following information for your "best" shareware program. (This information is for the purpose of determining if the criteria of a "nontrivial, non-demo program" have been met.)

Program name ......

Shareware price ......

Type of program ......

Where a copy of the program may be obtained for review: (e.g., CompuServe Forum, BBS name and phone number, by mail, etc.)

Major program features and capacities (limits): (e.g., for a database program, how many fields, records, etc. are allowed; for an editor, how many lines. Add as many lines of text as necessary at this point to completely describe your software.

Does the "registered version" have features or additional documentation which the "freely distributed version" does not?
(Y/N) _____ Check Y or N.

If Yes, add as many lines of text as you need at this point to COMPLETELY describe the differences.

Membership requires that you understand and agree to the following:

I _____ certify

- that the above information is correct;
- that I will abide by the standards of the ASP;
- that if I should ever decide to no longer abide by those standards or by new standards which the ASP may adopt in the future, I will cancel my membership immediately;
- that the ASP may cancel your membership using criteria and procedures specified in the bylaws; and
- that upon cancellation of membership by either party, I will discontinue using any materials. logos, claims of membership, or other benefits which are intended solely for members of the ASP.

Signed, _____ Date _____

The Association of Shareware Authors (ASA)

If you live in the United Kingdom, the counterpart to the ASP is the Association of Shareware Authors—UK (ASA-UK). The ASA-UK has essentially the same goals as the ASP except that it is dedicated to raising the quality and quantity of shareware orginating in the U.K.

The goals of the ASA-UK include:

- Setting standards for product quality, support, and documentation for shareware distributed by its members. ASA-UK members must document all of the software's functions, the author must acknowledge all registrations within 21 days, and the author must provide support for the registered versions they sell.
- Establish a Code of Conduct for shareware authors which specifies, amongst other things, that shareware distributed by its members will not be crippled.
- Establish standards for disk distributors that require distributors who are members of ASA-UK to clearly explain the nature of shareware in their catalogs and advertising.

To contact the ASA-UK for additional information or for a membership application write to:

ASA-UK
P.O. Box 26
Bracknell
Berkshire
RG12 4WA

Other software associations

I also recommend that you join other associations that may help you make useful business contacts or learn more about software publishing. If there is a software association in your state, you will find it very helpful to join that group. Only a few states have software associations at this time. These are:

California
Software Entrepreneur's Forum
P. O. Box 61031
Palo Alto, CA 94306
(415) 854-7219

Georgia
Southeastern Software Assoc.
P. O. Box 467190
Atlanta, GA 30346
(404) 458-3835

Illinois
Illinois Software Assoc.
c/o Richard A. Reck, President
KPMG Peat Marwick
303 E. Wacker Dr.
Chicago, IL 60601
(312) 938-5052
(312) 938-0449 (fax)

Massachusetts
Massachusetts Computer Software Council
581 Boylston St.
Boston, MA 02116
(617) 437-0600
(617) 437-6297 (fax)

Minnesota

Minnesota Software Assoc.
c/o Tom Kolbo, President
P. O. Box 14965
Minneapolis, MN 55414
(612) 331-8844

New Mexico

Software Entrepreneurs and Developers Assoc.
c/o Karl Smith, President
3825 Academy Pkwy. South, NE
Albuquerque, NM 87109
(505) 344-8891

Oregon

Software Asso.of Oregon
Ken Maddox, Executive Director
1600 NW Compton Dr., Suite 345
Beaverton, OR 97006
(503) 690-1395

Washington

Washington Software Assoc.
18804 North Creek Pkwy., Suite 112
Bothell, WA 98011
(206) 483-3323
(206) 485-8475 (fax)

14
Software you can use

This chapter looks at some software that you might find useful in running your business. I have tried to focus on programs that are helpful in running a software business instead of programming tools and utilities. In future editions of this book, I hope to expand this section to include new programs and updates of existing software. (Yes, I hope this book will have updates, just as software does. After all, the software reviewed here will change and I will need to keep the reviews up to date.)

I am very interested in your thoughts and comments on the shareware programs you use—or would use if they were available through shareware. I encourage you to write to me. Please feel free to write not only comments about this section, but also comments regarding anything I have written in this book. My address is given elsewhere, but I will provide it again here:

Steve Hudgik
c/o HCP Services, Inc.
P.O. Box 974
Tualatin, OR 97062
CIS 71450,254

Shareware recommended by other authors

My survey of shareware authors asked them to list both their favorite shareware programs and their favorite retail software. The results of both of those questions are summarized in this chapter. I will start with the list of authors' favorite shareware.

I use the term "mention" here and in chapter 15, which provides a summary of all the results from my surveys. A "mention" is when the answer to a survey question mentions the specific name of something. For example, in response to the question: "What shareware programs have you found useful in your shareware business?", one author responded with TAPCIS and Procomm. This is counted as two mentions because two programs were mentioned. If a second author responded by writing in TAPCIS, PKzip, and QEdit, then there would be a total of five mentions, two of which were for TAPCIS.

Survey results

The following list is arranged with the program most often mentioned at the top of the list. The number of mentions each program received is listed to the right of the program name. The column on the far right shows the percentage of times this program was mentioned. I apologize if I have misspelled a program name or incorrectly shown a trademark. I have done my best to find the correct spellings, but in most cases, I copied the program name exactly the way it was written on the survey form. Please feel free to write and correct me.

This listing shows the shareware programs that shareware authors said they used. There were a total of 240 mentions.

PKzip	36	15%
PC Write:	15	6%
Procomm	14	6%
PC File	13	5%
List	13	5%
QEdit	12	5%
Telix	7	3%
TAPCIS	7	3%
CopyQM	7	3%
LHARC	4	2%
4DOS	4	2%
QModem	3	1%
As-Easy-As	3	1%
4PRINT	3	1%
Windowboss	2	1%
RBBS-PC	2	1%
Operator	2	1%
Galaxy	2	1%
Grab Plus	2	1%
Flue Shot	2	1%
Telemate	2	1%
Can't Read Handwriting	2	1%
dbf-DOC	1	
Zipkey	1	
ZIP	1	

Window Boss	1
WHEREIS	1
VPIC	1
VDE Editor	1
ULTRA UTILITIES	1
Turbo Copy	1
Thedraw	1
The Rock Utilities	1
TextDraw	1
Tapmark	1
TXT2COM	1
TP&ASM	1
ShareSpell	1
SWAPDOS	1
SST	1
SHEZ	1
SCAN	1
READ&RUN	1
Quanalyst	1
QModem	1
QMail	1
Q Cache	1
Puma	1
Protocol	1
Present	1
PolyCopy	1
Point & Shoot Home Mgr	1
Point & Shoot Backup	1
Point & Shoot	1
Phoenix Word Processing	1
Penpal	1
Pak	1
PICEM	1
PCED	1
PC-BROWSE	1
PC Type	1
PC Forms	1
PC Fast Type	1
P4UP	1
Operator	1
Mass Appeal	1
Litecomm	1
LabelMagic	1
LZHarc	1
LZE Shell	1

BITIXZ	1
Index	1
Imprint	1
HyperHelper	1
Hexedit	1
HDM IV	1
Grab+	1
GT Power	1
Format Master	1
Flu-shot	1
Fast Invoice Writer	1
Fast Copy	1
FANSI-CONSOLE	1
F	1
Extended Batch Lang.	1
EZ Spread	1
EZ Copy-Lite	1
EIS BBS	1
Dupdsk	1
Dup	1
Doorway	1
DiskDup	1
DISK	1
DSZ	1
Checkup	1
CUT-EM	1
CLEAN	1
CHASM	1
Boot.SYS	1
Autocon	1
AutoMenu	1
Area Code	1
Address Partner	1
ASC2COM	1
ARC512	1

In addition to asking authors to list the shareware they used, I also asked them to send me the shareware version of any software they publish that other authors might find useful. I was surprised at how few disks I received. I was also surprised that most of the disks that authors did send were not things useful for running a business. I received games, Bible-study software, investment software, and other programs that are certainly very useful, but were not specifically things a shareware publishing business could use. What I was hoping to receive were disk copying and formatting software, communications software, invoicing software, and other small-business software.

I am shocked! As an author, anytime that you have the opportunity to send a disk to someone that might review your program—*send them a disk!* Do not pass up an opportunity for free publicity. For example, someone that has gotten a lot of free publicity is Scott Miller. Scott is the most successful shareware publisher of game software. Here is what he said in my telephone interview:

> *Exposure is important. Authors need to send their disks out to magazines. If I see a writer who is reviewing a shareware program or product similar to mine, the first thing I do is that night I'll send that person a letter with my program. If you do that, it really helps. It's like a blitz approach. If you blitz everyone, one or two will come through and write about your software. You've got to do the marketing. If you don't do the marketing, you won't get the exposure.*

If you have a program other authors can use in their business, please send me a copy. And by the way, when you send copies of your shareware to reviewers, include a printed copy of the documentation. When I started receiving a flood of disks after the first edition of this book, I found that I was much more inclined to look at programs that came with the documentation already printed. I would also like to hear from you if you have any comments that you would like to make about shareware you use or have tried to use. Please send me a note and tell me about your experiences.

When reviewing software, I am somewhat slow and thorough. I like to test the software I review by using it in my shareware business for a month or two. This provides me with a chance to get to know how well the software works under "live" conditions. Less than 20% of the programs that I looked at survived more than a day or two. In a minute, I will list the best and most useful of the surviving 20%.

What were some of the deficiencies that placed software in the group of 80% that almost immediately were rejected? First was crippled shareware. I always started by reviewing the shareware version of a program. If it was crippled, it was rejected. The second most frequent cause for software to be rejected was inadequate documentation. I was surprised by the number of programs that did not include even enough information to allow me to get started. The third most frequent cause was software that did not run on all the machines used for testing. All software was tested on a 386 VGA machine, 8088 composite color, 8088 CGA color, 8088 monochrome, and 8088 LCD portable. I used a Panasonic KX-P1091i, Epson FX, and Hewlett-Packard LaserJet IIP for testing the printing capabilities of software.

In reading my reviews, please keep in mind that, unlike magazine reviews which might be published within four or five months of when the software is reviewed, there might be a year or more between when I looked at the software and when you read the review. Problems that I mention in a review might be fixed by the time you read the review. That is why I recommend shareware! If you see something interesting, pick up a shareware copy and try it for yourself.

I do recommend all of the software reviewed here as being worth looking at. If I did not feel a program was worthwhile, it did not get reviewed. There are also many worthwhile programs that did not get reviewed. There are many programs I have not yet seen. I still have a stack of shareware here that I have only looked at briefly. I hope to be reviewing these programs in future magazine articles or possibly in a newsletter I might publish.

There are some types of software you will not see reviewed here. It is not because there was not any good software in a particular category. In many cases, there is too much good software. Probably the best examples of this are hard-disk menu/DOS-shell programs. In the past three months, I have received over 20 hard-disk menu/DOS-shell programs. I have looked at a few and several are very good. However, I just have not had time to test most of them. With software such as this, it is easy for you to find a good program, and the differences which favor one program over another are highly dependent upon personal tastes. So, try a few until you find the one you like. In the following reviews, I will be focusing on software that provides the biggest "bang for the buck" toward improving your productivity.

Shareware reviews

Fast Invoice Writer V4.7 (shareware)
H&P Software
218 Newman Ave.
Pueblo, CO 81005
(719) 561-0810
Registration: $39.95

If you are running a business, you need to print invoices both for your own records and as receipts for your customers. Fast Invoice Writer is the software that handles that task with ease.

I was immediately pleased with Fast Invoice Writer because I was able to get it running in just a few minutes. The 20-page manual is complete and easy to read. Once I figured out that the word "sheet" meant "invoice," I found the prompts on the main screen to be easy to understand. Figure 14-1 shows the Fast Invoice Writer main screen. Selecting "New Sheet" allows you to start a new invoice. "Edit Sheet" lets you modify the invoice. The reference to "MXL" is related to another program called Multifile-XL, which is a mailing-list manager.

You start using Fast Invoice Writer by going through an initial setup that enters your company's name and address, plus any customization you wish to include. For example, you can automatically include a set percentage for sales tax or print a customized message with, for example, your payment terms. Once customization is complete, you can start making out an invoice by selecting the "New Sheet" option.

```
INVOICE No.: 1001            Lines Available: 15         03-07-1991

  ┌─────────────────────────────────────────────────────────────────┐
  │  New Sheet                    MXL Not Being Used  CUST.COUNT: 0   │
  │  Print Sheet                  MXL Not Being Used                  │
  │  Edit Sheet                   Reset Serial No.                    │
  │  Add Item                     Labels and Insert                   │
  │  Down Pmt/Deposit             Cashbook Not Used                   │
  ├─────────────────────────────────────────────────────────────────┤
  │  F1 Help   Q Quit   F3 Clear Sheet    F4 Change Date  F5 Setup  F6 Dir. │
  ├─────────────────────────────────────────────────────────────────┤
  │  JOHN M. DOE                                                      │
  │  1234 Main Street                                                 │
  │  My City, State  00000                                           │
  │  SALE: CREDIT CARD                              RE: ORDER         │
  └─────────────────────────────────────────────────────────────────┘
              [F8] Load Data     Save Data [F9]
            [ALT S] Save to Customer File [ALT G] Get Customer Name
```

14-1 This shows the Main menu screen for *Fast Invoice Writer*. With the word "sheet" trans-
lated to mean "invoice" this software becomes easy to use.

To make out an invoice, the software will step you through a series of
prompts that ask for the: ship to name and address, item description,
quantity, unit price, and other key information. Once the first item is
entered, you can add the next one or exit to the editor. When all the items
are entered, you are given a chance to edit the invoice before printing it.

The printed invoice is clean and professional-looking. The customer's
name and address are positioned so that they will show in the window of a
#10 window envelope. You can also print a separate cut-and-paste address
label and an insert for a #10 window envelope, if you wish.

After an invoice is printed, push Alt–S to save it. A nice feature that I
especially appreciated is that a customer's name and address can be saved
and called back from an address book for use in another invoice. I also like
the way a new invoice is started. The new invoice can be based on the information entered in the previous one. You can reuse the customer name and
address or the information about the product(s) shipped. This can save
you a lot of time because you will not have to type the description and
price of your software over and over as you process 20 to 30 orders a day.

I like to throw unexpected keystrokes at software just to see what it
does. I was able to put Fast Invoice Writer into an error condition, but it
never caused a problem. The software recovered from errors with no problems.

If you run a consulting business in addition to your shareware business, a nice feature provided by Fast Invoice Writer is that you can post the
information you type on an invoice to a statement file. The statement
allows you to keep track of the balance forwarded, charges during the past
month, payments, and other information. All of this information is automatically added to the statement when you print an invoice.

Resident-TaskManager V2.1 (shareware)
WetZoft Applications
788 Martin Ct. West
Severn, MD 21144-2213
(301) 969-9385
CIS 75166,3200
Registration: $30

I used to have a problem. When a user called to request a copy of my software catalog, I would write his name and address on an index card. When a user called to report a problem, I would promise to fix it and put his name and address on an index card. When a user called to register one of my programs, I would write the information on an index card. Then, I would become deeply involved in solving a programming problem and I would forget about the rest of the world. The index cards would slowly merge into a growing pile of notes, reference books, and program listings and were soon lost and forgotten. Not until a few days later, or sometimes a week later, I would clean my desk and, one by one, my index cards would emerge. Each with a message about something that I might or might not have already done.

If you are going to be successful in running your business, you have to be professional. Being professional means not losing phone messages. Staying in business means you cannot misplace customers' orders. And misplacing customers' orders, even temporarily, is not a professional way to run a business.

The solution to the problem is Resident-TaskManager (RTM), published by WetZoft Applications. RTM creates and organizes to-do lists, notes, appointments, and project schedules. What is particularly nice about RTM is that it is quick and easy to use. I find the simplicity and ease of use of paper and pencil to be difficult to beat, but once I tried RTM I was hooked. My registration payment for this software was in the mail.

Resident-TaskManager can be loaded as a normal DOS program or as a memory-resident TSR. When run as a TSR, it only uses about 6K of memory. I run very few other TSRs on my computer, with my primary TSR being a keyboard buffer that tends to lock up the computer whenever any other TSR is loaded. RTM happily co-existed with my keyboard buffer. I also found RTM to be very well behaved in how it treated the primary program I was using. For example, it does not pop up during critical operations, such as when the hard disk is being accessed.

Once RTM is loaded as a TSR, you push Alt – T to pop it up. Figure 14-2 shows the main RTM screen with my to-do list. Pushing F10 displays a menu bar across the top of the screen. The menu provides selections from drop-down menus. But, you can also directly use the main functions without going through the menus. For example, a new item can be entered simply by pushing the letter ''A'' and typing in the information about the

```
Resident-TaskManager 2.11  Using: D:\RTM\RTM.DAT          08/22/91  02:41:23 pm
= Task ================================= Project =Date Due==Left=Pri=
Outline User's Manual for GET ORGANIZED! Sftwr.  NEW SFTR   08/20 Tue   -2  B
Return Mark Johnson's call                       BUS        08/22 Thu    0  A
Run errands                                      BUS/PER    08/22 Thu    0  A
USER SUPPORT - answer mail                       SUPPORT    08/22 Thu    0  A
USER SUPPORT - return Carla Smith's call         SUPPORT    08/22 Thu    0  A
Clean garage                                     PERSONAL   08/24 Sat    2  C
Send new ad copy to Goldmine Magazine            MARKETING  08/25 Sun    3  A
Complete GET ORGANIZED! user's manual            NEW SFTR   08/26 Mon    4  A
Arrange for babysitter for 8/30 (fri)            PERSONAL   08/26 Mon    4  B
Send out GET ORGANIZED! beta test versions       NEW SFTR   08/27 Tue    5  A
Check on status of new catalog (with FRANK)      MARKETING  08/29 Thu    7  A
CLEAN FILTERS IN FURNACE                          PERSONAL   09/02 Mon   11  C
Send new catalog to be proof read                MARKETING  09/03 Tue   12  A
Complete press release for GET ORGANIZED! Softwr NEW SFTR   09/04 Wed   13  A
================================ 3 of  14 =================================
= ↓ Attached Description ↓ ================================================
1. Shipping bags at ARVEY's (2 cases, #1 Jet Pack)
2. Pick up mail
3. Blank disks at KAO
4. Groceries: milk, donuts, cheetos, ice cream, chips & snacks
5. Deposit VISA receipts

F1-Help  F10-Menu  A)dd  M)od  D)el  Q)uit  Screen: ↑↓ PgUp PgDn  Dates: →← C
```

14-2 This is the main *RTM* screen. It shows fourteen scheduled tasks, one of which is two days late. The "run errands" task is currently highlighted and displays its attached description in the box on the lower half of the screen.

task. You can enter the "task" name, due date, priority, project name, and a five-line description. Push F2 and the information is immediately stored and displayed in sorted order.

RTM automatically provides multiple-level sorting based on the criteria you select. I find sorting my to-do list by due date and then by priority provides me with a listing that tells me at a glance what I need to do each day. You can also sort your list by different combinations of task name, priority, due date, and project name. If you need to change the sorted order, just push the letter "S" to pull down a Sort menu and select one of the eleven possible sorting combinations. Your tasks will instantly be rearranged based on the new sorting criteria.

If you fall behind, RTM flags items that are past due. When you pop up RTM, the past-due items cause your computer to beep and a box appears showing the number of past-due items. I found this feature to be a convenient, gentle reminder that there was something I needed to take care of.

When tasks are complete, they can easily be deleted from your list by pushing Alt–M. If you wish, deleted items can be saved in an audit file. This provides a handy record of what was completed. For example, the audit file is ideal for tracking software improvements and bug fixes. When you become aware of a bug, enter it in RTM as a task. When it is fixed, delete the task and save it in the audit file. You now have a complete and ongoing record of the changes you made. I also found the audit file useful for looking up phone messages that I thought I would never need again.

Resident-TaskManager has a short manual that is complete, but could use some improvement. Although I like short manuals, I would not complain about this one if it were made a little longer to include some examples. Yet, I was using RTM within 15 minutes and feeling fully comfortable after a day of use.

What I like the least about RTM is that it keeps reminding me of things I should have done several days ago. But, I guess that is why I entered them in RTM in the first place. I need a reminder every now and then or I will forget. And, if I wanted to, I could use RTM's editor to reschedule the past-due items for some date later in the future.

What I like best about RTM is that it is convenient and easy to use. Just pop it up whenever you need it. When I am talking on the phone, it does not matter what software I am using, I can pop up RTM and make notes as I talk. That is convenience. (It will not pop up over a graphics screen, though.) There are fancier note-taking programs with more features and capabilities, but the Resident TaskManager is a perfect fit. It is a program that makes your life easier and that is the type of software I like.

CopyQM V2.25 (shareware)
Sydex
P.O. Box 5700
Eugene, OR 97405
(503) 683-6033
(503) 683-1622 (fax)
Registration: $50 ($15 for personal use)

Even though you can use a bulk-duplicating service for most of your disk-copying needs, a good, fast disk-copying utility is handy to have. If you have discovered that disk-duplicating services can be expensive, a disk-duplicating utility you can use on your PC is just what you need. CopyQM might be that utility. CopyQM quickly formats, copies, and verifies multiple copies of a disk. It is fast and easy to use.

When I look at disk-copying utilities, I have four criteria the utility must meet.

1. It must be able to store an image file on a hard disk.
2. It must be able to copy 5¹/₄″ 360K and 1.2Mb disks, and 3¹/₂″ 720K and 1.44Mb disks.
3. It must be easy enough so that nontechnical people can use it.
4. Verification must be performed on all copies.

CopyQM meets and improves on these. For example, not only will it store an image file, but it stores the image in a compressed format. For most of my disks, 288K or less was used to store the image for a 360K disk. I can save the images of six disks in the space I would normally use for five. Although I am using a 100Mb hard drive, the additional space is important and welcomed.

CopyQM is command-line driven. The command words are simple, intuitive, and even somewhat humorous. For example, "SHUTUP" disables the audio warning tone. To make an image file, all you need to do is type the words RECORD=<filename>. To copy disks using the image file, you "playback" the recording you made by typing PLAYBACK=<filename> on the command line.

If you have someone working for you that has to be able to copy disks, CopyQM can shine brightly. Although CopyQM by itself is not a program a computer novice can quickly master, when combined with a menu system, it becomes easy to use. My hard-disk menu system, Your Menu, made a perfect front-end for CopyQM. I was able to set up a page of menu selections for making image files and a second page for copying disks. Once it was set up, my employees could easily select the disk they wanted to copy from the menu, enter the number of copies they needed, and then start feeding disks into the computer.

On the negative side, CopyQM does have one problem. When CopyQM is used on a computer with a TSR that includes a keyboard buffer, it might make bad copies. This problem can be serious because CopyQM might report a good copy has been made, but there will be nothing on the disk. In my testing, I found that this problem occurs at unpredictable times, making the copying process unreliable. The documentation does not provide any warning about using keyboard buffers. I was only able to determine that the keyboard buffer was the source of the problem when I called Sydex for support.

I like short user's manuals that get to the point. This is what you get with CopyQM. The 13-page manual is complete and allows you to start copying disks two to three minutes after the manual is printed. Everything you need to know is explained in simple, concise language.

When I was discussing shareware disk distributors, I said that identifying each distributor with a serial number will help you determine which distributors sell disks that result in registrations. CopyQM has the capability to put serial numbers on disks as it makes copies. This feature makes it easy for you to have a unique identification number for each distributor.

Although CopyQM does have some problems, it is excellent software. Since you can try shareware before you buy it, I recommend that you pick up a shareware copy of the latest version of CopyQM and try it for yourself.

TAPCIS V5.2 (shareware)
Support Group, Inc.
Lake Technology Park
P.O. Box 130
McHenry, MD 21541

(800) USA-GROUP
(301) 387-4500
(301) 387-7322 (fax)
CIS 74020,10
Registration: $79

If you use CompuServe, this software will save you money—lot's of it! There is no doubt that, once you learn to use TAPCIS, you can reduce your CompuServe bill by several orders of magnitude.

First, what is TAPCIS (The Access Program for the CompuServe Information Service)? It is software that automates most of what you do on CompuServe. If you have a modem, you should be using CompuServe, if for nothing else than to listen in on the ASP discussions in the ASP shareware forum (GO SHARE). With ordinary telecommunications software, you might spend an hour reading the ASP messages. With TAPCIS, and its ability to automatically retrieve new messages from any forum(s) and section(s), you will spend maybe three minutes on-line and then be able to read the messages off-line at your leisure.

Although I recommend TAPCIS as a must-have program, I do have one warning for you. I found TAPCIS difficult to learn. I blame this on the documentation. It is long (173 pages) and seems to wander around a lot without getting to the point of telling the user, in simple language, how to use the software. The main screen also keeps count of how many days it has been since you first booted TAPCIS, by displaying a warning message that says: "You are in the _____ day of a 21-day evaluation period." At the end of the 21-day period, two delay screens appear when you boot TAPCIS. They cannot be bypassed, and although they eventually time out and allow access to the software, the delay is so long that the software becomes essentially unusable. I recommend staying away from this type of registration "encouragement" as you'll probably lose more users who do not continue to use the software (and thus never register) than this "encouragement" gets you.

Because I first tried TAPCIS the day before I left for COMDEX, I was in the 12th day of the 21-day evaluation period on the second day I was using it! I found that very irritating. Software with messages like this and manuals that are difficult to understand usually end up in my trash bin. However, TAPCIS was highly recommended by several CompuServe users, so I continued working with it. It turned out to be worth the aggravation and extra effort.

Once you learn how to use TAPCIS and get it properly set up, it is easy to use. Figure 14-3 shows the main TAPCIS menu. Just push the letter "N," and TAPCIS goes on-line, sends any forum messages that you have written, picks up any new messages since you last visited that forum, and then logs off. Once off-line, you can read the forum messages by pushing the number associated with that forum (the forum number is shown in a list on the lower portion of the screen). The up/down cursor keys can be used to page through the messages. If you want to send a reply, just push the letter "R," type your reply, push F7 to exit (TAPCIS uses WordPerfect interface conventions), and then read the next message.

Based simply on the fact that it will save you money, TAPCIS is worth the time and effort required to learn how to use. It easily makes it onto my recommended buying list.

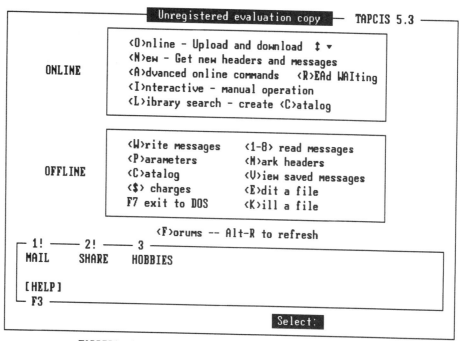

```
┌──────────────────── Unregistered evaluation copy ── TAPCIS 5.3 ──┐
│              ┌─────────────────────────────────────────────────┐ │
│              │ <O>nline - Upload and download ↕ ▾              │ │
│              │ <N>ew - Get new headers and messages            │ │
│   ONLINE     │ <A>dvanced online commands    <R>EAd WAIting    │ │
│              │ <I>nteractive - manual operation                │ │
│              │ <L>ibrary search - create <C>atalog             │ │
│              └─────────────────────────────────────────────────┘ │
│              ┌─────────────────────────────────────────────────┐ │
│              │ <W>rite messages      <1-8> read messages       │ │
│              │ <P>arameters          <M>ark headers            │ │
│   OFFLINE    │ <C>atalog             <V>iew saved messages     │ │
│              │ <$> charges           <E>dit a file             │ │
│              │ F7 exit to DOS        <K>ill a file             │ │
│              └─────────────────────────────────────────────────┘ │
│                  <F>orums -- Alt-R to refresh                     │
│   ┌─ 1! ──── 2! ──── 3 ─────────────────────────────────────────┐│
│   │ MAIL    SHARE    HOBBIES                                     ││
│   │                                                              ││
│   │ [HELP]                                                       ││
│   └─ F3 ─────────────────────────────────────────────────────────┘│
│                                              ┌─────────┐          │
│                                              │ Select: │          │
│                                              └─────────┘          │
└──────────────────────────────────────────────────────────────────┘
```

TAPCIS(tm) - Copyright (c) 1990, Support Group, Inc.

14-3 This is the main *TAPCIS* screen. Once *TAPCIS* has been set up, you just need to push the letter "N", for <N>ew, to automatically send all of the messages you have written and retrieve any new messages. The exclamation points next to the numbers 1 and 2 indicate that there are messages to be sent via Email (#1) and to the shareware forum (#2).

TextOut/5 (shareware)
CrossCourt Systems
1521 Greenview Ave.
East Lansing, MI 48823
(517) 332-4353
Registration: $20

I used to fight with WordPerfect, trying to get it to save a document as an ASCII file while retaining the document's formatting. I would always end up losing the margin settings and the text would all be shifted to the left. As a result, I had to do a lot of additional work to get my shareware manuals into a professional-looking form that could be included on a disk. TextOut/5 has solved that problem.

TextOut/5 converts WordPerfect 5.0 and 5.1 document files to ASCII and it preserves most aspects of page formatting, such as left margins, top margins, page breaks, and line spacing. It translates text, captions, footnotes, endnotes, and equations from graphics boxes. TextOut/5 also translates over forty of WordPerfect's special characters to ASCII (WordPerfect will translate 15). Overall, this is the ideal software to convert the WordPerfect file you used to create a printed manual to a file that can be used as the manual on a shareware disk.

The 12-page manual provided on the TextOut/5 shareware disk is clear and it gets to the point. The software is run from the DOS command line and is easy to use. This is not a program that you can use without reading the manual because there are many possible options when converting a file. However, because the manual gets right to the important information, you can easily begin using TextOut/5 five or six minutes after you load it on your hard disk.

CrossCourt Systems also publishes software to convert files from other word processing software such as IBM's DisplayWrite.

PowerBatch V1.4 (shareware)
Computing Systems Design, Inc.
P.O. Box 566484
Atlanta, GA 30356-6009
CIS 72701,155
Registration: $30

PowerBatch is a compiler for batch file "type" commands. I say batch file "type" because the current version does not compile standard DOS batch file commands, although these can be included in a compiled PowerBatch .EXE file. PowerBatch provides over forty commands that function only as part of a PowerBatch source file (they will not execute in a standard DOS batch file). In most cases, these PowerBatch commands are more powerful than similar commands in a DOS batch file, plus there are commands not available for use in a DOS batch file.

Any valid DOS executable command (.EXE and .COM), as well as any of the DOS intrinsic commands, can be included in a PowerBatch source file. The DOS commands will be "compiled" into an .EXE file created by PowerBatch. When the .EXE file is run, the DOS commands will be executed via a shell and the PowerBatch .EXE program will continue execution with the next compiled statement following each shell command. The result is a completely stand-alone .EXE file that executes without support modules.

The documentation supplied with PowerBatch is excellent. The 60-page indexed manual completely describes how to use the software in an easy-to-understand manner. Each command is explained and illustrated with a sample of commented source code.

PowerBatch provides several advantages over conventional batch files. First, the PowerBatch commands provide more functions and flexibility than the commands available in a conventional DOS batch file. This is particularly true for screen design. PowerBatch gives you control of the screen colors, has commands to draw boxes, automatically centers text, and can place text in specified locations anywhere on the screen. Figure 14-4 shows a screen created when installing PowerBatch.

```
┌─────────────────────────────────────────────────────────────┐
│                    Installation Program                      │
│                       POWERBATCH                             │
│                          by                                  │
│ Monday           Computing Systems Design, Inc.   05/06/1991 │
└─────────────────────────────────────────────────────────────┘

There are two groups of files on the PowerBatch installation disk. One
group contains the modules necessary to create PowerBatch programs and
one group contains documentation, examples, and informational files.

The modules necessary to create PowerBatch programs MUST be on your DOS
search path. The other files you may locate in a directory not on your
search path.

Enter the drive letter where the PowerBatch install modules are located




            ─┤ Press Ctrl-Break To Terminate The Install Process ├─
```

14-4 One of the installation screens for *PowerBatch* illustrates the flexibility and additional power this software provides. This two-color screen with boxes is easy to design using a *PowerBatch* batch file.

PowerBatch programs cannot be changed without making machine-code modifications. This means additional security for distributed batch files. If you have an installation batch file, you do not want users to tinker with it. Compiling it using PowerBatch will protect the file. However, this also has a down side. There have been many instances when I have had to look at and modify batch files in order to get software to install on my system. If the installation file is a PowerBatch file, I would not have been able to "fix" the installation procedure. So, if you compile your installation batch files, be sure you have considered every circumstance they can encounter during the installation of your software.

Also, PowerBatch programs can be created quickly because the Power-Batch command set is a very high-level language.

PowerBatch files will execute faster than conventional batch files. Conventional batch files are read one line at a time from the disk as they are executed. A PowerBatch file is completely loaded into memory and then executed. This provides another advantage if your program uses more than one disk. Using batch files to install software that comes on two disks usually means having identical batch files on both disks. With Power-Batch, you only need to put the installation "batch" file on the first disk.

Creating a PowerBatch source file is easy. Use a text editor to create an ASCII file, just as you would do to write a DOS batch file. Then use the compiler to create an executable file.

Some of the PowerBatch commands not available to DOS batch files include:

?CURRDIR—Retrieves the current drive and directory name from the system. This command can also be used to retrieve the current directory name for any drive.

?DIREXIST—Checks for the existence of a specified directory.

?DISKSPACE—Determines the total disk capacity and the total unused space on any specified drive.

?DRIVEEXIST—Checks to determine whether or not a specified drive exists.

?FILEEXIST—Checks to determine whether or not a specified file exists.

BOX1—Draws a box on the screen whose size, location, and color can be specified. Single-line, double-line, and large solid-line boxes are available.

CENTER—Automatically centers text on the screen.

CLEAR—Replaces the DOS CLS command and improves on it because the CLEAR command not only clears the screen, but new foreground and background colors can be specified.

CLEARBOX—Clears the screen within the interior of a box.

CLEARLINE—Clears a specified line.

READKEY—Reads a single keystroke from the keyboard and identifies keystrokes as either normal characters or special keys, such as the function keys, PgUp/PgDn, and cursor keys. The PowerBatch file can then be designed to branch and take various actions based on which key was pushed. Another command gets multiple characters from the keyboard.

As you can see from these few examples, PowerBatch provides much greater flexibility and power than a conventional DOS batch file. Power-Batch essentially provides a small programming language that allows you to quickly design .EXE files to replace many of your batch files.

4DOS (shareware)
J. P. Software
P.O. Box 1470
East Arlington, MA 02174
(617) 646-3975
(617) 646-0904 (fax)
CIS 75300,210
Registration: $50

This is a gem of a program and I am surprised it is not included with every computer sold. If Microsoft wants to provide a better version of DOS, they should license 4DOS to be included as a part of every version of DOS they sell.

With an introduction like that, what else is there to say? This is a useful program. 4DOS replaces the functions normally provided by COMMAND.COM. Once installed, 4DOS is totally transparent. All that you will notice is that your DOS commands have been enhanced and you now have over forty additional commands not provided by DOS.

There is so much in 4DOS that I can only cover a few of my more favorite features here. Figure 14-5 shows one of them. Figure 14-5 shows a listing of the files in my 4DOS directory. This is the listing you get when you type DIR at the DOS prompt. You might have noticed something different about this listing. PKUNZIP.EXE has a description attached to it. 4DOS allows you to include a description, of up to forty characters, for any file or directory. To add a description to a filename, all you need to do is type:

DESCRIBE [drive letter:][path]FILENAME "the description"

```
Volume in drive G is unlabeled
Directory of  G:\4DOS\*.*
 .              <DIR>      3-10-91   11:56
 ..             <DIR>      3-10-91   11:56
4DOS.DOC        344020     9-07-90    3:02
4DOS.ICO           766     9-07-90    3:02
4DOS.PIF           545     9-07-90    3:02
4DOSM.ICO          766     9-07-90    3:02
ALIASES           8164     9-07-90    3:02
COMPAT.DOC       70603     9-07-90    3:02
DOS.HLP         119826     9-07-90    3:02
HELP.EXE         45632     9-07-90    3:02
HELPCFG.EXE      15968     9-07-90    3:02
ORDER.FRM        21213     9-07-90    3:02
PKUNZIP.EXE      17931     9-07-90    3:02 Decompression program for ZIP files
README.DOC       18150     9-07-90    3:02
SHELL2E.COM       1212     9-07-90    3:02
SHELL2E.DOC       4718     9-07-90    3:02
SUPPORT.BBS        342     9-07-90    3:02
UPDATE30.DOC     40472     9-07-90    3:02
      749,568 bytes in 18 file(s)
      126,976 bytes free

G:\4DOS>
```

14-5 *4DOS* provides many features not available in DOS such as the ability to attach descriptions to filenames.

The description will stay with the file when you COPY, MOVE, RENAME, or ERASE it and it will be displayed anytime you type DIR. For people that lose track of files, this is a super feature.

I also like the 4DOS HISTORY feature. This feature keeps track of the commands that you have entered. You can move backward through a listing of previous commands by pushing the up arrow key. Pushing the down arrow key moves you through the more recently entered commands. You can immediately go to any previously entered command by typing the first few letters of the command and pushing the up arrow key. This feature is a great time saver when you need to re-execute the same, or a similar series of, commands several times.

Another great time saver is the LIST command. LIST replaces the DOS TYPE command for displaying ASCII text files. What is nice about LIST is that, unlike the TYPE command, you can use the cursor and PgUp/PgDn keys to move around in a document.

4DOS replaces the COMMAND.COM file that comes with all versions of MS-DOS and PC-DOS. It is an incredible program that provides all the capabilities normally provided by COMMAND.COM and does a better job. Plus, it provides a wide variety of functions not available in COMMAND .COM. For example, there is a FIND function that will search and find matches for any word or phrase you specify. You can also print a file from within LIST. This is exactly the type of feature you need if you are checking out shareware disks by looking at the documentation file.

I did find one area in which the DOS TYPE command is still useful. LIST will choke on any file that contains characters other than alphanumeric characters. For example, I regularly use TYPE to look at the dBASE-compatible indexes my database software creates. LIST was unable to display these files.

The 4DOS ALIAS feature is a unique and very useful feature. I try to automate my computer work as much as I can by writing batch files. However, there are times when loading an editor to write a batch file is too much effort. This is where the ALIAS feature comes into play.

An ALIAS is a new name for a command or combination of commands. For example, I could define the following ALIAS that, when "4D" is typed, would change disk drives, then change directories and list files in the 4DOS directory:

ALIAS 4D 'G: ^ CD \ 4DOS ^ DIR'

The one complaint I have is that the 4DOS error messages are more cryptic than DOS's. For example, when trying to rename a file to use a filename that already exists, you will get an "Access Denied" error. This is not very helpful in trying to figure out why you cannot rename the file.

4DOS has a good manual that is complete and easy to use. Although I had trouble understanding some of the explanations, lots of examples helped me get started with each 4DOS command. The manual is primarily arranged as a reference manual. Commands are listed in alphabetical order, allowing you to look up what you need, when you need it. A command summary at the front of the manual helps you determine which command you need.

Surprisingly, 4DOS requires less than 4K of memory for its resident portion. You will hardly know it is there.

FormatMaster V4.7 (shareware)
New-Ware
8050 Camino Kiosco
San Diego, CA 92122
(619) 455-6225
(619) 455-5226 (BBS)
Registration: $20, $30 for a TSR version

Formatting a disk should be quick, simple, and easy. FormatMaster is the software that makes formatting disks what it should be. John Newlin has written a top-notch disk-formatting program that easily beats DOS's FORMAT command.

FormatMaster can either be menu operated or run from the command line. Menu operation makes this program very easy to use. When you first boot FormatMaster, it will automatically configure itself for the drives in your computer. I tested it with several computers and it correctly detected the disk drives on all but one. My old Toshiba T-1100 has one internal 3 1/2-inch drive and an external 5 1/4-inch drive. FormatMaster saw both of these as 5 1/4-inch drives. Fortunately, this is not a problem. All I had to do was select the "Set Drive Table" option on the Main menu, and I was able to quickly set the correct drive configuration.

FormatMaster provides a variety of options. Figure 14-6 shows the Main menu. One of my favorite features is the ability to format a series of

```
Format and/or verify a 5¼" or 3½" floppy disk
```

```
──────── Main Menu ────────
  Format/Verify a Disk
  DOS Format/Verify
  Simultaneous Format/Verify
  Define Drive Table
  Enter DOS
  Transfer System         OFF
  Add Volume Label        ON
  cYcle Format            OFF
  Beeps                   ON
  Rapid Format            OFF
  800K Format             OFF
  Verify                  ON
  oNly Verify             OFF
  Check Disk
  Print Registration
  Quit to DOS
  @ Configure FM
```

14-6 The menu-driven user interface in *FormatMaster* makes this software a pleasure to use.

FormatMaster Shareware Evaluation Copy

disks and automatically add a volume label. What is nice about this feature is that the volume label can be used to put serial numbers on your disks. FormatMaster will automatically increase a number included as a part of the volume label by one for each disk it formats.

The formatting status screen is an excellent feature that keeps you informed about what is happening better than any other formatting software that I have seen. As shown at the bottom of the screen in FIG. 14-7, it provides both error and advisory messages. I tried using FormatMaster to format a variety of known bad disks and it correctly reported errors for all of them.

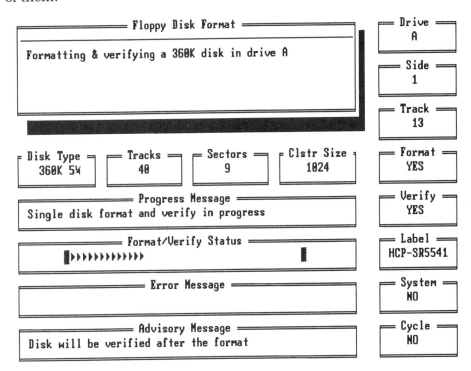

14-7   The *FormatMaster* status screen keeps you appraised of the selections you have made and the status of the formatting process.

Another feature I like about FormatMaster is its ability to perform repetitive formatting on any one or two floppy drives. This feature is referred to as "Cycle Format" on the Main menu. All you need to do is start FormatMaster and then feed it disks. It will format one after another and keep track of how many have been formatted.

I have always said that to have successful software, your software must include some extra or unique feature that the competition does not have. With the great features and smooth user interface provided by FormatMaster, it does not need to offer anything extra, but it does. The extra provided by FormatMaster can more than double the capacity of your 5¹/₄″ 360K disks. You can toggle into an 800K format mode and, if you are using high capacity 1.2Mb drive, format a 360K disk to use 80 tracks with 10 sectors per track. This provides a disk with an 800K capacity.

I do not recommend making 800K disks for distributing your software, because these disks might not work on all computers or with certain versions of DOS. However, this is an excellent way to squeeze a little more out of your machine. If your machine has a problem using 800K disks, FormatMaster includes a TSR that will enable your machine to format and use 700K disks. That is still almost double the capacity of the original disk.

I feel that with utility programs such as FormatMaster, you should be able to use the software in under fifteen minutes. I had no problem getting started in less time than that. FormatMaster is so easy to use that a manual of five or six pages would be all that is needed. The FormatMaster manual, at twenty pages, is longer than needed. It contains a lot of technical information and the first six pages are filled with legal terms, a discussion of shareware, and other information not related to using the software. However, if you skip over these pages, you will be up and running quickly.

Retail software

In looking to find software that you could use in your shareware business, I did not limit my search to just shareware. In my survey of shareware authors, many authors reported using lots of retail software because there was no equivalent available in shareware. This next list shows the retail software shareware authors said they use. There was a total of 192 mentions.

WordPerfect	17	9%
Microsoft QuickBasic	15	8%
Turbo Pascal	10	5%
Borland Turbo C	8	4%
Clipper	6	3%
Paradox	6	3%
Word	6	3%
dBASE	5	3%
FoxBase	5	3%
TurboPower OPro	5	3%
Borland Turbo C++	4	3%
Microsoft C	4	3%
Quattro	4	3%
Ventura Publisher	4	3%
Avery Label Pro	3	2%
Lotus 1-2-3	3	2%
PC Tools	3	2%
RBase	3	2%

WordStar	3	2%
Bascom 6.0	2	1%
Basic PDS 7.0	2	1%
Borland All	2	1%
Brief	2	1%
Couldn't read handwriting	2	1%
Crescent Software Libraries	2	1%
Page Maker	2	1%
Turbo Basic	2	1%
Ability	1	
Alpha Four dbms	1	
BROWSE	1	
Borland Pascal Tools	1	
Borland Turbo Assembler	1	
Computer Handholders Lib.	1	
DAC Easy Accounting	1	
Deskview	1	
Dr. Halo	1	
Epsilon	1	
Excel	1	
FastForms	1	
FastPak Mail	1	
Flash Up	1	
Fontasy	1	
FoxPro	1	
Goscript	1	
Hotshot	1	
Inset	1	
JPI Modula-2	1	
KEDIT	1	
Key Mailer	1	
M.E.I. Micro Marketing	1	
MKS Toolkit	1	
Meridian Ada-Vantage	1	
Microhelp Utilities	1	
Microsoft Assembler	1	
Microsoft Fortran	1	
Money Counts	1	
Multiplan	1	
Norton Utilities	1	
OPTASM	1	
PC Paint	1	
PCX Programmers Toolkit	1	
PDQ	1	
PFS Word Processing	1	
Paint Brush	1	

PeachText	1
Polylibrarian	1
ProBas	1
Prof. File	1
Prof. Write	1
Publish It!	1
Q&A	1
Quick C	1
Quicken	1
Quicksilver	1
Qume Presentations	1
SPRINT	1
So Mtn Sofwr Libraries	1
Soff Codel	1
Speed Screen	1
Sprint	1
Super Duper	1
SuperCalc	1
Turbo Assembler	1
Windows 3.0	1
Word For Windows	1
Works	1
ZipKey	1
dBMan	1
uLISP	1

Retail software reviews

Fast-Dup V2.3 (retail software)
LogiCom, Inc.
P.O. Box 27465
Lakewood, CO 80227
(303) 986-6651
Price: $39

As with the disk copying utility I reviewed in the shareware section of this chapter, Fast-Dup provides all of the features that I feel a good disk-copying utility must have: it stores an image file on a hard disk; it can copy all disk formats; it is fairly easy to use; and it verifies all copies.

I feel Fast-Dup offers an advantage over CopyQM in that it does not have problems working with TSRs and it correctly detected every bad disk I tried. Because I can count on Fast-Dup to make good copies and because it reliably rejects bad disks, it has become the disk-copying software I use every day. In other areas, CopyQM comes out ahead. For example, CopyQM compresses image files, saving disk space and, when combined with a menu system such as Your Menu, CopyQM is easier to use than

Fast-Dup. Unfortunately, having to combine CopyQM with a menu system results in a cost for CopyQM of $75, which is almost double Fast-Dup's $39.95 price.

What I would like to see is a disk-copying utility that combines the best of Fast-Dup and CopyQM and is menu operated. For now, however, I will stick with the one with the greater reliability and that is Fast-Dup.

Fast-Dup is menu operated. Figure 14-8 shows the main Fast-Dup menu. To copy a disk, you first make an image file by selecting "Image Files" on the main menu and then selecting "Generate Image File" and giving the image file a name. You can also copy a disk directly by specifying the drive that has the source disk.

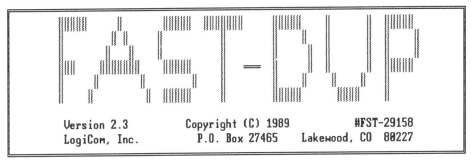

Version 2.3   Copyright (C) 1989   #FST-29158
LogiCom, Inc.   P.O. Box 27465   Lakewood, CO 80227

Image File Path: F:\MAIN\
      Source Drive: A   Options
Destination Drive: A   Verify: Data
Current Disk Type: Double Sided, 9 Sector (360K)   Format: On

1 - Change Source Drive   6 - Image Files
2 - Change Destination Drive   7 - Options
3 - Change Disk Type   8 - Begin Copying
4 - Change Image File Path   9 - Exit Program
5 - Turn Bell Off

                    Enter Choice:

14-8 *Fast-Dup's* Main menu allows you to quickly start copying disks. First, push number 1 and enter the name of the image file you want to use. Then push number 8 to start copying.

Once the image file is made, you specify the name of the image file to be used and select "Begin Copying" from the menu. The software will stay in the copying mode and provide a count of the number of copies made until ESC is pressed. If you have two drives, Fast-Dup will alternate between them, making the copying process even faster.

The one complaint I have is that you must remember the filenames that you have used for image files. The software does provide a way to look at a directory listing, but it is not convenient and, if you have a lot of disks, it can be difficult to remember which filename is used for a specific disk.

Although not fancy, the 27-page manual is complete and easy to read. I was able to quickly start using Fast-Dup with few problems.

Fast-Dup is the disk-duplicating software that I use everyday. Its menu-driven user interface makes it easy to use and the $39 price makes it an outstanding value. But, the key factor is that Fast-Dup provides quality disk duplication. When duplicating disks, anything less than 100% error-free copies is not acceptable. Fast-Dup provides that quality.

CompuServe's Information Manager V1.1S (retail software)

CompuServe Information Service
5000 Arlington Centre Blvd.
P.O. Box 20212
Columbus, OH 43220
Price: $24.95 (plus shipping)

In the shareware section, I discussed a program for accessing Compu-Serve. CompuServe publishes their own GUI-based program that makes accessing CompuServe easy. The program is called CompuServe's Information Manager (CIM). This program comes with a $15 CompuServe usage credit, making the effective cost of the software $10—a bargain that is hard to pass up.

CIM is, in many respects, the opposite of TAPCIS. It is very easy to use, but you will run up higher bills for connect-time charges. CIM places a GUI between the user and CompuServe. Figure 14-9 shows the overlapping menus used by CIM. To use CompuServe, all you need to do is to make selections from these pull-down windows. Unlike TAPCIS, which requires you to know where you want to go and what you want to do, CIM is an excellent program for browsing. For users new to CompuServe, CIM provides an easy-to-use interface that allows you to become productive almost immediately.

In many respects, CIM appears to be an unfinished program. Some of the menu selections are not available and it is missing features that are essential. For example, CIM allows you to quickly retrieve and send Email with minimal connect time. You can then read your Email off-line. However, if you want a hard copy of an Email message, there is no way to print it.

Another problem is that CIM continually dumps you out of the function you are working in and returns you to a blank screen. For example, when you compose an Email message and save it to your out-box, instead of staying in the message-writing function, you are returned to the main screen. To write a second message, you have to re-enter the mail system and select the "Create A Message" function again.

An essential feature missing from CIM is the ability to print your Email and forum messages. If you want a hard copy of a message, you cannot get it with CIM. I find this frustrating because, when someone sends me something important or interesting, I like to put a paper copy in my

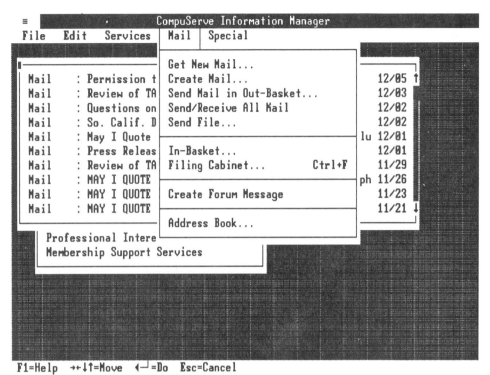

≡ · CompuServe Information Manager

File   Edit   Services   Mail │ Special

```
┌─────────────────────────┐ Get New Mail...                        ┌─────
│                         │ Create Mail...               12/05 ↑
│ Mail  : Permission t    │ Send Mail in Out-Basket...   12/03
│ Mail  : Review of TA    │ Send/Receive All Mail        12/02
│ Mail  : Questions on    │ Send File...                 12/02
│ Mail  : So. Calif. D    │                           lu 12/01
│ Mail  : May I Quote     │ In-Basket...                 12/01
│ Mail  : Press Releas    │ Filing Cabinet...    Ctrl+F  11/29
│ Mail  : Review of TA    │                           ph 11/26
│ Mail  : MAY I QUOTE     │ Create Forum Message         11/23
│ Mail  : MAY I QUOTE     │                              11/21 ↓
│ Mail  : MAY I QUOTE     │ Address Book...
│   ┌─────────────────────┘
│   Professional Intere
│   Membership Support Services
```

F1=Help →←↓↑=Move ◄─┘=Do Esc=Cancel

14-9 *CIM* uses overlapping pull-down menus which make accessing CompuServe easy.

files. CIM does provide an on-disk filing cabinet, but it is inconvenient to use. If the CIM filing cabinet stored messages as ASCII files, I would be happy because I would be able to print them using my word processor. However, these files include a lot of control characters which make the file unreadable. At least it was unreadable until I found pEDIT by Terry Muench. This program editor was able to read and print the CIM filing cabinet files. It would just be a lot nicer if CIM could directly print copies of the messages.

With all these negative things I have to say about CIM, why am I talking about it? Because I still find CIM useful. I particularly like CIM for uploading and downloading files. Its GUI allows you to see what is going on. With CIM, it is easy to browse through a library and pick out the files you want. For the low price CompuServe charges for CIM, it is worth having around for the few things it does better than TAPCIS.

Pizazz Plus V2.0 (retail software)
Application Techniques, Inc.
10 Lomar Park Dr.
Pepperell, MA 01463
(800) 433-5201
Price: $149 (plus shipping)

Most manuals that I have seen produced by shareware authors have very few illustrations or screen shots. Screen shots showing the user what they should be seeing when they are performing the functions described by the text of the manual are a big advantage in helping users understand your software. It becomes a lot easier for users if they can read a description and see what the screen should look like at the same time. One of my manuals that was highly rated by reviewers had screen shots on every even-numbered page. Pizazz Plus provides an easy and convenient means of capturing screen images to include in your manual.

Pizazz Plus runs as a memory-resident program. When you push SHIFT-PRINT SCREEN, instead of getting the DOS print screen function, you get the Pizazz Plus screen. It is a well-behaved TSR. I have been using this software for three years and have never had a problem with Pizazz Plus conflicting with another TSR.

With Pizazz Plus, you have a lot of flexibility. For example, you can set the size of the printed image to fit the available space. Enter one dimension, such as the width, and Pizazz Plus will calculate the height. Or, you can manually enter the second dimension and distort the image to appear however you would like it to appear. Images can be rotated and rough edges smoothed.

Figure 14-10 shows the Main menu. The size of the image can be set by selecting the Width or Height options. Once you have entered one of these dimensions, the other can be automatically calculated, or you can manually set it. By entering a manual setting for both dimensions, the image can be "stretched" vertically or horizontally.

I have found the shading function to be very useful. This allows you to adjust the gray-scale shading (shown in the lower right box in FIG. 14-10) used to represent each color on the screen. Pizazz Plus will automatically select gray scales, but at times I have found that I get a clearer image by changing these selections to increase the contrast.

Pizazz Plus will save images in files that can be imported into desktop publishing documents. PCX, TIF, IMG, WPG, PCX, BIT, or Spinnaker Software Splash (SS) file formats are supported. This makes including a screen image in your manual very easy. Just save the image in the appropriate format, then incorporate it into your manual using your word processing software. If your word processing software does not have this capability, just print the screen image and paste it into the appropriate spot in your manual. If you wish, you can also save screen images as ASCII text files.

I have only had one problem with Pizazz Plus. I have not always been able to print screens generated by TSR software. For example, to print the screen shown in the Resident-TaskManager review, I had to run RTM in its non-resident mode. In general, I do not feel that this is a big problem, it is just an inconvenience.

The 160-page manual is designed as a reference manual, allowing you to find what you need, when you need it. Although the publisher, Application

Techniques, provides technical support, I never needed to call them. The manual provided everything I needed to know.

The bottom line is that Pizazz Plus does what it is supposed to do in a simple straightforward manner. It requires little of the user and that is what I like in software.

```
┌─────────────────────────{ Pizazz Plus Main Menu }───────────────────────┐
│ ▐Print▌ File  Crop  StYle  Shading  Width  Height  PosItion  View  Rotate │
│ SMooth  CopiEs  Top  SettinGs  Units  Quit                               │
│                                                                          │
│ Print or Transfer a screen image (While printing, press ESC to Stop) p.33 │
└──────────────────────────────────────────────────────────────────────────┘
```

```
┌─────────────────────────────┐  ┌─────────────────────────────────────┐
│ Print Settings ( PZP    )   │  │     Print Shades (Absolute)         │
│ ─────────────────────────   │  │     ───────────────────────         │
│       Width - 3.50"         │  │  0 - Black          8 -             │
│      Height - 2.63"         │  │  1 - Gray # 14 (E)  9 -             │
│ Left Margin - Centered      │  │  2 -                A -             │
│  Top Margin - 0.00"         │  │  3 - Gray # 8       B - Gray # 3    │
│  Form Width - 8.00"         │  │  4 - Gray # 12 (C)  C -             │
│   Form Feed - Yes           │  │  5 -                D -             │
│      Rotate - No            │  │  6 -                E - Gray # 1    │
│      SMooth - No            │  │  7 - Gray # 5       F - White       │
│      Copies - 1             │  │ Black and White Print Colors Reversed│
│       Style - Black & White │  │       Installed Hardware            │
│               Presentation  │  │       ─────────────────             │
│        Cropped Area         │  │ Display Card - IBM VGA (Video Graphics)│
│        ────────────         │  │       Printer - HP LaserJet Series II│
│   Top - 0     Left - 0      │  │ Printer Port - LPT1:                │
│ Bottom - 399  Right - 719   │  │  Environment - Overlay              │
└─────────────────────────────┘  └─────────────────────────────────────┘
```

14-10 The *Pizazz Plus* Main menu displays both the options you have and the current status. Notice that the help message across the bottom of the upper box includes a reference to a page in the manual. All of Pizazz's help messages include a similar reference that allows you to quickly find more detailed information.

15

Survey results

During the summer and fall of 1990, I conducted the first of what I hope will be a series of annual surveys. I sent questionnaires to over 800 shareware authors, over 200 disk distributors, 96 magazine editors and writers, and over 500 users and user groups. The objective of these surveys was to determine the current state of the shareware industry, learn how shareware authors did business, identify the differences between successful and unsuccessful authors, and determine the press' and users' perceptions and feelings about shareware.

To help make responding to the survey easy, all survey forms included a pre-addressed return envelope with a stamp on it. As a way to encourage people to complete and return the surveys, everyone that responded was promised a free copy of a summary of the survey results.

This chapter summarizes the answers to the questions on these surveys.

Shareware author survey

This section provides the results of my survey of shareware authors. Survey forms were mailed to 812 authors. At the time the data was tabulated, I had received 210 completed survey forms. There were 19 questions; however, some authors did not answer all questions. I continue to receive completed survey forms, but these have not revealed any significant changes to the data.

I have divided the results into five groups by the authors' annual sales. The groups are:

Group 1—Over 50,000 in annual sales (20 authors)
Group 2—$10,000 to $50,000 in annual sales (26 authors)
Group 3—$2000 to $10,000 in annual sales (75 authors)
Group 4—$0 to $2000 in annual sales (62 authors)
Group 5—did not report annual sales (27 authors)

In some of the tables, the information is formatted as follows: The number of authors responding to the question is in parentheses, the values over which answers ranged are shown as $nn - nn$, and the average is shown followed by the "avg." Other tables are labeled to identify the information. For questions to which the answers could not be quantified, I have summarized four or five of the most common answers. I list each question as it appeared on the survey form and then provide a summary of the answers that I received.

Background information   The first part of the survey asked authors to provide some background information about themselves or their companies. This information is summarized in TABLE 15-1. Although the annual sales figures are for shareware only, the numbers of full-time and part-time employees might not accurately reflect the number of people solely involved in shareware. Several of the Group 1 and Group 2 companies reported they were involved in consulting and their employees worked in both the consulting side and the shareware side of their business.

Table 15-1

Background information summarizing the type of author/company responding to the shareware author survey in each of the five groups.

	Group 1	Group 2	Group 3	Group 4	Group 5
Avg. annual sales	$428,611	$23,421	$4757	$294	NA
Full-time employees	(18) 1 – 18 4.3 avg.	(14) 1 – 3 1.3 avg.	(20) 1 – 4 1.5 avg.	(12) 1 – 4 1.7 avg.	(12) 1 – 2 1.2 avg.
Part-time employees	(18) 1 – 4 2.0 avg.	(16) 1 – 2 1.7 avg.	(42) 1 – 4 1.3 avg.	(26) 1 – 4 1.3 avg.	(23) 1 – 6 2.6 avg.
# yrs. publishing shareware	(18) 2 – 7 4.5 avg.	(20) 1.5 – 7 3.6 avg.	(66) 0.5 – 6 2.9 avg.	(57) 0.5 – 6 2.1 avg.	(25) 0.5 – 13 4.5 avg.
# programs published	(18) 1 – 31 4.9 avg.	(21) 1 – 21 5.4 avg.	(66) 1 – 12 2.5 avg.	(57) 1 – 12 2.0 avg.	(27) 1 – 10 2.9 avg.

Question 1   For your top three selling programs, provide the registration price, number of registrations you have received, the year the program was first released, and the type of software. (Note that because of the low number of responses for some categories of software, the pricing information might not truly reflect the market.)

TABLE 15-2 summarizes the answers to this question. In software categories with more than two responses, notice that business software has the highest average registration price. Also notice that the more successful shareware publishers (Groups 1 and 2) charge more for their software.

Table 15-2

A shareware pricing summary of average prices charged
for registered versions of software in various categories in 1990.

	Group 1	Group 2	Group 3	Group 4	Group 5
# programs	37	47	125	84	48
Average registration	$7.50–$220 $58.50	$10–$500 $57.50	$2–$399 $40.50	$0–$100 $26.20	$10–$395 $59.40
Avg. # of registration per program	13,856	946	209	21	NA
Years since release	3.3	2.3	2.1	1.7	NA
Business	(11) $70.30	(9) $125.00	(24) $86.00	(24) $36.80	(15) $80.70
Utility	(9) $47.70	(9) $35.40	(26) $23.20	(10) $35.00	(4) $36.25
Games	(3) $12.50	(8) $41.30	(14) $20.40	(7) $8.29	(4) $14.37
Communication	(1) $75.00	(1) $40.00	(5) $83.60	(0)	(2) $25.00
Programming	(2) $72.00	(5) $42.40	(7) $21.43	(5) $27.70	(4) $71.00
Word processing	(2) $103.00	(0)	(5) $30.80	(4) $20.00	(1) $39.00
Spreadsheet	(2) $55.00	(0)	(0)	(2) $15.00	(0)
Database	(1) $70.00	(3) $24.66	(12) $33.40	(5) $17.60	(3) $50.00
Graphics	(2) $72.00	(2) $57.50	(4) $32.50	(4) $13.75	(4) $41.00
Educational	(3) $36.70	(4) $22.25	(9) $21.90	(19) $14.40	(6) $24.00
Home	(1) $70.00	(6) $39.16	(9) $29.00	(1) $15.00	(0)
Other	(1) $40.00	(5) $51.20	(16) $35.10	(4) $18.75	(7) $94.10

This could be because they publish better software, which commands a higher price, or it might be that they have more sales because they charge more. This is where your marketing research is important. Look at competing shareware and do a realistic evaluation comparing the competition with your software. Is their software better than yours? Do they do a better job of marketing it? Then compare what they charge with the registration fee for your software.

Another trend I noticed is that games go against the trend of the more successful authors charging more for their software. In the games category, the most successful authors (Group 1) charge significantly less.

You might also notice that the mainstream categories of software, word processing and spreadsheets, seem to be dominated by a couple of leaders and the rest of the competition lagging far behind.

Question 2 Which of the following do you provide to registered users? This question then listed the items shown in the left column of TABLE 15-3.

Overall, the responses to this question show that printed manuals, the current version of the software, and user support are by far the most common benefits offered to registered users.

Table 15-3

Registration incentive summary showing that printed manuals, the current version of the software, and support are the registration incentives most authors offer.

	Group 1	Group 2	Group 3	Group 4	Group 5
Printed and bound manual	12	13	20	7	11
Photocopied manual	0	4	13	19	3
Current version	16	19	54	44	21
Source code	1	4	3	4	1
Free updates	4	9	28	15	9
Commissions	3	1	4	1	1
Free phone support	15	17	46	29	20
Free support via mail	15	16	56	32	22
Quick-reference card	4	2	1	0	0
Free newsletter	5	6	9	6	4
Other	2	7	19	7	8

Question 3 What is your software update policy? Here are the answers six authors wrote on their survey forms.

I provide free updates on the occasion of a serious bug fix.
I only send updates to people who complain about bugs.
All registered users are offered an update at a reduced cost.
My software is stable. I do not need to have updates.
I charge for the cost of media, handling and postage.
Free bug fixes, otherwise $10.

Most authors also provided the price that they charge for an update. TABLE 15-4 summarizes the pricing information for updates.

Table 15-4

What the average shareware author charges for an upgrade as a percentage of the normal registration price.

	Group 1	Group 2	Group 3	Group 4	Group 5
Range of answers	Free – 50%	5% – 58%	13% – 100%	18% – 100%	20% – 100%
Cost of upgrades as a percent of registration fee	30%	31%	40%	49%	45%

Question 4   What is your policy for major upgrades or for users who wish to get an update after their eligibility for free updates expires?

Fewer authors responded to this question than to Question 3. I wanted to find out whether or not authors treated major updates/upgrades differently than minor updates. Overall, the answers showed that most authors treated major and minor updates/upgrades in the same way.

Not established yet. I have not had any major upgrades.
Same update policy described in answer to Question 3.
The cost is based on the features and changes I make.

Several authors gave a response to this question that surprised me. Six authors, all of whom reported very low sales and expressed negative feelings about the effectiveness of shareware, reported that their software was stable and did not need to be updated. This type of answer is fine if the orders are pouring in, but if your software is not bringing in registrations, then something is wrong. Something needs to be changed.

These authors might have stable software from the prospective of there being few or no bugs, but from a marketing viewpoint, they should be changing their programs, adding features, working to make them easier to use, and most importantly, getting user feedback to find out what needs to be changed. When nothing is happening, it is time for you to shake things up, makes some changes, and make something happen.

Question 5   How do you inform registered users that a new update/upgrade is available?

The three common answers to this question were by postcard, by sending a letter, and by announcing the update/upgrade in a newsletter.

Question 6   What is your support policy?

This question presented a list of options that could be checked off. These are shown in the left-hand column of TABLE 15-5. The fourth item in the list, "Reg. Users Only" indicates those authors that provide support to

Table 15-5

	Group 1	Group 2	Group 3	Group 4	Group 5
This table shows that few authors use 800 numbers to provide support.					
800 number	2	2	2	0	1
900 number	0	0	0	0	0
Conventional phone	16	17	56	41	20
Registered users only	6	3	14	16	10
Anyone who calls or writes	10	16	48	35	15
Free newsletter	2	16	6	3	4
Other	3	9	16	8	2

the registered users. The most common answer in the "other" category was that support is provided via BBS.

Question 7 Do you sell/give copies of your shareware directly to the public?

My policy has been that if a user has a problem with any of my shareware, I will replace the disk with the current version at no charge. However, I am not in business to compete with the disk distributors, so I do not publicize that I give away free disks and many times I will ask users to send me their old disks.

TABLE 15-6 summarizes the responses to this question. I was surprised to see that the group that most actively gives away free disks is Group 3, authors whose sales average $4757. I was expecting to see the more suc-

Table 15-6

	Group 1	Group 2	Group 3	Group 4	Group 5
About 40% of authors offer to sell copies of their shareware disks direct to users at prices that range from free to the full price of their registered version.					
# of authors who give or sell copies of their shareware disks directly to users	10	13	37	16	8
Average disk selling price	$7.00	$5.33	$0.16	$4.17	$5.87
Range of prices charged	$0–$20	$0–$17	$0–$10	$0–$15	$0–$30

cessful authors giving away disks free because they could more easily afford the cost. From a marketing standpoint, however, this does make sense. If you are the up-and-comer, you need to do more to be noticed and recognized in the market. You have to work harder to build your market share. Giving away free copies of your shareware disk is a good way to do this.

Question 8   Have you ever purchased advertising? If so, in what type of publication? Was it worth the cost?

TABLE 15-7 summarizes the answers to this question. In general, most authors have never purchased advertising. Among those that have used advertising, a few reported good results, but most did not feel it was worth the cost.

Although the average rating of the value of advertising is less than 5 on a scale of 1 to 10, do not take this as a sign that you should never advertise. The reasons advertising did not work for many of these authors might be due to related things, such as the advertising being placed in the wrong publications or poor advertising copy.

Table 15-7

On a scale of 1 to 10, the most successful authors rate the value of advertising at 5.6.

	Group 1	Group 2	Group 3	Group 4	Group 5
# of authors who had advertised	14	13	44	8	10
Value of advertising on a scale of 1 – 10	5.6	3.9	1.3	3.1	4.0

Question 9   How many shareware distributors do you send your programs to? Do you charge for these? How frequently do you send updates to distributors?

TABLE 15-8 (at the top of the next page) shows the responses to this question. Notice that the Group 1 authors send their disks to an average of 268 distributors and dealers. This number declines dramatically when you look at Group 2 and then continues to drop with Group 3 and 4. What I find interesting is that Group 3, the group that tends to give away free disks to individual users, only sends disks to an average of 60 distributors. The most effective use of free disks is to send them to distributors, because one disk sent to a distributor can be multiplied by the distributor's efforts into several hundred disks going to users.

Question 10   How many BBSs do you upload new programs/updates to?

The responses to this question are summarized in TABLE 15-9. In general, authors who publish software related to telecommunications focused

Table 15-8

The number of disk distributors and dealers authors send disks to and the frequency at which disks are sent. While most authors send updated disks to distributors about twice a year, the more successful authors in Group 1 send their disks to a lot more distributors than any other group.

	Group 1	Group 2	Group 3	Group 4	Group 5
Range (# of dealers)	63–600	10–330	0–400	0–165	0–2000
Avg # of dealers authors send disks to	268	92	60	51	140
Frequency range (times/yr)	1–3.5	1–6	0.5–6	1–2	0–4
Avg Frequency (times/yr)	1.9	1.9	1.8	1.4	2.1

Table 15-9

The number of BBSs to which the average author uploads copies of their shareware. The use of BBss for distributing shareware varies quite a bit based on the type of software. Telecommunications-related software is heavily uploaded to BBSs while large business applications are more widely distributed using disk distributors.

	Group 1	Group 2	Group 3	Group 4	Group 5
Range (# of BBSs)	0–180	0–35	0–118	0–100	0–300
Avg # of BBSs	28.0	4.1	7.4	7.4	19.0

heavily on uploading their software directly to BBSs. One author even reported having written a program that automatically called BBSs during the night and uploaded copies of his software.

Most authors reported that they uploaded their software to fewer than three places. The most commonly mentioned places software is uploaded to are CompuServe and GEnie.

Question 11 Do you mail out press releases?

TABLE 15-10 shows the number of authors in each group that mail press releases.

Question 12 How long does it take from when you send out a new program until you get a significant number of registrations?

Some authors reported that they start to get registrations within a week or two of sending out their new shareware disks. However, except for

Table 15-10

Most authors do not send out press releases. While 13 of the 20 (65%) authors in Group 1 have used press releases, only 26 of the 75 (35%) authors in Group 3 have used them.

	Group 1	Group 2	Group 3	Group 4	Group 5
# of authors sending out press releases	13	10	26	9	7

the Group 1 authors, the average time between sending out a disk and getting registrations seems to be 6 to 7 months. My guess is that Group 1 reports a much shorter time because of the brand recognition of their company name. Their new programs are probably accepted by distributors quicker and users feel more comfortable with their software as a result of the brand recognition.

A summary of the response to this question is presented in TABLE 15-11.

Table 15-11

The average amount of time between when you send out a disk and when you start to receive registrations.

	Group 1	Group 2	Group 3	Group 4	Group 5
Range (weeks)	1–26	4–104	3–104	4–104	2–78
Average time (weeks)	9	34	36	26	24

Question 13 Do you limit or restrict the use of your shareware in any way?

Nearly all of the authors reported that they do not limit their software in any way, except Group 3, where 30% of the authors reported that they limited their software. However, I found it interesting to see that many of the authors that reported they did not limit their software also included notes in response to Question 2 that said registered users receive a version of the software that provided additional features. This implies there is a difference between their shareware and registered versions.

Question 14 Do you build anything into your software to encourage registration?

The answers to this question were consistent with Question 13. Most authors report that they use only an introductory screen that informs the user that the software is shareware. The most commonly used registration "encouragement" is a delay screen.

Question 15 Do you offer site licenses? If so, what do you charge for a site license?

Most authors offer site licenses, but few have sold a site license. The most common response concerning the price of a site license was that fees are negotiated on a case-by-case basis.

Question 16 What shareware programs have you found useful in your shareware business?

Chapter 14 provides the list of shareware programs that authors reported as being useful in their business.

Question 17 What commercial services/software have you found useful in your business?

See chapter 14 for the list of retail software that shareware authors reported using. The following is a list of the services authors reported using. There were 27 mentions.

CompuServe (information service)	13	48%
GEnie (information service)	4	15%
Sizzleware (shareware disk distributor)	2	7%
Whitehall Press (book printer)	2	7%
Calumet Carton (packaging/mailing envelope supplier)	1	
Data Northwest (disk services)	1	
Echo Data Service (disk services)	1	
Gemini Marketing (shareware disk distributor)	1	
Midwestern Diskettes (diskette supplier)	1	
Solomon Brothers (accounting)	1	

Question 18 What publications have you found useful in your shareware business?

There were 158 mentions. An asterisk (*) indicates a publication that is no longer published.

Shareware Magazine	28	18%
PC Magazine	25	16%
ASPects Newsletter	10	6%
Computer Shopper	8	5%
Programmers Journal	7	4%
Dr. Dobbs	6	4%
InfoWorld	6	4%
PBS Shareware Author's Booklet	6	4%
PC Computing	5	3%
Byte	4	3%
Inside Microsoft Basic	4	3%
PC World	4	3%
PSL News	4	3%
Home Office Computing	3	2%
Midnight Engineering	3	2%
PC Week	3	2%
PCM	3	2%

Compute!	2	1%
Computer Language	2	1%
Data Base Advisor	2	1%
Shareware Dealer Catalogs	2	1%
Best Bits & Bytes Catalog	1	
Boardwatch	1	
C Users Journal	1	
(Couldn't read handwriting)	1	
Computer Innovations	1	
Computer Language	1	
Dr. C	1	
Elite Computing	1	
Gorilla Marketing (book)	1	
Industry Specific Publications	1	
Micro Market Newsletter	1	
Microsoftware Marketing	1	
One Thousand	1	
PC Brand Catalog	1	
*PC Resource**	1	
PC Techniques	1	
PC Today	1	
*Programmers Update**	1	
Shareware, Try Before You Buy (book)	1	
Sizzleware Catalog	1	
TUG Lines	1	
Vulcan Computer Buyer's Guide	1	

If I may, I am going to slip in a short editorial comment here. Both in this listing and in the listings of the most popular software in chapter 14, I have included an item called "Couldn't Read Handwriting." In many cases, the writing on my survey forms was so bad that I could not make out what it said. Fortunately, after several people looked at these surveys, we were able to figure out what was written. However, a few were totally unreadable. This means that whoever wrote them wasted their time. Please, if you are going to take the time to respond to a questionnaire, try to type or write clearly.

Question 19 What advice do you have for new shareware authors?

Answers to this question are included throughout this book.

Shareware disk distributor survey

This survey was sent to 225 shareware disk distributors. A total of 60 survey forms was returned.

The answers to the following three questions are combined in TABLE 15-12.

Question 1 For which types of computers do you sell shareware?
Question 2 Approximately how many titles do you carry?
Question 3 Approximately how many disks do you sell per month?

Although I tried to include as many Apple and Macintosh disk distributors as I could find, only one distributor responded that sells just shareware/public-domain software written for computers made by Apple.

Table 15-12

The average number of different disks in the libraries of shareware distributors and the average number of disks they sell each month.

	IBM	Macintosh	Apple II	Atari	Commodore
# of distributors	59	5	8	3	7
# of titles carried	10–25,000 1727 avg.	2–1200 480 avg.	2–500 194 avg.	500–800 600 avg.	5–700 361 avg.
# disks sold per month	10–200,000 7856 avg.	200–4000 2100 avg.	5–500 189 avg.	1000 1000 avg.	50–1000 325 avg.
Total disks sold per month	377,070	4200	755	2000	1300

Table 15-13

Most shareware disk distributors use direct mail and magazine ads to sell disks.

	# of distributors using this method
Direct mail	45
Magazine ads	37
User groups	7
Swap meets	23
Computer dealers	15
Retail	10
BBS	5
Information servies	2
Other	

Fifty-nine distributors of IBM software responded. Some of these distributors also reported selling software for other types of computers.

From TABLE 15-12, you can easily see that, based on the number of disks shipped per month, the IBM market is dominant.

Question 4   How do you market/distribute shareware?

TABLE 15-13 shows that the primary means of distributing shareware disks is through direct mail and magazine ads.

Question 5   What types of programs do you sell the most of?

Games, by far, are the most popular programs distributors sell. The responses to this question are summarized in TABLE 15-14.

Table 15-14

The answers to Question 5.
Distributors sell more games
than any other type of software.

Mentions	
Game	29
Education	17
Graphics	8
Home	6
Business	18
Utility	13
Other	20

Question 6   What can shareware authors do to help you?

This was one of the key questions on the distributor survey. I wanted to find out how authors and distributors could do a better job of working together. Both want to have a vibrant, healthy shareware industry and should be working together toward this common goal. Here is what Roger Jones, President of Shareware To-Go had to say about this in a telephone interview:

> *The relationship between the author, customer, and distributor is an important one. The author has certain responsibilities and the distributor has certain responsibilities. But, our customer is the reason why we exist. If we don't have customers, we don't have anything. It's our responsibility, both of us, to be reputable, professional in our approach, reasonable, and very careful not to give the customer a bad experience with shareware.*

The following is the list of things shareware disk distributors suggested authors could do to help them. The number to the right is the number of times this suggestion was made. The percentage shows the number of times this response was given compared with the total number of responses.

Better descriptions of disks	25	34%
Send timely updates	13	18%
Provide good documentation	5	7%
Stay in contact with vendors	5	7%
Keep up the good work	2	3%
Makes lots of new programs	2	3%
Answer questions on-line (i.e., CIS)	1	
Don't cripple programs	1	
Don't require permission letters from dealers	1	
Go to user group meetings	1	
Include "type GO" to start a program	1	
Join ASP to get dealer list	1	
Leave room on disk for dealer files	1	
Let vendor know if you get registrations	1	
Listen to feedback	1	
Make programs easy to use and install	1	
Make complete programs	1	
Nice screen shots for catalog	1	
Provide more on-disk documentation	1	
Provide bug-free software	1	
Put user survey on disk	1	
Put version number on disk	1	
Reduced registration fees for SW dealers	1	
Respond to customers	1	
Send updates to all ASP vendors	1	
Send programmers to smaller dealers	1	
Software that works on most computers	1	

Question 7 What do shareware authors do that you would prefer they not do?

This is the opposite of Question 6 and it is also a key question. What do authors do that upset distributors? Here is a list of the answers.

Put too many limits on programs	9	19%
Cripple shareware	5	11%
Let any disk distributor sell their disks	2	4%
Not respond to vendor letters	2	4%
Put threats on disk	2	4%
Require dealers to purchase disks	2	4%
Send disks without written descriptions	2	4%
Send incomplete programs	2	4%
Assume everyone has a hard disk	1	

Assume user knows enough	1
Delay mailing upgrades	1
Distribute buggy software	1
Give vendors a hard time	1
Have monthly updates	1
Not include phone number on disk	1
Not notify dealer when software is discontinued	1
Offer no exit to DOS when done	1
Refuse to help unregistered users	1
Relocate without notice	1
Require membership in a group	1
Send demo software	1
Send uncompiled BASIC programs	1
Specify low selling price for disks	1
Time limit shareware	1
Put too many limits on distributors	1
Use nonstandard interface	1
ZIP files without including UNZIP	1
Have limits without telling the dealer	1
Set to self-destruct after 90 days	1

Question 8   What can shareware authors do to increase the number of registrations that they receive?

There was essentially only one answer to this question. Nearly every distributor said the same thing, "Provide quality software."

Question 9   What new software would you like to see available as shareware?

With this question I was looking for ideas for new programs. Shareware distributors are on the front lines in dealing with users. I assumed that they would be aware of the software their customers were asking for, but which they did not have available. Here is a list of their answers.

Good desktop publishing	9	16%
Windows 3.0 software	6	11%
Educational/tutorial for 10-year-old+	4	7%
Education for under 10 years	3	5%
Educational software	2	4%
GUI applications	2	4%
Networking applications	2	4%
Point-of-sale inventory	2	4%
Quality games	2	4%
Spanish/English translator	2	4%
VGA software	2	4%
4GL development software	1	
Automatic cataloging software	1	

Bible study and research	1
Business applications	1
C++ utilities	1
CASE software for novices	1
Clip art	1
COBOL compiler	1
Cross stitch & quilting programs	1
Foreign language business software	1
Gambling games	1
Geographic information systems	1
Integrated packages	1
LaterJet utilities	1
Magellan-like programs	1
Medical dictionary	1
Scientific graphics	1
Simulators	1
Utilities	1
Writing tutorials and guides	1

Question 10 What shareware programs do you feel shareware authors would find useful?

I asked this question because I hoped distributors, who have the opportunity to see almost every shareware disk released, might have suggestions as to useful software for shareware authors. The most common response to this question was that distributors do not know what software authors need.

Question 11 Do you offer any products/services shareware authors could use?

Distributors that answered this question are included in chapter 16.

I have lumped the next two questions together. Most distributors said they did not know which programs get registered and which do not. However, a couple of distributors include coupons on the disks they sell. When a user registers and gets the author to sign the coupon, the distributor gives the user a free disk. Based on the coupons returned to them, these distributors felt they had a fairly good feel for which programs were being registered.

Question 12 What type of shareware do you feel gets the most registrations?

Question 13 What type of shareware do you feel gets the least number of registrations?

The answers to Question 12 are summarized in TABLE 15-15. The answers to Question 13 are shown in TABLE 15-16.

Table 15-15

The software disk distributors feel get registered most often. Seventeen of the 60 distributors said that business applications are the most likely programs users will register.

Mentions

Game	4
Utility	6
Business	17
Education	5
Home	5
Word processing	9
Communication	2
Other	16

Table 15-16

The shareware disk distributors feel gets registered least often. Twenty-seven out of 60 distributors said that games are the least likely programs to be registered.

Mentions

Games	27
Business	2
Home	4
Spreadsheet templates	6
Other	6

Magazine editor survey results

I asked 96 magazines editors and writers to complete a survey about shareware. Unfortunately, only 13 completed the survey and returned it to me. Of these 13, several were only half completed. This is not a sufficient return rate to give valid results, but they did have some interesting comments. I have included some of the comments from editors throughout this book. Here are three more.

> *Much of the best shareware eventually goes commercial. Also, there's A LOT of junky software out there. It's frustrating to waste time installing it.*

> *I get lots of programs for review that are excellent in concept, but difficult to use—awkward commands, inconsistent commands or menus, technically complicated manuals. I rarely review these programs because my readers are typically not sophisticated enough (or patient enough) to sit down and figure it all out. The non-tekkie public wants programs that are easy to use. I broke this rule once with AFRO1, an investment program, because it filled a niche that none of the commercial programs filled. But I had readers complain that it was impossible to use.*

> *When you send a press release, include a short bio of the author. Most authors are very talented, but are not known in the business.*

It was interesting to note that 12 of the 13 editors said that they would like to see copies of the shareware program included with press releases. All of the publications reported that they have published either articles, reviews, or commentary about shareware and plan to continue to do so in the future. Seven editors reported that they felt their coverage of shareware would increase in the future. One said coverage would decrease and five either did not know or said there would be no change.

User survey results

The return rate on our user survey was also too low to provide valid results. In general, almost every user that responded had registered at least one shareware program and expressed a high level of satisfaction with shareware. However, there were some complaints.

- Users had a problem with shareware authors that moved or went out of business. Several users reported that they had sent checks or letters with questions to authors and either got them back as undeliverable or never heard from the author.
- A complaint that several users had is that many authors do not provide phone numbers on their disks.

- Users also complained about timed software that stopped working in 30 days. They found it frustrating to get a "trial period up" message before they had learned to use the program.
- Users had complaints about distributors that sell crippled software. If they are buying from a major distributor, they feel they should be able to feel confident that they will not get crippleware.
- My survey also went to users outside the U.S. and I had a fairly good return on these international surveys. Users in other countries had similar complaints to those voiced by U.S. users. The most common additional complaint was that shipping charges are sometimes too high.
- Over 90% of users in Europe and Australia prefer to pay for shareware using a credit card.
- An area I thought might be a problem was support for international users, but every international user reported that they were satisfied with the support they got.

16
Resource directory

This chapter provides a listing of suppliers for the material, equipment, and services you might need as a shareware author. Although I have used many of these vendors, I am not endorsing any of them. I am only providing a listing that you can use when looking for suppliers. I can say that I know of no problems or of anyone that has had a problem with the companies listed here. However, you should contact these suppliers and make your own decisions concerning quality, service, and value. For more information, contact each supplier and ask for a catalog.

This directory provides addresses for mail-order companies. I also feel it is a good idea to have local sources for some of the materials you need. Should you be in a bind and need something fast, there is nothing better than being able to drive to a supplier and pick up what you need.

This directory is not intended to be complete. There are many more vendors that supply these services, equipment, and materials. A good place to look for supplies is in *Computer Shopper* magazine or *PC Sources*. The purpose of this directory is to help you find what you need to run your business, if you do not know where else to look. If you have experience with a company not listed here, please let me know about them so I can add them to this directory.

I have divided this directory into types of materials, equipment, or services and it is listed in alphabetical order. After each heading, I have provided a short description of the type of material, equipment, or service you will find in that category.

Bookbinding

See Manual printing on page 301.

Bookbinding supplies

Three-ring binders, folders, GBC binding machines, and covers.

Vulcan Binder & Cover
P.O. Box 29
Vincent, AL 35178
(800) 633-4526
(205) 672-7159 (fax)

American Thermoplastic Co.
622 Second Ave.
Pittsburgh, PA 15219
(412) 261-6657

Bulk diskettes

Blank and preformatted diskettes, and disk sleeves.

Midwestern Diskette
509 W. Taylor
Creston, IA 50801
(800) 221-6332

Bulk-mailing service

These are vendors that will handle your bulk mailing for you. For example, you can send them your shareware disk, a set of mailing labels for distributors, and any inserts you wish to have included and they will duplicate, label, package, and bulk mail your disks.

Sunshine Software Services
4255 S. Channel 10 Dr. #38
Las Vegas, NV 89119

AP-JP Enterprises
P.O. Box 399
Islip, NY 11751-0399

Diversified Systems Group
P.O. Box 1114
361 NE Gilman Blvd.
Issaquah, WA 98027
(206) 392-0900

Business cards

See Stationery on page 303.

Catalog printing/production

These companies specialize in printing catalogs. If you have a small manual, they can also produce saddle stitched manuals.

Dinner Klein
600 S. Spokane St.
Seattle, WA 98134
(206) 682-2494

Catalogs America
1840 Michael Faraday Dr.
Reston, VA 22090
(703) 689-4680

Color printing

This is a company specializing in printing color brochures and flyers.

American Color Printing
1731 N.W. 97th Ave.
Plantation, FL 33322
(305) 473-4392

Computer supplies

Suppliers of general computer supplies and equipment.

Inmac
2465 Augustine Dr.
P.O. Box 58031
Santa Clara, CA 95952-8031
(800) 547-5444

QC Distributors
6011 Westline Dr.
Houston, TX 77036
(800) 888-2290

Lyben Computer Systems
1150 E. Maplelawn
Troy, MI 48084
(313) 649-4500

Dealers who sell registered versions

PC-SIG
1030D East Duane Ave.
Sunnyvale, CA 94086
(408) 730-9291

Disk duplication and labeling

These companies supply disk-duplication and labeling services.

FailSafe Media Co.
236 Egidi Dr.
Wheeling, IL 60090
(800) 537-1919

Ultimate Data Technology
7751 Hickory Ln.
Findlay, Ohio 45840

Monogram Media, Inc.
206 Parallel St.
Beaver Dam, WI 53916
(800) 527-2389

Diversified Systems
P.O. Box 1114
361 NE Gilman Blvd.
Issaquah, WA 98027
(206) 392-0900

Disk-duplication equipment

If you want to do your own duplication, this is where you can buy disk-duplication equipment.

Micro-Technology Concepts, Inc.
258 Johnson Ave.
Brooklyn, NY 11206
(718) 456-9100

Disk mailers

Flat- and folding-carton disk mailers.

Calumet Carton Co.
P.O. Box 405
16920 State St.
South Holland, IL 60473
(708) 333-6521
(708) 333-8540 (fax)

DiskSavers
14023 N. 57th Place
Scottsdale, AZ 85254
(800) 528-2361

Mail Safe
4340 W. 47th St.
Chicago, IL 60632
(800) 527-0754

G R A
3800 Monroe Ave.
Pittsford, NY 14534
(716) 385-2060

Legal Services

Help with copyright and trademark problems.

Lance Rose
Greenspoon, Srager, Gaynin, Daichman & Marino
825 Third Ave.
New York, NY 10022
(212) 888-6880

Magazines and periodicals

I assume that you are aware of the computer magazines available, thus they are not included in this listing. The following magazines are ones you might not have known about. They all are related to marketing, mail-order businesses, and the use of technology in business. Write and ask for a sample issue of any that you are interested in.

The Alternate Software Bulletin
P.O. Box 757
Brooklyn, MI 49230
News and information about high-quality shareware, freeware, and public-domain software.

Office Systems 90
Box 4097
Woburn, MA 01908
Includes advice for small- and medium-sized businesses and articles about office use of computers and software, in addition to other office-automation equipment.

Inbound/Outbound
12 West 21 St.
New York, NY 10010
A magazine for people who use technology to build sales and deliver customer service.

Telemarketing
One Technology Plaza
Norwalk, CT 06854
(800) 243-6002
Information about direct marketing.

Telecomputing
2625 Pennsylvania NE
Albuquerque, NM 87110
(505) 881-6988
BBS use, products, and services.

C Gazette
1341 Ocean Ave. #257
Santa Monica, CA 90401
(213) 473-7414
(213) 479-5472 (fax)

Computer Language
P.O. Box 53525
Boulder, CO 80322
Practical information for programmers and reviews of programming tools.

Mailing lists

Research Projects Corp.
Pomperaug Ave.
Woodbury, CT 06798
(800) 243-4360

Sunshine Software Services
4255 S. Channel 10 Dr., #38
Las Vegas, NV 89119
Author/shareware user lists.

Apogee Software
4206 Mayflower
Garland, TX 75043
Provides a mailing list of over 475 shareware distributors.

Manual printing and binding

Whitehall Printing Co.
1200 S. Willis Ave.
Wheeling, IL 60090
(708) 541-9290

Mailing, international services

Alternative service for overseas bulk mailing and shipping.

TNT Mailfast
12560 N.E. Marx
Pacific Business Center, Bldg. 4
Portland, OR 97230
(800) 558-5555

Office supplies

This category includes folders, binders, paper, and general office supplies.

Visible
3626 Stern Ave.
St. Charles, IL 60174
(800) 323-0628

RTJ Associates
1601 Paterson Plank Rd.
Secaucus, NJ 07094

Packaging products

Tape, boxes, shrink-wrap machines and supplies, poly bags, and shipping supplies.

Chiswick Trading, Inc.
33 Union Ave.
Sudbury, MA 01776-2246
(800) 225-8708
(508) 443-8091 (fax)

Premiums and incentive gifts

Custom-imprinted promotional merchandise such as coffee mugs, jackets, pens, and hats. (Also look in your local phone book under "Novelties.")

Nelson Marketing
210 Commerce St.
P.O. Box 320
Oshkosh, WI 54902-0320
(800) 722-5203

Sales Guides, Inc.
10510 N. Port Washington Rd.
Mequon, WI 53092-5500
(414) 241-3313

Best Impressions
P.O. Box 800
LaSalle, IL 61301
(815) 223-6263

Printed disk sleeves

Data Envelope
490 Division St.
Campbell, CA 95008
(408) 374-9720

Printer ribbons (color)

Ramco Computer Supplies
P.O. Box 475
455 Grove
Manteno, IL 60950
(800) 522-6922

Proofreading

Discover Software
P.O. Box 818
Castroville, TX 78009

Rubber stamps

Pre-inked custom and standard stamps.

Shachihata, Inc.
23705 Crenshaw Blvd.
Torrance, CA 90505
(213) 530-4445

Shipping boxes

Iroquois Products
2220 W. 56th St.
Chicago, IL 60636
(800) 453-3355

Shrink-wrap machines

Chiswick
33 Union Ave.
Sudbury, MA 01776
(800) 225-8708

Software packaging services

Leahy Press, Inc.
79 River St.
Montpelier, VT 05602
(800) 639-6011
(802) 229-5149 (fax)

PakStar USA
2909 Langford Rd.
Suite A400
Norcross, GA 30071-1506
(404) 446-7363

Stationery

Letterhead, business cards, envelopes, and mailing labels.

Stationery House
1000 Florida Ave.
Hagerstown, MD 21741
(800) 638-3033

A
Using the Shareware Mailing List Manager

At the end of this book is a coupon for ordering a disk containing a shareware program called The Shareware Mailing List Manager. This is a program that I have used for several years for maintaining various mailing lists, including my registered user list and my list of disk distributors.

To use this software, copy the SWMAIL.EXE file to your hard disk or a floppy that has at least 550K of space available after SWMAIL.EXE has been copied to it. Then, change the DOS prompt so it is set for the hard disk and directory or the floppy drive into which SWMAIL was copied. Type SWMAIL and the program will automatically be de-archived. No further installation is required. The installation procedure described in the manual can be used to install the software on a hard disk, if you de-archived it onto a floppy. However, it is primarily intended to just serve as an example of an installation procedure.

Included with The Shareware Mailing List Manager is a set of data files. They contain mailing lists of shareware disk distributors and magazine editors and writers. These files are:

EDITORS.DAT and EDITORS.MDR   Contains the names and addresses of editors and writers of computer-related magazines to whom you should send press releases.

NEWS.DAT and NEWS.MDR   Contains the names and addresses of editors and writers of non-computer news publications to whom you might wish to send press releases.

SHARE.DAT and SHARE.MDR   Contains the names and addresses of shareware disk distributors and dealers.

The files ending with "DAT" contain the actual data. The files ending with "MDR" contain the current settings and custom field titles for the associated data file. All data is stored in ASCII.

Quick-start instructions

This section provides a brief introduction to the basic functions of The Shareware Mailing List Manager so that you can quickly get started. The software is completely menu operated, with prompts on every screen, so it is easy to use. To start the software, type MAIL and push ENTER.

Let us start by looking at one of the mailing lists provided with this software. With the Main menu on the screen, push #2. Then enter #1 as the entry number to be edited. This will bring up the first name on the mailing list of magazine editors and writers. With the first name on the screen, push F2 to go to the second name. Each time you push F2 the display will advance by one name. Push F1 to back up by one name.

Push Esc or F10 to return to the Main menu.

There are two other mailing lists included with this software. To change to another mailing list you need to change the filename setting. With the Main menu back on the screen, select #5—Filename. (The current setting of the filename is shown in brackets.) A list of filenames already used will be displayed, followed by a prompt asking for the filename you wish to use. Enter either SHARE, EDITOR, or NEWS depending on which you want to look at. Type SHARE and push Enter.

Next, to print a list of disk distributors' names and addresses. Select # 3 on the Main menu to go to the Search/Printed Reports Screen.

At the bottom of the Search/Printed Reports Screen you will notice a prompt that says, "F2—[MONITOR]." This shows where the results of a search or listing will be sent. The default setting will display the information on the monitor. Push F2 to change this setting. The available settings are:

1-7/16 Prints names and addresses on $3^{1}/2''$-$\times$-$1^{7}/16''$ labels.

15/16 Prints names and addresses on $3^{1}/2''$-$\times$-$^{15}/16''$ labels.

DISK Prints the names and addresses to a ASCII disk file.

LINE-CP Stands for single-LINE report on Continuous Paper. It prints the name, city and state, and zip code on one line and lists 50 names per page. (Nice for quick reviews of the names on your mailing list.)

LINE-DSK The same type of report as LINE-CP except it is stored in an ASCII disk file.

MONITOR Lists the names on the screen, one at time, so that you can page through them.

To get a listing of names and addresses in order by zip code, push F2 until the type of report you want is selected. In this case, select $1^{7}/16$. Then push F4 for a listing of all entries for this filename. (Push F1 to see a help screen that describes each prompt in more detail.) When you push F4, a small menu will appear in the lower right corner. Next, push F1 to start the listing by zip code. Your printer should start printing.

After a few names have been displayed on the screen, push F10 to stop this report. For now, there is no need to use up a lot of paper.

To search for a specific name, use the down cursor key to put the cursor on the NAME line. Push F2 to select the type of report you wish to get. Type (in all caps—the names I have supplied are always in caps) the name you want to find, for example, PC-SIG. Push F6 to start the search.

Push F10 to return to the Main menu.

To add new names to the mailing list, select #1 on the Main menu. Figure A-1 shows the screen you will see. Start by entering the zip code, which is the first field at the top of the list. The zip code is generally used as an identifying code for each person. It is usually the quickest way to find a specific name, since names can sometimes be hard to spell correctly. That is why it is placed at the top of the page.

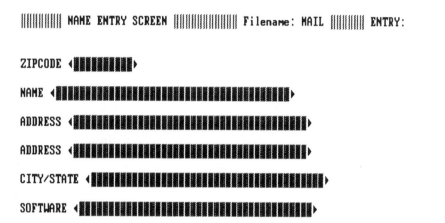

A-1 This shows the data-entry screen in *The Shareware Mailing List Manager*. The zip code is the first line because using a zip code is the most convenient way to look up a user.

Next, type in the name and address. If a comma is included in the NAME field, the printed reports will automatically reverse the information in this field when a label is printed. Everything typed after the comma will come first when the name line is printed. For example: DOE, JOHN will print on the label as JOHN DOE.

The final line is titled SOFTWARE. It is intended to be used to list the software that you send to a distributor (i.e., name and version number) or the software and version registered by a user. Anything typed on this line will be printed across the top of the label as a header. For users, I generally put an abbreviation for the program name, the version number, the disk size, and the month and year the software was registered on this line. When you print address labels, you will then be able to quickly see which program(s) and version numbers each user has and the disk size they need.

Once the name and address is entered, push F5 to save it. Push F10 to return to the Main menu.

Using the mailing list

The software is designed to keep the important information about each name on the first screen. Additional screens are available if you need to record or catalog additional information.

The zip code is listed as the first item because I have found that using zip codes is an easy way to quickly identify people that have called on the phone. When users call, I ask for their zip code and use it to look up their name. I have found this approach is easier than asking for a name because I then do not have to figure out how to spell the name. I have also noticed that users do not always give you the same name on the phone as they use to register the software. No, they are not using aliases. People usually use their legal name when they register software and might use a nickname when they call.

With The Shareware Mailing List Manager, I can quickly look up a name and address. If a user needs a new disk or information on one of my other programs, I can push Alt-P and get a mailing label.

I also include people that have asked for information about my software, but who have not yet registered in the same mailing list as my registered users. I identify them as unregistered by putting the word INFO on the bottom line along with the month and year they requested information. That way, when users register the software, I do not have to retype their name. I just change INFO to whatever abbreviation I am using for the software they purchased. If I want to do a mailing to unregistered users, I just include INFO on the SOFTWARE line as a part of the search criteria.

I also like to track people to whom I have sent a shareware disk, but who have not registered. For these people, I put INFO SW plus the month and year of their request on the SOFTWARE line.

Index

Other Bestsellers of Related Interest

MAC-GRAPHICS®
Octogram

This book illustrates clearly the possibilities of producing quality printed matter with the Macintosh. It puts together the key elements in pre-press production, including type, tint, color, grayscale, image, rule halftone, process color, and graduated color, and shows you how they relate to each other in the process of graphic design. Technical language is kept to a minimum; the visual nature of the book enables even beginners in the field to make the fast and accurate graphic decisions. 288 pages, 160 full-color pages + 128 2-color pages.

Book No. 3864 $49.95 paperback only.

MICROSOFT® WORD FOR WINDOWS® REVEALED
Herbert L. Tyson

Tyson concentrates on Word for Windows' more advanced aspects, including the program's WordBASIC macro language, page composition functions, field types and applications, and printer setup procedures. Special sections cover hot-linking to Excel spreadsheets, working around the "Command Not Available" message, and writing single-keystroke macros on the fly. Tyson even includes time-saving macro programs for printing envelopes, turning on "smart quotes," performing multifile search-and-replace, shading graphics on laser printers, and more. 568 pages, 82 illustrations.

Book No. 3799 $24.95 paperback only.

LOTUS® 1-2-3® SIMPLIFIED, RELEASE 3.1
David Bolocan

This helpful guide, completely revised to include Lotus® 1-2-3® Release 3.1, has made learning this latest release painless for thousands of users. Bolocan presents over 300 commands, functions, and macros in a logical, step-by-step format—basic commands are explained before more complex ones. You'll explore Release 3.1's built-in publishing functions . . . mouse support . . . scalable fonts . . . real-time editing . . . page layout . . . on-screen formatting . . . and drawing features. Updated illustrations reflect the program's fresh look and improved user interface. 448 pages, 261 illustrations.

Book No. 3772 $19.95 paperback only.

THE LOTUS® 1-2-3® FINANCIAL MANAGER: 60 Models
Elna R. Tymes, Charles E. Prael, and Patrick J. Burns

Designed for quick reference, this book presents 60 ready-to-use spreadsheet templates for personal, business, and statistical applications. Each template comes complete with command sequences, cell-by-cell data listings, and screen illustrations. Plus, all model instructions and cell listings are included on a FREE companion disk! This is the largest, most comprehensive collection of spreadsheet templates available today for users of Lotus 1-2-3 Releases 2.01, 2.2, and 3.0. 336 pages, 152 illustrations.

Book No. 3721 $39.95 hardcover only.

NORTON UTILITIES® 5.0: An Illustrated Tutorial
Richard Evans

Now DOS users and programmers can learn how to take charge of their systems wit the new features of release 5.0. Evans covers all the latest utilities and explains the consolidation of older utilities into compact modules. All illustrations have been changed to reflect the new look of Norton's screens. To ensure technical accuracy, Norton Computing, Inc., has reviewed the book. Each of the utilities is described in detail with its command line switches and parameters. 359 pages, 238 illustrations.

Book No. 3720 $26.95 hardcover only.

WORKING WITH ORACLE® DEVELOPMENT TOOLS
Graham H. Seibert

Speed up online inquiries and simplify updates. Make data input and manipulation, menu access, form design, and report formatting and layout easier than ever. Discover new approaches to everything from relational data linking to laser printouts. Do all of this and more with the help of this new desktop reference. It contains detailed instructions for using Oracle's SQL*Forms, SQL*ReportWrite, and SQL*Menu to solve a variety of database management problems. 256 pages, 172 illustrations.

Book No. 3714 $36.95 hardcover only.

BUILD YOUR OWN POSTSCRIPT® LASER PRINTER AND SAVE A BUNDLE
Horace W. LaBadie, Jr.

If you can plug in boards and handle a soldering iron, you can build your own high-powered, high-quality laser printer, at about half the cost of the retail model with this book. LaBadie shows you the best way to collect the parts and assemble a low-cost machine that works as well as—perhaps better than—an off-the-shelf printer. He explains how to convert a stock Canon CX or SX laser engine to full PostScript capabilities. 176 pages, 124 illustrations.

Book No. 3738   **$26.95 hardcover only.**

OPTIMIZING MICROSOFT™ C LIBRARIES
Len Dorfman

Designed for novices as well as experienced programmers, this book outlines the newest features of the Microsoft C 6.0 compiler—the C compiler that also supports Windows 3.0. It shows you how to make the most of the program's optimizing features while planning and building a multi-model, optimized C library. All library functions are completely explained and documented with demonstration programs. Code and examples that you can use on your own system are included. 352 pages, 138 illustrations.

Book No. 3735   **$34.95 hardcover only.**

Prices Subject to Change Without Notice.

Look for These and Other TAB Books at Your Local Bookstore

To Order Call Toll Free 1-800-822-8158
(in PA, AK, and Canada call 717-794-2191)

or write to TAB Books, Blue Ridge Summit, PA 17294-0840.

Title	Product No.	Quantity	Price

☐ Check or money order made payable to TAB Books

Charge my ☐ VISA ☐ MasterCard ☐ American Express

Acct. No. _____ Exp. _____

Signature: _____

Name: _____

Address: _____

City: _____

State: _____ Zip: _____

Subtotal $ _____

Postage and Handling
($3.00 in U.S., $5.00 outside U.S.) $ _____

Add applicable state and local
sales tax $ _____

TOTAL $ _____

TAB Books catalog free with purchase; otherwise send $1.00 in check or money order and receive $1.00 credit on your next purchase.

Orders outside U.S. must pay with international money order in U.S. dollars.

TAB Guarantee: If for any reason you are not satisfied with the book(s) you order, simply return it (them) within 15 days and receive a full refund.   **BC**

Writing and Marketing Shareware
—Revised and Expanded 2nd Edition

If you are intrigued with the possibilities of writing your own shareware programs, you should definitely consider having the Shareware Mailing List Manager mentioned in *Writing and Marketing Shareware* by Steve Hudgik (TAB Book No. 3961). The program, which contains more than 200 addresses for shareware distributors, is guaranteed free of manufacturer's defects. (If you have any problems, return the disk within 30 days, and we'll send you a new one.) Not only will you be able to use and examine a sample shareware program, but you also will have a large database of shareware distributor addresses at your disposal. Interested?

Available on disk for the IBM PC at $24.95 for each set, plus $2.50 shipping and handling.

YES, I'm interested. Please send me:

_____ copies 5¼″ disks (#6788S), $24.95 each . . . . $ _____

_____ copies 3½″ disks (#6789S), $24.95 each . . . . $ _____

_____ TAB Books catalog (free with purchase; otherwise send $1.00
in check or money order and receive coupon worth $1.00 off your next
purchase) . . . . $ _____

Shipping & Handling: $2.50 per disk in U.S.
($5.00 per disk outside U.S.) $ _____

Please add applicable state and local sales tax. $ _____

TOTAL $ _____

☐ Check or money order enclosed made payable to TAB Books

Charge my ☐ VISA ☐ MasterCard ☐ American Express

Acct No. _____ Exp. Date _____

Signature _____

Name _____

Address _____

City _____ State _____ Zip _____

TOLL-FREE ORDERING: 1-800-822-8158
(in PA, AK, and Canada call 1-717-794-2191)
or write to TAB Books, Blue Ridge Summit, PA 17294-0840
Prices subject to change. Orders outside the U.S. must be paid in international money order in U.S. dollars.

TAB-3961